Upon the Doorposts
of Thy House

Also by Ruth Ellen Gruber

*Jewish Heritage Travel: A Guide to East-Central Europe,
Updated and Revised Edition* (Wiley)

Upon the Doorposts of Thy House

Jewish Life in East-Central Europe,
Yesterday and Today

Ruth Ellen Gruber

John Wiley & Sons, Inc.
New York • Chichester • Brisbane • Toronto • Singapore

To
Henry Leonard,
Jonah Joseph,
and
Zoë Rebecca

Acknowledgments

⤮

It would have been impossible to write this book without the encouragement, support, companionship, advice, technical assistance, and good will of many, many people: friends, family, colleagues, experts in their fields—and combinations thereof. It is a pleasure to be able to thank them for all they have done.

My brother, Samuel D. Gruber, director of the Jewish Heritage Council of the World Monuments Fund, fits into all the categories and was behind, beside, and ahead of me every step of the way. Our parents, too, were unstinting in their support, and our brother, Frank J. Gruber, also contributed valuable insights and critique. Edward Serotta was a sympathetic confidant, counselor, and *compagno di viaggio*. Barbara Walsh Angelillo took time from a very busy schedule to run her critical eye over many of these pages, and I would have been lost without the hospitality extended to me (and mine) by her and her family.

In Hungary, Péter Wirth, Agnes Böhm, Ilona Seifert, and Marika Rapcsak were more than generous with time and advice, and the staff of the Rabbinical Seminary Library were patient and helpful. Thanks, too, to Miklós and Antonia Haraszti, László Rajk, Tamás Raj, Gina Bőni and Ernest Beck, and Adam Bager. Particular tribute must be paid to Lajos Lőwy and János Gerle.

In the Czech Republic, Daniel Rexa and the entire Rexa/Zapotocký family again provided not only a home away from home but assistance on every level. Arno Pařik and Jiří Fiedler again were generous with their expertise and friendship. I thank, too, Dr. Josef Klánský for sharing his memories and insight, as well as Rabbi Karol Sidon, Tomáš Kraus, Alice Marxová, and the others at the Jewish Community.

In Poland, I was buoyed by the invaluable support of old friends as well as the interest and generosity of new ones. Kostek and Małgosia Gebert and Staszek and Monika Krajewski once again provided the warmth, hospitality, advice, and instruction for which I have turned to them many times over the years. Drusilla Menaker shared her time, her insights, and her observations. Sylwia Tempel and Rev. Marek Głownia afforded me assistance that went beyond the call of duty. I thank, too, Joachim Russek, Henryk Halkowski, Jonathan Webber, Sonia Lucas, Franciszek Piper, Jurek Bebak, Mirek Ganobis, and Jutta Renner; also, Janusz Smolski, the staff of the International Culture Center in Cracow, and the Jogałła family. I would like to make particular mention of Archbishop Henryk Muszyński, who has been unflagging in his efforts to overcome historical evils.

Many friends, relatives, and colleagues were kind enough to read and comment on sections of this work in progress, to obtain reference materials for me, to help with translation, to discuss issues, to guide me through difficult passages, or simply to give me a pat on the back or a place to sleep. In particular, I would like to thank Geoffrey Wigoder, Jerry and Diane Rothenberg, Victoria Pope, Cal and Sonia Greenbaum, Liz Nash, Elmer and Lois Miller, Linda Richardson and Isaac Kleinerman, Miriam Weiner, Tadeusz Konopka, Michael Menkin, Sylvia Poggioli and Piero Benetazzo, Sam and Dorothy Schankler, Fay Peel, Gilbert Levine, Sheri Allen, Jonathan Stein, Lucyna Gebert and Rudi Assuntino, Bogdan Turek and Pat Koza, Robert Rothstein, Jonathan Lax, Michel Złotowski, and my other colleagues at the Jewish Telegraphic Agency, and George Jahn, Teddie Weyr, and the entire Associated Press bureau in Vienna.

A special note of thanks goes to Susan Birnbaum for allowing me to share her mother's recollections and to Herman I. Morris, along with a welcome to Shirley and a tribute to Aunt Judy, who is greatly missed by us all.

Several organizations and their representatives were especially kind in a number of ways. I'd like in particular to mention Amir Shaviv and Yitzhak Zohar of the American Jewish Joint Distribution Committee, Rabbi A. James Rudin of the American Jewish Committee, Rabbi Leon Klenicki of the Anti-Defamation League, Jerome Chanes of NJCRAC, Karen Strauss of United Jewish Appeal, and Elan Steinberg of the World Jewish Congress. I am especially grateful to the World Jewish Congress for helping with some of my communications expenses. I also thank Rabbi Jack Bemporad, Gunther Lawrence, and their colleagues associated with the Center for Christian-Jewish Understanding at Sacred Heart University in Fairfield, Connecticut, for enabling me to be along on their mission. And thanks to Marilyn Shubin and the Atlanta Jewish Federation for including me on their visit to Budapest.

Finally, I can't go without thanking Steve Ross for helping me find the right direction to take, Upton Brady for helping me to take it, and Hana Umlauf Lane for getting me there.

Some of the experiences recounted in this book have appeared, in different form, in articles published in *The Oberlin College Alumni Magazine, The Jewish Telegraphic Agency, The Philadelphia Jewish Exponent,* and the *Jewish Chronicle* (London).

Contents

❦

Introduction
Mezuzahs

◆

. . . every stone, every beam, every morsel of tooled silver, hammered brass, figured embroidery, painted wall, fretted stucco, and illumined parchment evokes its own moment in the long drama of Israel. Looking behind each morsel we shall find a man; and with little effort we may see the drama re-enacted. Our ears properly attuned, we shall hear history repeating itself.
—Marvin Lowenthal
A World Passed By

 HEN I WENT TO VISIT the office of a little Jewish community in western Hungary a few years ago, I first had to locate the synagogue, which long since had been transformed into a concert hall. I found a strikingly ornate, Moorish-style building with two chimneylike towers; symphony music from a rehearsal was flowing in lush waves from its windows. Nearby, at the edge of a parking lot, stood a Holocaust memorial commemorating the forty-two hundred local Jews deported to Nazi death camps. The present-day prayer room and office for the hundred or so Jews who still lived in the town were in a building next door.

In the office, I introduced myself as an American Jew, a writer interested in learning about the community and its history. The community's treasurer, a dour-faced man who looked to be in his seventies, eyed me suspiciously for a moment from behind a small desk where he was going over accounts. Suddenly, he picked up a prayer book, opened it apparently at random, and thrust it in front of me, pointing to the Hebrew writing on the page.

"Can you read that?" he asked. The few other people in the room went silent; I knew it was a sort of test. "Yes," I replied. I took the book and began easily to read the prayer that he had indicated. I could have chanted it, or even recited it from memory:

Shema Yisroel Adonai Elohenu Adonai Echod. . . . Vee aw hav taw ays a don ai el oh he haw. . . .

Hear, O Israel, the Lord our God the Lord is One. . . . And thou shalt love the Lord thy God with all thy heart, with all thy soul, and with all thy might. And these words which I command thee this day shall be in thy heart. And thou shalt teach them diligently unto thy children, speaking of them when though sittest in thy house, when thou walkest by the way, when thou liest down and when thou risest up. And thou shalt bind them for a sign upon thy hand, and they shall be for frontlets between thine eyes. And thou shalt write them upon the doorposts of thy house and upon thy gates.

The passage, from the book of Deuteronomy, is the *Shema,* one of the key Jewish prayers. It embodies the essence of Judaism—the basic profession of Jewish faith in one God—and also sets out the commandments, still followed by observant Jews, that men pray while wearing *tefillin,* or little boxes containing these prayers, bound on their forearms and foreheads, and that *mezuzahs,* or containers holding slips of parchment on which the Shema is written, be affixed to the doorposts of Jewish homes.

This book is about mezuzahs. Not so much the little boxes themselves, but rather what they symbolize, and where they were, and what is there now.

The Hebrew word "mezuzah" originally simply meant "doorpost." Today, on the doorposts of countless houses in countless towns and villages throughout East-Central Europe, where few if any Jews have lived since the Holocaust half a century ago, it is still possible to distinguish the places where mezuzahs had once been attached, marking these houses as Jewish homes. On some doorposts there are actual scars—empty, often very neat, gouges in the wood left when the mezuzahs were removed. On

(Facing page)

TARNÓW: A doorway in Tarnów, southern Poland, showing the place where a mezuzah once was.

some doorposts there are nail holes. On some, a faint outline of an oblong shape; a thickening of paint.

More than that, though. In countless towns and cities and villages throughout East-Central Europe, there are today a host of what I call *symbolic* mezuzahs, too: the hundreds and thousands of synagogue buildings, abandoned Jewish graveyards, and Jewish *shtetl* and ghetto buildings that still, despite deliberate Nazi destruction and Communist-era neglect, denote not houses, but villages, towns, and cities that were once homes to Jews. And in a way, the few remaining Jews themselves are also mezuzahs, flesh-and-blood reminders of vibrant Jewish communities that otherwise have disappeared.

Less tangible mezuzahs linger, too: memories. Memories encapsulated in fictional and historical writings; in letters, in superstitions; in folk tales and family stories handed down through the generations; in the archives and artistic collections that managed to survive the war; in the recollections of local non-Jews about their vanished neighbors; in the persistence of anti-Semitism in places where there are no longer any Jews to hate.

This book is about some of these places, some of these people, some of these memories, and some of the ways in which they are perceived today. It is a book of exploration, a book of journeys to places—like that little town in western Hungary—where Jews once lived and where, for the most part, only symbolic mezuzahs remain.

These journeys are the fruit of repeated visits to four post-Communist countries in East-Central Europe: Poland, Hungary, the Czech Republic, and Slovakia. Nearly five million Jews lived in these countries before the Holocaust. They were Orthodox and Reform; traditional and secular; *Hasidic* and assimilated; desperately impoverished and fabulously wealthy. They lived in big industrial cities and tiny small-town shtetls; for part of their history they were segregated in ghettos. They were bankers, factory owners, writers, and architects; housewives, merchants, tavern keepers, and students; rabbis, peddlers, shopkeepers, and beggars. Today, in these four countries, live few more than 120,000 Jews. As many as 90,000 of them are concentrated in just one city, Budapest. The rest are scattered in small, tiny, and minuscule communities, the largest of which, in Prague, has not many more than 1,000 members.

During the war, in addition to their attempts to annihilate the Jewish people, the Nazis carried out a systematic program of destroying the places that Jews held most dear. They desecrated and demolished synagogues and uprooted Jewish cemeteries, often using the elegantly carved tombstones to pave roads or build pigsties. Later, during four decades of Communist rule, abandoned buildings and burial grounds were often bulldozed to make way for urban development, converted for secular use, or simply left as they were to drift into oblivion and deteriorate slowly from neglect. Those Jews who remained suffered repression and even persecution; most eventually left for Israel, the United States, or elsewhere.

Since 1989, I have traveled extensively in these and other countries to document surviving traces of Jewish life. Some of this documentation became a book, *Jewish Heritage Travel: A Guide to Central and Eastern Europe,* which was published by John Wiley & Sons in 1992. (The new edition of this book is titled *Jewish Heritage Travel: A Guide to East-Central Europe,* Revised and Updated [Wiley, 1994].) In my research for that book, research that has also continued since its publication, I sought out synagogues and graveyards, study houses and ghetto streets. I also met with Jews who still live in these countries, mainly Holocaust survivors and their children. Some, I found, were trying to forget the past; some were trying to preserve it. Some, particularly younger people, knew little or nothing about their ancestry and Jewish heritage but were now actively seeking to regain their Jewish identity and turn the dormant past into a meaningful present and future. In addition, I met local people—often not Jewish—who were engaged in Jewish research or in the preservation of Jewish monuments. And over and over again I confronted the troubling ways in which Jewish monuments, heritage, personalities, and historical associations were regarded or made use of today.

My intention in this new book was to return to some of the places I had visited in the past, and to examine them in much greater depth, both in historical terms and in their present state.

My aim was not to write a "Holocaust book," to re-evoke memories and retellings of the Holocaust per se, although the destruction by the Nazis of the centuries-old Jewish civilization in this part of Europe forms immutable and inescapable bedrock for any consideration of modern

KOLÍN: The author at the Jewish cemetery (photo by Daniel Rexa).

Jewish issues. Rather, I wanted to investigate the matrix—and the memories and perceptions of the matrix—in which the Holocaust happened and then to place this in the context of present-day circumstances.

I didn't want to ignore the Holocaust, by any means; but I preferred to write around that gaping, jagged hole in the tapestry of Jewish history, to examine instead the tapestry that surrounds it—particularly the broken, frayed, and unraveled threads at its edges.

Who lives now in the places where Jews used to live? What memories are retained about what it was like when there was a Jewish population? What do people born after the Holocaust know about the Jewish past? What use is made of synagogues and Jewish cemeteries? How do Jews feel about these sites? What do non-Jewish local people feel about them? Do they know what they once were? Do they even notice them? What knowledge remains, and what uses are made of Jewish memory and Jewish history? Have they left their mark anywhere, on anyone?

TWO PIECES OF WRITING greatly influenced the direction I followed in this project. One was an unpublished summary of an ethnographic research project carried out in 1988 and 1989 under the auspices of the Jagiellonian University in Cracow, which has a Jewish Research Institute. The other was a poem.

The research project, by Andrzej Paluch and Jonathan Webber, was entitled *The Jews of Galicia in the Memory of Local Communities,* and the summary I obtained on a visit to the Jagiellonian Center was a preliminary progress report on the results of interviews with 220 elderly people in southeastern Poland, a region in which, before the war, Jews had made up fifty percent or more of the population in many towns.

"What we are studying is not the Jewish community in Poland, but rather its image in social consciousness and the memory of those who have remained," the report said. "It is not a study of facts. It is a study of social consciousness. It may be said that the object of study is mythicized knowledge."

The field interviews—all of them with men and women old enough to remember the prewar Jewish population from their own experience—had involved six main topics: how Jews appeared in the consciousness of the gentile community around them; knowledge of Jewish religion and rituals; attitudes toward Jews; changes in attitudes because of World War II; memories of how Jews and Catholic Poles had interacted; and stereotypes of Jews.

I found the results both fascinating and deeply disturbing, a mixture of ignorance and superstition, stereotype and nostalgia, faded memories and fear:

> Jews lived almost exclusively in towns, which was caused by their preferred employment: trade. Jews who were met in villages were only innkeepers or leaseholders or peddlers. All mentioned Jewish traders; thirty-two percent claimed that Jews were exclusively merchants and dealers. Another Jewish occupation perceived as typical was craftsman, like shoemaking or tailoring. Some mentioned learned professions, and only three percent mentioned Jewish farmers, but as landowners or leaseholders who did not themselves work the land. This is more or less true.
>
> This occupational structure was perceived as being caused by Jewish predisposition to trade and a specific aversion to hard work such as agriculture or blacksmithery. They were said not to like work; they were involved in exploitation.

, It was said that a Jew could be recognized in the street by his dress and beard. A Jewess could not; they were, however, thought to be prettier than Polish women. . . .

All know that Jews do not recognize Jesus Christ; however, the majority admit that Jews believe in the same God as Christians. The difference is explained, if it is at all, by the fact that Jews are wrong. Nearly all define the Jewish Scripture as the Old Testament. The word "Torah" is unknown. However, the same informants claim that Jews keep in their synagogues a golden calf. . . .

All perceive the internal differentiations among Jews. Categories used most often for description are assimilated Jews (intelligentsia), rich Jews, poor Jews (who are seen as the most Orthodox). Hasidim are well known . . . and are perceived as a special Jewish group; their Tzaddiks are described as saintly rabbis, sometimes simply saintly men.

Today, [forty-five] years after the war, the large majority claim that Polish-Jewish relationships were smooth and without conflict. If conflicts happened, they were like other conflicts between people, usually economic. However, nearly fifty percent say that "we were different, we lived next door to each other, but not together." . . .

Generally, Jews are perceived as strangers, richer than Poles, not wishing Poles well. Exceptions are usually seen as only those who were known personally to informants: They were good and honest friends different from other Jews. The Holocaust is generally perceived as a human tragedy, [a tragedy] that Poles were helpless to prevent. But: Nearly thirty percent support "the final solution"; fifty-seven percent accept as good that Jews are no longer in Poland; eighty percent say that, considering everything, it is perhaps better that Jews are no longer in Poland.

The report said that all of the people interviewed had heard that Jews committed ritual murder—the ancient "blood libel" that Jews used blood taken from Christian children or young women in the preparation of matzos at Passover. Sixteen percent of those interviewed believed this; thirty percent said it happened "very long ago"—and five percent claimed personally to remember such incidents and even described the instruments used to drain blood from the bodies. They quoted nine lawsuits based on blood libel cases, but admitted that proof was never found that such crimes had been committed.

In addition, seven of the informants said that Jews had poisoned

wells and spread the plague—and nearly all of the people interviewed, the report said, "believe that Jews were nomads and perished
in the Holocaust because they had killed Jesus Christ. Eleven percent
said that it was God who cursed the whole Jewish nation."

These findings piqued my interest and gave me much food for
thought. I wondered how Jews were remembered in other places in
the region, not only in other little shtetls like those in Galicia but also
in cities where Jews had been more acculturated into society.

The second piece of writing that influenced me, the poem, was
in a sense a literary version of this ethnographic research. It is part of
a cycle of poems by Jerome Rothenberg, an American poet who
often uses Jewish themes. The cycle is called *Khurbn,* a Yiddish word
that means "total destruction" and that is used to refer to the Holocaust. *Khurbn* was based on Rothenberg's own first visit to Ostrów
Mazowiecka, the small town in Poland, just fifteen miles from what
became the Treblinka death camp, from which his parents had emigrated to America in 1920. Jews made up more than fifty percent of
the population of Ostrów Mazowiecka before the war. During his
visit, in 1987, Rothenberg sought out Jewish houses, Jewish streets,
the ravaged Jewish cemetery, and memories people might have about
his family—just as I myself had done when I visited the little town in
Romania from which my own grandparents had emigrated.

In one section of *Khurbn,* Rothenberg recorded conversations he
had had with local people, interspersed with the inescapable reflec-
tions about the destruction of local Jews—including many of his own
relatives—that simultaneously had flashed through his mind:

> . . . were there once Jews
> here? Yes, they told us, yes they were sure there were, though
> there was no one here who could remember. What was a Jew
> like? they asked. (The eye torn from its socket hung against
> his cheek.) Did he have hair like this? they asked. How did he
> talk—or did he? Was a Jew tall or short? In what ways did he
> celebrate the Lord's day? (A rancid smell of scorched flesh
> choked us.) Is it true that Jews come sometimes in the night &
> spoil the cows' milk? Some of us have seen them in the mead-
> ows—beyond the pond. Long gowns they wear & have no faces.
> Their women have sharppointed breasts with long black hairs
> around the nipples. At night they weep. (Heads forced in the

bowls until their faces ran with excrement.) No one is certain still if they exist. (Plants frozen at the bottom of a lake, its surface covered by thick ice.)[1]

In gathering material for this book, I found myself asking the same sorts of questions that both the poet and the researchers had asked. *Were there once Jews here?* I came across the same types of village ignorance and superstition, but at the same time I also met people whose minds were open, whose memories were full, and whose insights greatly enhanced understanding. Like Rothenberg, though, I at times had to stop a minute, shaken internally by Holocaust visions or simply by the great unanswerable question, "What if?"

EACH CHAPTER OF THIS BOOK is different and each is self-contained. Each became, as I have said, a journey of exploration to a place or group of places where Jews once lived and where few, if any, Jews live today. Each took me into the physical world of people and places and also into the shifting world of memory and perception. I found that memory is a very illusive factor. No two—or three or five or million—people will remember the same thing the same way. The circumstances recollected might be identical, but different things stand out; different emphases are placed. I encountered this cacophony of memory wherever I went, and conflicting perceptions became one of several themes that run through these chapters.

Most of the material I used for this book was gathered during trips made between the autumn of 1989 and the summer of 1993, and these chapters reflect circumstances as I found them then. Since completing my research and writing, I have made return visits to some of these places, and I have included some updated material in the notes at the back of the book.

In "A Circle Game," I explore Prague, the most famous Jewish center in Central Europe, on a number of different levels. These include the ways in which Jewish heritage and memory, in the same city, are exploited and exalted, but how they also have been stifled and buried in total oblivion.

In "Wine Merchants and Wonder Rabbis," I evoke the days when intrepid Jewish merchants carried wine from Hungary to Poland and when, along many of the same routes, Jewish *rebbes* carried Hasidism from Poland south into Hungary. It is a journey that weaves through three centuries and three countries, to remote places in the foothills of the Carpathian Mountains where isolated outposts of memory and belief serve still as symbolic mezuzahs.

"Synagogues Seeking Heaven" is something of a detective story, the chronicle of a personal obsession: my search for a turn-of-the-century Jewish architect whose magnificent synagogues were a symbol of his age and whose life and work became for me a metaphor for Hungarian Jewish history.

In "What's to Be Done?," about Cracow, I examine a problem touched on to a lesser degree in other chapters: What contemporary use should be made of abandoned Jewish buildings? How? By whom? And why?

Finally, "Snowbound in Auschwitz" is a diary of my own confrontation with the place whose name has become synonymous with the *Shoah*. It was an unexpected, unplanned confrontation, which in the end gave me a singular opportunity to reflect upon and consolidate the many themes I had been exploring during the long months I worked on this book.

It is a reflection that I hope will cause reflection, too, in others.

∾1∾

A Circle Game
The Golden City,
Fame-Crowned Prague

∾∾∾

Great men were once capable of great miracles.
—I. L. Peretz
The Golem

Prague doesn't let go. . . . This little mother has claws.
—Franz Kafka

N THE EVE of Rosh Hashanah—the Jewish New Year—
5753, a date that corresponded to Sunday, September
27, 1992, Karol Sidon was formally inaugurated as the
rabbi of Prague.

The midafternoon ceremony took place in the
Jubilee Synagogue, a gorgeously ornate temple built in 1906 and the
only synagogue in Prague (other than the historic Old-New Synagogue situated in the former medieval ghetto) that is still consecrated
as a Jewish house of worship.

The inauguration had been advertised on hand-lettered signs put
up around town in places frequented by the thousand or so
acknowledged members of Prague's Jewish community, and a stand-
ing-room-only crowd filled the opulent sanctuary, whose blue, gold,
and deep red arabesques shimmered in the diffused light from
stained-glass windows. The president of the community gave a

speech; the president of the Czech Jewish Federation gave a speech. The rotund little cantor chanted in his raspy, old man's voice. The local Jewish choir earnestly sang three songs to the equally earnest accompaniment of a violin and a guitar. Sidon, looking very rabbinical in his beard, glasses, dark, baggy suit, and fedora hat, gave a little talk. His teacher, from the seminary in Israel where he had studied, addressed the congregation in Hebrew (with Czech translation) and expounded upon Sidon's most illustrious predecessor, the legendary Rabbi Judah ben Bezalel Löw, who died in 1609.

Following the ceremony, the congregation moved directly into a brief—very brief—service initiating Rosh Hashanah and then adjourned, long before sundown, the time at which this service ordinarily should begin. Prayers ended so early, in fact, that several people arrived for Rosh Hashanah services only to find that they were already over.

Sidon's inauguration—the setting, the timing, and the persona of the new rabbi himself—represented a drawing together of the many threads that make up Prague's tangled, thousand-year Jewish history. It has been a history of piety, mysticism, scholarship, and survival. In medieval and Renaissance times in particular, Prague was one of the great, golden centers of Jewish learning, home to some of the most notable Jewish figures of the age. In more modern times, Jewish history here has been marked by less pious characteristics: secularism and assimilation, for example, and intellect and anxiety. More recently, there was the tragic history of the Holocaust and the virtual elimination of Prague Jewry. And more recently still, there was the torment of communism and the relentless repression of the small group of postwar Jewish survivors.

At times these various currents of history have meshed. For example, Franz Kafka, Prague's most famous assimilated, anxiety-ridden Jewish intellectual, became fascinated with East European Yiddish theater and studied Hebrew before his death at the age of forty in 1924. His contemporary and fellow assimilated Jewish Prague intellectual, the poet Mordechai Jiří Langer, embraced Hasidism and in 1913, at the age of nineteen, journeyed to the small town of Belz in far-off Galicia to become a disciple of Belz's revered Hasidic rebbe, Yissakhar Dov Rokeach, who (to complete the circle) was a descendant of Prague's most famous ancient sage, Rabbi Löw. Kafka's three sisters and various other family members perished in the Holocaust; his writings were all but banned outright under the Communists. Langer escaped from Nazi persecution to what was then Palestine, but died there in 1943 as a result of the hardships he had suffered en route.

All these currents meshed in Karol Sidon.

The new rabbi was once an assimilated Jewish intellectual and had suffered personally under both Nazism and communism. Heir to Prague's secular intellectual Jewish tradition, he had chosen a difficult road back to the Orthodox religion of his fathers and was heir now, too, to the long line of Prague rabbis whose scholarship, piety, and spiritual associations helped give Prague a special significance in Jewish memory.

For Sidon, the progression seemed preordained.

"All my life, I've been moving in a circle toward the inauguration," he told me a few days before the ceremony. "People do things unconsciously; they don't always consciously decide what to do; their subconscious leads them to it. It's a progression that I had to make, but that I didn't plan. . . . I came from the world of literature, cosmopolitanism, and so on, to Judaism. It's hard. You can't change into a different person. I have my personal history, I can't escape from it. I carry my life on my shoulders, but I'm trying to get my life to another place—it's very complicated, very difficult."

Sidon was born in 1942, the son of a Jewish father who died in the Terezín Ghetto concentration camp north of Prague and a gentile mother who survived the war and eventually married another Jew. Sidon himself spent the war years in a village where he was hidden by Christian relatives. As an adult, he became a playwright and an outspoken anti-Communist dissident who joined Václav Havel as one of the founders and guiding lights of the Charter 77 movement in the late 1970s.

According to Jewish law he was not considered a Jew since he does not have a Jewish mother, but, Sidon told me, he had always *felt* Jewish, and a number of his plays involved Jewish themes or characters. Since childhood, he had identified with a scholarly ancestor, Rabbi Simeon Sidon, the rabbi of Trnava, now in Slovakia, who lived from 1815 to 1892. "He wrote books," Sidon said. "When I was little, I knew he was important. I didn't have any idea that I would become a rabbi, but this was a man who influenced me."

Increasingly drawn to religious Judaism, Sidon underwent formal conversion in 1978. (Oddly enough, one of Rabbi Simeon Sidon's most noted treatises was an 1850 work concerning the laws of circumcision—a procedure that it is essential for a male convert to undergo.) At about this time, he was forced to leave Czechoslovakia for political reasons and went to Heidelberg, Germany, where he immersed himself in Jewish studies.

"I was a dissident, but I was the leader of the group, too," he told me. "I realized after awhile that I was teaching people things but that I didn't know enough to be a teacher. This was after I converted. The situation was difficult. I didn't want to leave Czechoslovakia unless there was a good place I could go to, to study. I had a lot of reasons to leave, but I didn't want to go until I had arranged this. . . . I knew ever since 1968, when the Soviets invaded here, that the situation in Czechoslovakia could go up and down. . . . I didn't think I had enough strength to become a rabbi; I thought I would complete my studies in Germany and then simply become a teacher."

The "Velvet Revolution"—the peaceful mass protests that began in November 1989 and swept the Communists from power in Czechoslovakia—changed everything. For forty years, the regime had carried out a policy of persecution aimed at stifling Jewish religious and cultural life. It had forbidden or strictly limited contact with international Jewish organizations; it had restricted both worship and secular activities; it had prevented regular contact with Israel. The state-appointed Jewish leadership had followed the party line and had routinely issued statements critical of Israel. They had also supported the state's use of force in putting down antigovernment demonstrations. Just six months before the revolution, in a letter to these local Jewish leaders, a group of young Prague Jews had warned that Jewish life in Czechoslovakia was "in danger of extinction."

As I sat in the congregation at Sidon's inaugural ceremony, I vividly recalled an earlier Jewish gathering in Prague. It had been in November 1989, less than one week before the Velvet Revolution, when Edgar Bronfman had made his first official visit to Prague as president of the World Jewish Congress. Bronfman, tall, tanned, and elegant in his beautifully cut suit, had addressed a small crowd of Prague Jews who assembled to meet him in the dark-paneled function room on the top floor of the the Jewish Town Hall. They were anxious and eager at the same time, and it was a touching, memorable moment. His brief spreech had sounded like an unrealistic pep talk, but given the events that exploded only a few days later, it had turned out to be uncannily prophetic.

"The winds of freedom are blowing across the world like a gale," Bronfman had said. "I don't like to use the word 'democracy,' but prefer to say that there is a new era dawning on everyone, that people won't be governed without their consent. In Eastern Europe, we see a non-Communist government in Poland. We see government in Hungary by a party that used to be Communist but now is not. In East Germany there is the promise of free elections under the eyes of the entire world. I have been told and am convinced that here too things will change along these lines. It is important that the Jewish people in Eastern Europe are beginning to feel closer together. It is heartbreakingly sad that there are so few Jews left, but we did meet in the synagogue and we did meet here. The Jewish world will go from strength to strength. We have a mission—to teach others the way of the Lord. I said a silent prayer for Jewish unity and the state of Israel. . . . Freedom is blowing, blowing for all of us."

One of the first acts of the new, post-Communist government led by President Václav Havel was to reinstitute full religious freedom. Jewish spiritual and cultural life embarked on a renaissance, and in April 1990, Havel became the first leader from the newly emerging East-Central European democracies to visit Israel. Then, in the summer of 1990, the incumbent rabbi in Prague, Daniel Mayer, was forced to resign after admitting that he had been a police informer under the Communists. The new, post-Communist Jewish community leaders called on Sidon to become the new rabbi and sent him to a seminary in Israel to complete his studies.

A stocky man with thick glasses, a thick brown beard, wide-spaced front teeth, and an infectious laugh, Sidon chain-smoked as we sat talking in a dusty little side office upstairs at the Jewish Town Hall. (His own office—the rabbi's big office—was undergoing renovation.) I had waited for him nearly two hours after the time we had set to meet, and he was apologetic about his lateness. He had had to go out to northern Bohemia to certify a margarine factory as *kosher* and had taken the opportunity to visit nearby Terezín, to pay homage at the place where his father and tens of thousands of other Czech Jews—

many of them so assimilated that they did not consider themselves Jewish until the Nazis rounded them up—had died or been incarcerated before being deported to Auschwitz and other death camps.

From Rabbi Löw on down, Sidon's rabbinical predecessors include many of the great names of Central European Jewry. Intellectually Sidon follows in the footsteps of Kafka and other influential writers of the nineteenth and twentieth centuries. He is aware of the power of this double lineage but drapes its mantle loosely over his baggy, dark suit. He himself undergoes transformations: When he chants the ancient prayers in the seven-hundred-year-old sanctuary of the Old-New Synagogue, enveloped head to foot in a blue-striped *tallis,* he blends with the medieval surroundings. You can feel the power of the past as he rocks and bows his body with the blessings. Yet he is a thoroughly modern man, too. Cigarette in hand, leaning against the counter of the community's kosher restaurant, and leafing through a newspaper, he looks like any other rumpled intellectual who simply dropped in for a meal.

"From one side," he told me, "you can look at all those big names who went before me, from Rabbi Löw on down—and then, here I am, so very small, like this"—he held finger and thumb so that they were nearly touching. "But given the situation now, I think I am the right person to be here. If a big rabbi, say from Israel or the United States, came here, he couldn't have the same connections with the community that I do. It wouldn't just be a language problem— he'd be like Gulliver, too big. Now, I don't think a big rabbi would come here and put on airs and act like 'I'm the most important one here and you should listen to me.' But for the people in the community it would still be hard. . . . And I know that *I* couldn't be a rabbi anywhere else. . . ."

SIDON DESCRIBED THE PROGRESSION of his life, his return to Judaism, his becoming rabbi of Prague, as a circle. To my eyes, that circle is one of many that make up Jewish Prague. During repeated visits, I have grown to view Jewish presence here as a series of circles, circles within circles: like a bull's-eye. I imagine them centered on the centuries-old medieval ghetto, where today's Jewish community still has its headquarters, and then stretching out, further and further, like widening ripples in water, to the very outskirts of town. Memory is concentrated in the center, in the Inner Circle: Here Jewish legacy is cultivated—even exploited—as part of the ancient fabric of the city. In the outer rings, memory dims, even dies.

Other circles exist, too—circles of intellect, circles of accomplishment, social circles, circles of tradition—that trace their own intersecting paths on top of the bull's-eye.

All these circles set my own pattern for the exploration of Jewish Prague. I started in the center and worked my way outward, moving away from the places where Jewish memory was strongest toward where it dimmed and disappeared. Prague was one of the most glorious Jewish centers in Europe and gave birth to some of the most famous Jewish legends. Today it has the continent's most celebrated complex of Jewish monuments and museum collections.

I wanted to discover just what traces of Jewish Prague still exist and how they had survived. Half a century after the Holocaust, a handful of years after the ouster of repressive communism, I wanted, too, to observe the role these traces played in the fabric and consciousness of the present-day city—the physical city of brick and stone, the living city at the pulse of post-Communist Europe, the metaphorical city of myth and loss and memory, the Golden City, fame-crowned Prague.

The Inner Circle

The heart of Jewish Prague beats close to that of Old Prague itself: the old Jewish Town, the ghetto, place of shadows and legend on the low-lying right bank of the Vltava—the Moldau—River near the Old Town Square, where Prague's Jews were compelled to live from the Middle Ages until the middle of the nineteenth century, when emancipation granted by the Hapsburg monarchs allowed them to move out of that decrepit, damp quarter into more salubrious parts of town.

This is "ground zero" for Jewish Prague: stomping ground for all the old heroes and villains, background setting for all the old legends, and—particularly since the Velvet Revolution helped make Prague one of the continent's hottest tourist destinations—Europe's all-time biggest Jewish tourist attraction. These days, it seems almost a theme park of Jewish life and lore, where the habits and ancient habitats of an almost extinct people can be viewed on the spot, and where contemporary specimens may be seen as they pray and consume kosher food and go about their other daily business.

Here, within the space of a few square blocks, are the handful of historic remnants that were left standing when a massive, turn-of-the-century urban renewal project transformed the medieval ghetto from a romantic, if slumlike, welter of crooked alleys, crowded shops, dank, dim courtyards, and atmospheric—if often dilapidated—old buildings into the proudly prosperous bourgeois neighborhood of broad streets and ostentatious dwellings (with modern plumbing) we see today.

Here stand the *Altneu,* or Old-New, Synagogue and the Old Jewish Cemetery, two of Europe's most precious Jewish relics. Here, too, stands the Jewish Town Hall, a dusty pink building whose famous clock has Hebrew letters rather than numbers and hands that move backward to point to the time. There are also four or five other synagogues in the immediate area. None but the Altneu, though, is used for services; the others now form part of the Jewish Museum, exhibition halls for Europe's richest collection of Judaica, a collection that has rightly become known as a "Precious Legacy."

A Jewish museum was founded in Prague in 1906, partly as a place to display the ritual and artistic objects from three ancient synagogues that were razed as part of the urban renewal project that destroyed the old ghetto. The present Jewish Museum owes its vast collection to the fact that the Nazis destroyed more than 150 individual Jewish communities in Bohemia and Moravia. As they systematically rounded up Jews and sent them to their deaths, the Nazis confiscated Jewish treasures from homes, libraries, synagogues, and study houses and brought them to Prague, where they planned to display them in what they foresaw as a "museum of an extinct people."

A group of Jewish scholars in Prague had urged the Nazis to collect this material, in the hope that Jewish treasures, if not the Jews who used them, could at least be saved. As fellow Jews around them were deported to the death camps, these scholars labored meticulously to document this trove of more than two hundred thousand objects—until they, too, like all the others, were shipped off to their doom.

After the war, the Communist regime took over this vast collection as the State Jewish Museum. The Nazis already had displayed a selection of the treasures in some of the synagogues in Prague's old Jewish Town. These synagogues, left empty by the destruction of Prague's Jews, were in turn taken over by the State Jewish Museum and converted into its galleries. Even the Old Cemetery passed from Jewish community hands to become simply a museum exhibit. Following the ouster of the Communists, the slow process of transferring museum property and premises back to the Jews was begun.

ON A LATE SUMMER MORNING in 1992, just before the museum's 10 A.M. opening time, I station myself on a street corner near the Old-New Synagogue and watch the tour groups begin to converge. One moment the streets are empty; the next moment it is as if a floodgate has been opened. They come from all directions; they seem to encompass all nations: Italian, French, German, American, English, Japanese. Old, young, middle aged, they make their way down the streets in flocks, in clumps, in droves, following guides hoisting umbrellas or colored flags in the air.

They have set routes: tour of the Jewish Town; tour of Old Prague. A stop at the Old-New Synagogue; a stop at the Old Jewish Cemetery; maybe a poke of the nose inside one of the other old synagogues to see the exhibition of Jewish silver or Jewish textiles, or the exhibit of drawings by children who died in the Terezín concentration camp. Then on to the next stop. Or maybe, at lunchtime, a meal at the kosher restaurant in the Jewish Town Hall, where local Jewish community members sit apart at reserved tables and pay a tenth of what foreigners are charged. Germans and Japanese, Italians and Americans eat chicken soup and overcooked brisket; an autographed photograph of Barbra Streisand—a souvenir from when parts of her movie *Yentl* were filmed in and around Prague—gleams benevolently in soft focus from a frame above the cash desk at the door.[1]

Rush, rush, rush.

The streets are full; it is hard to pass; groups and languages mingle. I can tag along with anyone and no one knows the difference. There is a jam at the entrance to the Altneu Synagogue, a crush waiting to enter the Old Cemetery. "*Andiamo, andiamo avanti!*—Come

PRAGUE: Crowds of tourists around the Old–New Synagogue.

on, let's go! Let's move on!" a perspiring Italian guide shouts to his charges, hustling them along; then he catches the eye of another guide and exchanges a sly glance.

Inside the Old-New Synagogue, there is a continuous fugue of tour groups. They come in through a gothic portal topped by a carving of a grapevine with twelve bunches of grapes, representing the twelve tribes of Israel. They stand at the same place for a few minutes; they hear the same guides' spiel in English, Italian, German, French, Czech; they move on in a clockwise direction around the gothic sanctuary. Men who do not have hats with them pick up pointed cardboard skullcaps at the door; one man instead covers his head with a paper napkin that lies flat on his bald spot; another piles a sweater on top of his head; boys pull up the hoods of their sweatshirts; one teenager covers his head with a Palestinian *keffiah*. The air is heavy with breath and the shuffling of bodies. Bored teenagers on school trips flirt behind the teacher's back. A bleached blond woman from the Jewish community stands at the door, shepherding people along: "Go on, move around, please!"

The synagogue is an austere gothic structure built nine steps below the level of the street, with a sharp, peaked roof decorated with brick gables and distinctive sawtooth edging. The oldest functioning synagogue in Europe, it was erected as the "new" synagogue, the second in the ghetto, in the late thirteenth century and many years later received its strange name, *Altneu—Alte Neu,* or "Old-New"—after still newer synagogues were built in the quarter nearby. (Legends popularized in the nineteenth century also suggested that the synagogue may have received its name from the Hebrew word *al-tenai,* meaning "conditionally," indicating that the synagogue was to be considered only temporary, until the Temple in Jerusalem should be rebuilt.)

The Altneu Synagogue was already old six hundred years ago, on the last day of Passover 1389, when a bloody pogrom was unleashed in the ghetto, touched off by the accusation that Jews had desecrated the Christian Host. Most of Prague's Jews, as many as three thousand or more people, perished in the carnage. Jews, the story goes, took refuge in the synagogue and were slaughtered there; it is said that the blood from the victims was left where it had splashed high on the walls until it faded away, to testify to the savagery of the massacre.[2] Rabbi Avigdor Kara—poet and scholar and adept at the mystical Kabbalah—was one of the survivors. The elegy he composed to commemorate the massacre, "All of the Hardships That Befell Us," is a classic lamentation and is still recited today during Yom Kippur services in the synagogue:

> More than one father killed his own son, and more than one mother slew the very child she had carried in her womb, to thus spare it from being forced to abjure the faith of its ancestors. It was, as it is written, a sacrifice of innocents, of innocent lambs.
>
> And so fell our [community leader], a man honored by all. And so fell the rabbi, a rare sage and benefactor, along with his brother and his only son. Let us remember him, along with his God! . . .

Too many fell to be named: young men and women, old men and babes in arms. . . . They even demolished the cemetery, the place of eternal freedom where the bones of my ancestors lie at rest. . . .

So much torment has engulfed us—yet we have not forgotten the name of God! . . . The days of hope must come! Injustice and desolation must be driven out! Let us return together from exile and . . . let the prophecy of Isaiah, our constant comfort, come to pass: "For my salvation is near to come, and my favor to be revealed."

The synagogue's double-naved sanctuary is centered on a *bimah,* or reading desk, standing in the middle of the hall between two lofty pillars and surrounded by a cagelike, late gothic wrought-iron grille whose uprights are topped with burnished balls; wooden pews with flip-up seats line the walls around the room. Ornate chandeliers descend on long cables from the steeply vaulted ceiling.

Above the bimah hangs a stiff, faded red banner, descendant of the one originally presented to the Jews of Prague by King Charles IV in 1357, who granted to them the right of bearing it as a sign of their independence. The present banner is a restoration of the already patched original that was carried out in 1716 to honor the birth of the then-Emperor's son, as a Hebrew text proclaims in fittingly lofty language:

> Deputies of the Lord, the whole land is full of His glory. In 1357 the Emperor Charles IV granted the Jews of Prague the privilege of carrying a banner. This banner was repaired during the reign of the Emperor Ferdinand. Damaged in the course of long years, it has now been repaired in honor of our lord the Emperor Charles VI. Praise be to His Majesty on the occasion of the birth of his son, the Archduke Leopold. May his glory be raised to happiness. In the year of Tikon may his Empire be strong. Year 1716.

The banner bears the representation of the three-cornered hat medieval Prague Jews were at times compelled to wear, but more important, it also bears a six-pointed Star of David, "the Shield of David," which became the official symbol of the Prague Jewish community. It was the first time the Star of David was used as the official symbol of any Jewish community, and it was from Prague that the practice spread to become universal.

In the center of the east wall, in the direction of Jerusalem, five steps lead up to the Ark—the *Aron ha Kodesh*—which holds the Torah scrolls in a niche behind an iron door surrounded by carved pillars and a pediment decorated with sculpted grapevines.

Six days a week this synagogue is a tourist attraction; morning services are held before the ten A.M. opening. Only on Sabbath and Jewish holidays are the crowds barred completely; then men wrapped in vast prayer shawls perform their devotions in the ancient sanctuary, while women, segregated in a side hall according to Orthodox practice, watch through tapering narrow slits that give distorted visions of the room—distant, as if seen from the wrong end of a telescope, as if looking back through time to the Middle Ages.

ALL AT ONCE, as if by magic, all the tour groups make an exit together; it's like those odd moments at a party when everyone suddenly stops talking. For a few minutes, only a handful of people remain, seated in the pews around the edges of the room. In the respite before the assault begins anew, I feel the old building sigh. It's a building that *would* sigh, a building that over the centuries has developed a persona that has made it rich subject matter for artists, storytellers, dreamers, and poets.

According to one of the legends connecting the name *Altneu* with the Hebrew word *al-tenai* ("conditionally"), the synagogue was constructed by angels using stones from the Temple of Jerusalem *on the condition* that the stones were to be returned when the Temple was rebuilt; another legend says angels brought it directly to Prague from Jerusalem, *on the condition* that it never be changed or repaired. Still another legend says that the angels came back, in the form of doves (or a dove), during a devastating fire that swept the ghetto in 1558: The doves (or dove) perched on the synagogue's roof (or hovered over the synagogue), fanning away the flames with their (or its) wings and saving the synagogue from the conflagration.

Rabbi Judah ben Bezalel Löw (or Loew), the legendary *MaHa-RaL*— "Most Venerated Teacher and Rabbi"—of Prague, the most famous of all Prague's long line of famous rabbis, preached and studied here. The mystic and possibly magical philosopher and scholar lived from about 1512 to 1609 and served as Chief Rabbi of Prague during the reign of the eccentric, melancholy Rudolf II, Holy Roman Emperor and King of Bohemia, whose preoccupation with the realms of art, science, magic, and alchemy stamped the Prague of his age as a city of wonder, mystery, and imagination—an image that has endured for four centuries and is still kept quite deliberately alive.

Looming against this background, Rabbi Löw's dramatic figure has become a leading protagonist in the folk tales of both Jewish and gentile Prague to such an extent that, for most people, the legends have usurped the memory of his importance as a scholar, teacher, and writer on Jewish religion and philosophy. Rabbi Löw is said to have dabbled in alchemy and magic and to have used supernatural powers, for example, to halt a plague that killed only Jewish children. On another occasion, it is said, an angry mob hurled rocks and mud at him, but these turned to flowers in the air before they fell. He is also supposed to have received a visit from the Emperor in his old, cramped house in the ghetto: Instead of dark rooms and dank corridors, the Emperor magically found himself in a palace.

The legends grew up long after Rabbi Löw died and may have been spawned by a mysterious audience he seems really to have had with Rudolf II. David Gans, a friend and contemporary of Rabbi Löw and a brilliant mathematician, historian, and astronomer, recorded this audience—said to have taken place on February 16, 1592—in his memoirs, but revealed nothing about the subject of the discussion between the two great men. Whatever Rudolf and the rabbi talked about, Gans wrote, remained a closely guarded secret—"closed, sealed and concealed," as he put it—and thus open to centuries of storytelling and speculation.

It was here in the Old-New Synagogue itself, according to the most famous legend about him, that Rabbi Löw magically breathed life into clay and created the *golem*, an automaton, a humanoid robot, a man without a soul who served as the rabbi's assistant and defended the Jews from attack until he escaped from control and wreaked havoc and destruction with his supernatural strength. It is here, according to the stories, in the attic of this synagogue, that the rabbi hid the clay body of the golem after he removed the magical amulet bearing the magic word that had brought it to life. As Yiddish writer I. L. Peretz recounted in one of the numerous versions of the golem legend that have come down over the years:

PRAGUE: Models of golems lined up for sale on a stand in Old Jewish Town.

To this day the golem lies hidden in the attic of the Prague syna-gogue, covered with cobwebs that extend from wall to wall. No liv-ing creature may look at it, particularly women in pregnancy. No one may touch the cobwebs, for whoever touches them dies. . . . The golem, you see, has not been forgotten. It is still here! But the Name by which it could be called to life in a day of need, the Name has disappeared. And the cobwebs grow and grow, and no one may touch them.[3]

When the journalist Egon Erwin Kisch, a friend of Franz Kafka, went up into the attic to investigate in the early part of this century, he found nothing but dust and gravel and a bat hanging upside down: "If the clay creature of the great rabbi Löw is buried there, it is buried there until judgment day. If it were exhumed, the house of God would collapse."[4]

The golem myth became attached to Rabbi Löw only in the nine-teenth or possibly the late eighteenth century—more or less two cen-turies after his death. The creation of artificial life has had its place in Jewish mystical writing—the Kabbalah—since ancient times; there is even a mention of the creation of an artificial man in the Talmud. The concept blossomed from the early Middle Ages onward, when there was much learned discussion about specific recipes and incantations for bringing clay to life; most of these involved combinations of Hebrew letters and the sacred name of God.

Rabbi Löw, however, was not the first sixteenth-century scholar credited with actually creating a golem. In the middle of the seventeenth century, published accounts described how the Polish Kabbalist, Rabbi Eliahu of Chełm, the Ba'al ha-Shem (Master of the Name), who died in 1583, brought an artificial man to life but had to destroy it when it got out of control. Many years later, two of Eliahu's descendants vigorously debated the pros and cons of whether a golem could be considered a man, and thus form part of a *minyan,* the ten-man quorum required for Jewish services. After much philosophical consideration, they brought in a verdict: "No."

Somehow and at some point, these early legends about Rabbi Eliahu were transferred to Rabbi Löw, possibly because of all the other legends about him and, possibly, as the Czech scholar Vladimír Sadek has suggested, by followers of Hasidism in Eastern Europe, who considered Rabbi Löw a precursor of the Hasidic movement and who enthusiastically studied his religious and philosophical teachings.[5] Followers of Hasidic rebbes delight in telling stories about the miracles wrought by their masters. What would have been more natural than to weave stories, too, around such a towering figure as Rabbi Löw?

There's no historical evidence that Rabbi Löw ever tried to bring an inanimate being to life or that he was involved in any magical activity. On the contrary, he condemned sorcery in the strongest of terms and even wrote that anyone who used magic for worldly reasons deserved to die. In the very same treatise, however, he stressed that anything is possible in the name of God. Since God's name figured prominently in various recipes for bringing a golem to life, this passage, too, may have suggested Rabbi Löw as a golem maker.[6]

In whatever way the connection was first made, by the latter part of the nineteenth century Rabbi Eliahu of Chełm was all but forgotten. Rabbi Löw instead was indelibly identified as the mystical and mythical golem maker—and had become a prominent figure in the dozens and dozens of stories, plays, films, novels, and visual works of art inspired by the golem story up to this very day.[7] So intimately linked with Prague was this connection that the city fathers erected a striking statue of Rabbi Löw as part of the decoration of its art nouveau New Town Hall, built in 1910 a few steps from both the old ghetto area and Old Town Square. The sculpture shows the ancient, long-bearded rabbi recoiling in horror as a muscular, nude young woman—representing death—clings to his robes and tries to gain hold of his arm.

IN THE OLD-NEW SYNAGOGUE, one of the pews to the right of the Ark is bigger than the others and is marked with the Star of David: This, legend has it, was where the great Rabbi Löw had his seat. When Jerome Rothenberg, the American poet whose Holocaust poem, "Khurbn," had such an impact on me, visited Prague in the mid-1980s, he sat in the venerated pew and found himself thinking of legend and history and the ghosts of all the tens and thousands and millions of Jews who had lost their lives in waves of persecution from earliest times through the Holocaust. The tangle of thoughts became a poem, "Golem & Goddess":

> into the dark of Prague
> the golem walks
> backwards in the familiar stride
> empty of longing
> a madman takes   o Loew Loew
> in your chair I sat
> the shadows in your books
> so heavy
> hurt my eyes & brought
> memories of the children
> changing to skeletons
> you my old rabbi couldn't
> bring to life again
> though with your stones I spoke
> & heard
> old voices through old cities
> the victims of the century
> that the century will bring together
> will offer their own flesh to the hill

somewhere beyond the city
the goddess once built with
the bones of dogs & children
a thousand cities spring from
over europe   & the goddess
still waits above the moldau
the daughter of the morning star
who feeds her son the moon
with children's blood[8]

Rabbi Löw's extraordinarily long life (he was close to one hundred when he died) led to the legend that he battled mightily with the Angel of Death, who finally tricked him by masquerading as a rose.

The rabbi is buried in the Old Jewish Cemetery, toward the back, near the wall, in a massive tomb that also contains the grave of his wife, Perl. The tomb is shaped like a little house with tall facades masking the gables and is decorated with carvings of a pine cone, bunches of grapes, and a lion—the symbol for the Tribe of Judah or the name Judah, as well as for names like Loeb, Leib, or Löw, which mean "lion" in Hebrew. There are legends even about this tomb: It is said, for example, that the spirit of the rabbi managed to move the monument a little so that the monument of his grandson, Samuel, who died in 1655, could be squeezed in alongside—and there indeed is Samuel's tomb, a small, narrow tombstone tilted over, next to the tomb of his ancestor.

Rabbi Löw's tomb is a place of pilgrimage for thousands who have elevated the rabbi to the sphere of the mystic. Every possible ledge of the tomb is covered with pebbles placed in remembrance. Every crack and crevice is stuffed with kvittleh, slips of paper on which the pious, or merely superstitious, have written supplications: "Peace." "Hope." "Long Life."

Avigdor Kara, too—the "beloved elegist" and survivor of the 1389 massacre—is buried in the Old Jewish Cemetery. The epitaph on his tomb describes him as "a man who understood sweet songs, taught the Torah in public and in private, and was well versed in the teachings of all the books of wisdom and the Holy Writings." Kara died in 1439, and his tombstone is the oldest identifiable gravestone in what became the final resting place for countless thousands of

PRAGUE: The Old Jewish Cemetery.

Prague Jews from the time it opened in the early fifteenth century to the last burial in 1787.

Some twelve thousand remaining gravestones crowd the irregular, walled-in patch of ground. Eroded, tilted, crammed together in clumps, they riot over the hummocky earth where, for lack of space, the dead were buried layer upon layer, as many as twelve layers deep. Trees grown up over the years shade meandering paths through the hilly forest of tombstones. The monuments—to scholars, to tailors, to pharmacists, to merchants, to faithful wives, to pious makers of ritual fringes—comprise an eerie archive chiseled in stone of Prague's Jewish history from the Middle Ages to the threshold of modern times. Witness this list of the occupations of seventeenth-century Jews in Prague, compiled from epitaphs:

Tailors (many), shoemakers, tanners, dyers, furriers, hatmakers, glovemaker, harnessmakers, saddler, butchers, carpenter, locksmiths, hatchetmakers, nailmaker, tinman, ironmongers, glaziers, potters, quiltmaker, upholsterer, candlemaker, writers, hospital nurses, domestic servants, cooks, citron importers, porters, innkeeper, pastrycooks, vintners, publicans, spirit-dealers, tobacconist, watchmen, street police, toll-keeper, woodcutters, timber-merchant, horse-dealer, charcoal burner, architect, painters, musicians, singers, string-maker, goldsmiths (many), pearl-setters, lace-maker, stone-graver, optician, glass polisher, wheelwrights, wagon-makers, doctors (many), barbers, apothecaries, midwives, printers (many), booksellers, bookbinders.[9]

Crowds swirl among the graves, along the winding paths, amid the hummocks and hollows.

For well over one hundred and fifty years artists and lovers of the unusual have been captivated by this bristling forest of stones. Nineteenth-century painters sketched romantic views here of crooked tombstones lost amid rampant vegetation; old pictures show visitors in frock coats and top hats solemnly admiring the wild scene as if lost in some strange wilderness, pointing at the beautifully carved epitaphs, the sculpted reliefs that often reflect the deceased person's name or profession, or the rich ornamentation denoting wealth and position.

Today it is the turn of tourists en masse. It is said that one million tourists—or more—come each year now to Prague's Jewish Town, and all of them go to the Old Jewish Cemetery. So many tourists make their way to this legendary place that even they themselves have spawned legends: I was told—quite seriously—by one visitor that he had been told by someone at the Jewish community office that the ground level of the cemetery had sunk by half a meter due to the tramping feet of the tourist traffic. At the entrance, a sign in several languages warns visitors of pickpockets.

"It really put me off Prague," said Adam, a Jewish student from Harrow, England, who was making a tour of Jewish places in Eastern and Central Europe. "I looked in the Old Cemetery and walked right out because of all the tourists there. It was offensive. It made me sick. There they were; they were climbing on the gravestones, taking pictures. I saw a German tourist write a kvittel on a bus ticket or something and laugh while he was doing it. I picked it up after him; I couldn't read it, as it was in German, but it was obviously offensive, so I threw it away."[10]

ON THE SIDEWALK of the street leading from the Old-New Synagogue to the cemetery, stallkeepers sell postcards and compact discs, little etchings of Jewish sights, miniature plaster golems, and golems made out of gingerbread, all identical, all modeled on the golem as it appeared in the 1952 Czech movie *The Emperor and the Golem*: a menacingly massive and clumsy, almost headless form held together

PRAGUE: A woman sells pebbles painted with Stars of David in the Old Jewish Town.

by bolts and a big belt. The vendors sell *yarmulkes* (bobby pins included), mezuzahs, pieces of honey cake, and necklace pendants made from tiny bottles containing, according to the labels, "soil of the old Jewish Ghetto of Prague."

Souvenir shops sell pop-up postcards of the Old Jewish Cemetery and T-shirts bearing a variety of Jewish or pseudo-Jewish designs: Hebrew letters, candlesticks, abstract renditions of Rabbi Löw's tomb, the massive golem, and at least four representations of Franz Kafka. A few new boutiques sell high-quality Jewish souvenirs, including antique candlesticks and seder plates, and Kiddush cups in Bohemian crystal.

A woman sits puffing a cigarette behind a sidewalk stand that displays execrable kitsch at exorbitant prices: simple pebbles painted with Jewish symbols and advertised in various languages as "Stones for Luck, hand made," "Stones of David," and "Stones and Paperweights for Happiness." ("Jewish pet rocks," comments an American tourist looking over my shoulder.) Prices range up to ten dollars and more.

I take a picture, and the woman is outraged. "You can't take a picture of me without asking first!" she fumes. Facing her, my back to the jostling crowd that fills the street, the tourists shuttling back and forth from the synagogue to the cemetery to the Kafka museum to Old Town Square to the next stop, cameras click-click-clicking miles of film of anything that looks old—of graves, of museum halls that were once synagogues whose last congregrants were herded away to their deaths—I only glare. Deliberately, I take another picture of her, then slowly turn and walk away.

AROUND THE CORNER on the edge of the Old Cemetery, the orange-yellow Pinkas Synagogue, the second oldest surviving synagogue in the ghetto, stands as a memorial to Czech victims of the Holocaust, and here I find an unexpected respite from the crowds and commercialism.

While hordes throng the Old Cemetery and clog the entrance to the Old-New Synagogue, only a few hushed individuals enter what is one of the most impressive, and one of the most subtle, monuments in Old Jewish Town. Originally built in the fifteenth century as the private prayer house of the wealthy Horowitz family, the synagogue was enlarged and embellished in the 1530s. It was, as a Hebrew plaque in the entranceway, now translated into several languages, attests, "a jewel of an edifice."

And it still is today. The stark emptiness of the gothic sanctuary, bathed in pastel colors and a cool half-light from stained-glass windows, is offset by a riotous decorative iron railing enclosing the bimah in the center of the hall. Through the pale-colored glass of the tall windows, shadowy silhouettes of trees—and even gravestones—can be made out. They merge with the shadows of ancient frescoes on the walls—dim flowers, each petal distinct, and dim echoes of Hebrew inscriptions. There is an underwater quality to the light and atmosphere; it is as if submerged. The few visitors speak in whispers; they point; they crane their heads up at the vaulted ceiling; their footsteps echo on the stone floor.[11]

The Pinkas Synagogue was reopened to the public in 1991 after having been closed for more than twenty years during a drawn-out restoration process that many charge was deliberately prolonged by the Communists to bar visitors from a building that had been transformed after the war into a Holocaust memorial: On the interior walls had been inscribed, one by one, all the names of the 77,297 Bohemian and Moravian Jews killed by the Nazis.

The synagogue was closed in 1968, the year after Czechoslovakia and most other Communist states broke off relations with Israel following the the Six Day War. The official reason for the closing was to repair damage caused by ground water soaking into the foundations and rising into the walls; due to its low-lying position and poor drainage, the synagogue had been flooded a number of times over the centuries. The building then remained closed after vaulted underground chambers, including an ancient *mikvah,* or ritual bath, were discovered during the waterproofing process.

During the waterproofing, reconstruction, and archeological work, the 77,297 names painted on the inner walls were removed. The official reason was that they too had become damaged by damp, and/or that they had to be removed in order to waterproof the walls anyway. Years of discussions went on about how—or even whether—the names should be replaced. Nonetheless, during the entire time the synagogue was closed to visitors, some twenty-three years, guidebooks continued to list it as a memorial to the victims of Nazi persecution, and periodic progress reports were consistently optimistic that it would be reopened soon.

"After having finished the restoration of the stonework, which is not going to take much more time, the interior of the synagogue will be painted and the names of the Jewish victims of the Holocaust will be inscribed on the walls again," stated an article in 1983 in the State Jewish Museum's bulletin, *Judaica Bohemiae*. Three years later, the "final phase" of restoration was said to be "under way," but the names had not been reinscribed. Three years after that, in 1989, the walls were still bare; the synagogue was still closed; and officials told me the museum was looking into a plan to print the names on sheets of Plexiglas and hang these on the walls.

The restoration of the synagogue—and particularly the Holocaust memorial—became an emotional, and more than an emotional, issue.

"It was closed. I couldn't get in when I visited Prague," an American woman whose grandparents had been killed by the Nazis told me. "I was upset. My grandparents are not buried in any grave; this would have been their only memorial place, the only place I could have said Kaddish for them."

"It's a political question," Jewish intellectual Desider Galský told me in November 1989, a week before the Velvet Revolution. Galský, who less than a month later became president of the Jewish community—a position he held until his death in a car accident in November 1990—at that point was unwilling to speak on the record or be quoted by name in the foreign press. Under the Communists, what we were talking about—the restoration of a monument to Czech Jewish victims of the Holocaust—was virtually a taboo subject. "The Plexiglas idea is crazy," Galský complained. "It would be like hanging up posters. They are trying to convince us that this is the best way because the colors of the names printed on Plexiglas would be better. It would be better if we simply had the names painted in black, right on the wall."

Work finally began on reinscribing the 77,297 names in August 1992, nearly three years after the ouster of the Communists: They were being painted, one by one, in the same script and in the same way as they had originally been painted in the 1950s, directly onto the walls of the sanctuary. The official explanation of why the names had been removed in the first place had changed, however: They had been, according to a notice in the synagogue, "mostly unnecessarily removed during the reconstruction."[12]

"The official reason to remove the names was the humidity," Tomáš Kraus, secretary of the Czech Jewish Federation, told me. "But someone, somewhere, said that it was because of Israeli aggression [in the Six Day War]. No one has written proof of this, but it is in the framework of official anti-Zionist policy of the Communist government."

Said Jewish Museum director Dr. Lyudmila Kybalová, "Under the Communists, they didn't want to speak of Jewish victims."

Outer Circles

The outer circles ringing Prague's Jewish bull's-eye stretch from the borders of ancient Jewish Town all the way to the farthest edge of today's city. They include integral parts of historic Prague, as well as distant suburbs that until the early part of this century—or in some cases, even later—were independent villages.

Jews settled in some of these communities as early as the sixteenth and seventeenth centuries; indeed, these places served as havens of refuge for thousands of Prague Jews when expulsion orders, fires, floods, or epidemics drove Jews from Jewish Town itself. Early Jewish industrialists had already established factories in a few inner suburbs in the early nineteenth century, but the Jewish population of suburban communities mushroomed only after the ghetto was abolished a few decades later. At that time, Jewish Town was formally united with Prague's four historic "cities"—Old Town (Staré Město), New Town (Nové Město), Lesser Town (Malá Strana), and the Castle (Hradčany)—simply as Prague's Fifth District, Josefov, named after Josef II, the first Hapsburg emperor to grant Jews formal, if limited, civil rights.

More than ten thousand Jews lived in Prague in the mid-nineteenth century, making it one of the largest Jewish communities in Central Europe. The Jews who moved out of the old ghetto into the suburbs and other more prosperous neighborhoods were joined by Jews from small provincial towns and villages who flocked to Prague and other big cities in such numbers that many historic rural Jewish communities had vanished altogether by 1890, leaving little Jewish ghost towns all over Bohemia and Moravia. By that year, about twenty-seven thousand Jews lived in and around Prague. Fewer than one-quarter of the residents of old Jewish Town were Jewish, but seven distinct Jewish communities flourished in various new and old suburbs.

Splendid new synagogues with domes, towers, choir lofts, and organs reflected the prosperity and worldliness of the increasingly assimilated Prague Jews. They included the exuberant Moorish-style Spanish Synagogue, built on the site of the former Old Synagogue at the edge of Jewish Town, sumptuous synagogues in the industrial suburbs of Karlín and Smíchov, and the massive twin-towered synagogue in the posh new neighborhood of Vinohrady, just outside the city center. Built in 1896–1898 by architect Wilhelm Stiassny, it was the largest synagogue in Prague. It was destroyed in an air raid during World War II.

Stiassny's Jubilee Synagogue, where Karol Sidon was inaugurated as rabbi, was formally named the Emperor Franz Josef Jubilee Synagogue in honor of the Hapsburg emperor. The decision to build it was made in 1898, the fiftieth anniversary of Franz Josef's ascension to the throne. It was erected in 1905–1906 and was dedicated by loyal Jewish subjects in 1908 to honor the sixtieth year of the emperor's reign. Located on a stolidly bourgeois little side street between Wenceslas Square and the main train station, it was a replacement for the three ancient synagogues torn down in the urban renewal project that razed the ghetto. The street is called Jeruzalémská (Jerusalem Street), and the red-and-orange-striped facade, with its teal blue, Moorish-style horseshoe arches, false battlements, and slim-domed side turrets, stands out like an apparition under its layer of soot, a monument to the worldly assimilationist dreams of turn-of-the-century Prague Jews. "Do we not have one father? Were we not created by the same God?" reads a hopeful egalitarian inscription over the door. The wrought-iron gates are entwined with intricately worked wrought-iron grapevines, and Stars of David tip flagpoles.

The outer communities had their cemeteries, too, where expensive black marble obelisks, fancy mausoleums, and sculpted funerary monuments marked the final resting places of businessmen and

PRAGUE: Ornate, Moorish-style stripes and horseshoe arch of
the Jubilee Synagogue.

bankers, lawyers and merchants, artists and writers, doctors, teachers, and civil servants. Many of these people were leading figures of their day. Some achieved knighthood or other honors bestowed by the Hapsburg rulers; quite a few gained international renown.

FEW TOURISTS (and I would venture to say few people, Jewish or gentile) either know or care today about these outer Jewish settlements and their relics. Synagogues stand empty and unmarked, or now fulfill other functions. Vines and thick undergrowth shroud the fine tombstones; their only recent visitors, in some cases, have been vandals.

All of these forgotten and semiforgotten places, however, bear witness to important phases of Jewish history in Prague, and I felt it an important duty to seek them out. They are metaphorical mezuzahs documenting a past quite different from that of Rabbi Löw and Avigdor Kara. It is the past of a Jewish community whose attitudes and practices paralleled in many ways those of many contemporary American Jewish communities, including the one in which I grew up.

Many of those Prague Jews had emigrated to the big city from provincial villages where they—or at least their parents—had led traditional Orthodox lives, based on the home, the synagogue, and the marketplace, much the way my grandparents had lived before they came to America. These Jews of nineteenth- and twentieth-century Prague were increasingly secularized. They were, to a great extent, solidly middle or upper middle class, hoping to move higher; many were "four-day Jews," who went to services only during the High Holy Days and then again on the emperor's birthday, and that was it. They did not keep kosher or light the Sabbath candles; they did not know Hebrew or Yiddish. Intermarriage, as in present-day America, was endemic (by the 1930s, about one-quarter of all Bohemian Jews married out of the faith), and many Jews, trying hard to assimilate but still either coming up hard against the wall of anti-Semitism or at least never finding full acceptance, faced serious identity crises.

Dr. Kurt Wehle was secretary general of the Council of Jewish Religious Congregations in Bohemia and Moravia after the war from 1945 to 1948 and now lives in the United States. "I didn't go to synagogue regularly at all," he told me. He came to Prague in 1926 as a youth from a provincial town and lived in Vinohrady, the prosperous neighborhood with the biggest synagogue in the city. "My wife's parents went to synagogue sometimes, and we also went sometimes to the big *shul.* But we had no contact with the old Jewish Town. In the 1930s, my Jewish life was completely limited. I was a bank clerk, and I was studying law."

His wife, Hana, added, "I had a cousin who was Czech, Czech, Czech—he didn't want anything to do with Judaism. After he survived the concentration camp, he didn't want to read anything about the war, or anything like that. He was still totally non-Jewish. Then his children grew up, and he made a trip back; he visited Poland and Auschwitz. He began to teach, to feel, to be Jewish."

The Wehles and their generation grew up in the Czechoslovakia of Tomáš G. Masaryk, the philosopher and politician who spearheaded the cause of independence during World War I and in the waning days of the Austro-Hungarian Empire and became its first president when the independent Czechoslovak state was founded in 1918. Masaryk has his special place in Czechoslovak history, but also occupies a unique place for Jews. He wrote candidly that during his childhood in a small village on the Slovak-Moravian border he grew up in an atmosphere steeped in anti-Semitism. In 1914 he wrote:

> In the 1850s, every little Slovak in the region of Hodonín was educated in anti-Semitism by his family, school, church, and all society. Mother forbade us to go near the Lechners. The Jews, we were told, used the blood of Christian children for their Easter holidays. Like all my comrades among the youth of [the village], I always made a big circle around the Lechners' house. Every now and then I was warned against the Jews in school, as well as in the church . . . the superstition about the use of Christian blood was so deeply instilled in me that whenever I chanced to meet a Jew I never went close to him. I always stared at his fingers to see if there was blood on them. This stupid habit remained with me a long time.[13]

Despite this upbringing, Masaryk became a champion of Jewish rights and an outspoken opponent of anti-Semitism; as president of Czechoslovakia he even visited Jewish settlements in Palestine. In his most famous attack on anti-Semites and anti-Jewish superstition, Masaryk in 1899 boldly defended Leopold Hilsner, a Jewish ne'er-do-well accused of murdering a Christian girl near the southern Bohemian village of Polná and draining her blood for use in Jewish ritual. The case whipped up anti-Semitic hysteria that was manipulated by right-wing and clerical Czech nationalist politicians. As a result, Masaryk himself became the target of anti-Semitic mobs, but his courageous stand helped win him his reputation for integrity and the lasting admiration and gratitude of Jews.

"I grew up under Masaryk," said Mrs. Wehle. I'm glad that I lived twenty years under his leadership. I got a taste of love, respect, and admiration for the head of state. Masaryk was the one who, during the Hilsner affair, said that he would be ashamed to be the leader of such a nation that would believe such nonsense. He had the courage to stand up. He told how he had grown up in an anti-Semitic environment but also told that once, when he saw a Jewish boy praying at sunset, a respect for the Jewish faith suddenly hit him. After that, he philosophized about it and fought for justice."

FRANZ KAFKA'S FATHER, Hermann, an exact contemporary of Masaryk, was the upwardly-mobile-Jewish-businessman-from-the-provinces par excellence. The son of a dirt-poor kosher butcher in the Bohemian village of Osek, he went on the road as a peddler when he was a teenager and after serving in the Austrian army landed in Prague, where he eventually became proprietor of his own fancy-goods shop on the Old Town Square. As Franz Kafka's biographer Ernst Pawel has recounted, he named his first son in honor of the Emperor Franz Josef.[14]

Franz Kafka and his father had, to put it mildly, a difficult relationship: Hermann was a big, earthy, rather vulgar man who overwhelmed his delicate, introverted, oversensitive son. At the age of thirty-six, Franz Kafka let all the anger, hurt, frustration, and misdirected love spill out in an extraordinary fifty-page "Letter to His Father" that was never sent but that became one of Kafka's most famous autobiographical writings. In it he castigated Hermann, the son of pious Jews, for, among other things, carrying on a lip-service observance of Judaism, which Franz considered a spoiled legacy. Colored by pain, bitterness, and accumulated neurosis, the letter is a vivid portrait of the offhand Jewish practice of Prague's secularized turn-of-the-century Jewish bourgeoisie:

. . . as a boy, I could not understand how, with the insignificant scrap of Judaism you yourself possess, you could reproach me for not (if for no more than the sake of piety, as you put it) making an effort to cling to a similar insignificant scrap. It was indeed really, so far as I could see, a mere scrap, a joke, not even a joke. On four days of the year you went to the synagogue, where you were, to say the least of it, closer to the indifferent than to those who took it seriously, patiently went through the prayers by way of formality, sometimes amazed me by being able to show me in the prayer-book the passage that was being said at the moment, and for the rest, so long (and this was the main thing) as I was there in the syn-agogue I was allowed to hang about wherever I liked. And so I yawned and dozed through the many hours (I don't think I was ever again so bored, except later at dancing lessons) and did my best to enjoy the few little bits of variety there were, as for instance when the Ark of the Covenant was opened, which always reminded me of the shooting-stands where a cupboard door would open in the same way whenever one got a bull's-eye, only with the differ-ence that there something interesting always came out and here it was always just the same old dolls with no heads. . . . That was how it was in the synagogue, and at home it was if possible even more poverty-stricken, being confined to the first evening of Passover, which more and more developed into a farce, with fits of hysterical laughter, admittedly under the influence of the growing children. . . . And so there was the religious material that was handed on to me, to which may be added at most the out-stretched hand pointing to "the sons of the millionaire Fuchs," who were in the synagogue with their father at great festivals. How one could do anything better with this material than get rid of it as fast as possible was something I could not understand; precisely getting rid of it seemed to me the most effective act of "piety" one could perform.

. . . You had really brought some traces of Judaism with you from that ghetto-like little village community; it was not much and it dwindled a little more in town and while you were doing your mili-tary service, but still, the impression and memories of your youth did just about suffice to make some sort of Jewish life. . . . At bot-tom the faith that ruled your life consisted in your believing in the unconditional rightness of the opinions prevailing in a particular class of Jewish society, and hence actually, since these opinions were part and parcel of your own nature, in believing in yourself. Even in this there was still Judaism enough, but it was too little to be handed on to the child; it all trickled away while you were passing it on. . . . It was also impossible to make a child . . . understand that the few flimsy gestures you performed in the name of Judaism, and with an indifference in keeping with their flimsiness, could have any higher meaning.[15]

In the frenzy of identity seeking that exploded in Prague in the wake of the Velvet Revolution, Franz Kafka became not so much Franz Kafka the writer or even Franz Kafka the Jew, but Franz Kafka the native son; Franz Kafka the symbol; Franz Kafka the tourist attraction; Franz Kafka the nightmare figure constructed, sort of, out of someone's promotional idea of what he and his writings were about.

Kafka spent almost all of his short life in the city and had a rather morbid, love-hate fascination with the place that has become legendary. "Prague doesn't let go," he wrote to his friend Oskar Pollak in a celebrated (and much quoted) letter of December 20, 1902. "Neither of us. This little mother has claws. We ought to set fire to it at both ends, on the Vyšehrad and on the Hradčany, and maybe then it might be possible to escape."[16]

Kafka's works were all but banned outright in Communist Czechoslovakia except during a short period of officially sanctioned rehabilitation in the 1960s, centered on and after a conference in 1963 marking the eightieth anniversary of Kafka's birth. The door was slammed shut again after the Soviet invasion in 1968. Books and articles worldwide on Kafka total well over fifteen thousand—but few were allowed to be sold or published in his native city. The door had begun to crack open a little in the late 1980s—there were a few theater productions based on his works, and an edition of some of his letters was planned—but the Velvet Revolution and its aftermath resurrected Kafka with a vengeance: The "little mother" embraced him with a tenacious grasp as a maligned local son and elevated him onto a pedestal atop which Kafka himself probably would have swooned from acrophobia.

"Kafka's name is connected with Prague in every possible way. Kafka and Prague are almost two inseparable ideas nowadays," asserts a booklet put out in 1991 by the Franz Kafka Center, an organization founded in 1990 to further studies on Kafka as a symbol of

Central European—and Central European Jewish—culture. The center is in a palace on the magnificent, tourist-packed Old Town Square. A note beside its door reads: "Making pictures and films from the windows of our office must be arranged beforehand. Thank you."

I walk through the city, through the labyrinthine streets of the Old Town; I pause in the Old Town Square, stroll along the fashionable pedestrians-only Na příkopě. Franz Kafka is indeed everywhere, but in ways neither he nor any of the people who knew him or read his works would have ever thought possible. His hollow-eyed face, or rather caricatures of his face, peer out from postcards, T-shirts, posters, souvenir mugs, banners, and even graffiti. "The commercialization of memory," I write in my notebook. "The creation of memory. The creation of perceptions of history and people. The perception of memory."

Kafka was born in 1883 at the edge of old Jewish Town, in a house that was pulled down during the urban renewal project a few years later. All that remained was the grand front doorway, which was incorporated into the subsequent building put up on the spot. On the corner of this building, a plaque incorporating a larger-than-life-sized bust of Kafka was placed in 1965, commissioned by the Communist authorities during that brief period of rehabilitation before the Soviet invasion. The bust, with its pointy, stylized features, doesn't really look a lot like Kafka, but until the ouster of the Communists in 1989, this was the only evidence of Kafka in downtown Prague.

In 1991, as witness to the change, a museum dedicated to Kafka's life and work was installed on the ground floor of the building at Kafka's birth site. It combines worshipful resurrection with the blatant commercial exploitation of a new myth. The museum has a well-mounted exhibition of text, photographs, and some original objects; it illustrates the author's life, provides an introduction to his writing, and includes a thoughtful exposition of the Jewish intellectual and bourgeois world from which he came.

But almost more impressively, one entire side of the hall is taken up with a souvenir display and shop, all painted in basic black—because, apparently, everything about Kafka must be dark. Ghoulish, caricaturish busts of Kafka with a long, skinny neck and an outthrust chin stand in rows. Ranging in dimension from miniature to almost life size, they remind me of the plaster popes or Beethovens on sale in other countries, or of the multiple sculpted golems for sale at Jewish Town sidewalk stands. There are Kafka postcards, Kafka T-shirts, all sorts of Kafka pamphlets, maps of Kafka's Prague, Kafka posters, Kafka videos, even Kafka wrapping paper: cryptic black splotches that look like ink spots from an old-fashioned pen that doesn't work (symbolizing writer's block?). The display is—dare I say it—Kafkaesque.

A short walk away, a huge banner is draped across Pařížská Street, one of the elegant thoroughfares constructed when the old Jewish Town was destroyed. The street leads from the Old Town Square to the river. Kafka lived in his parents' apartment on Pařížská Street, in one of the fancy new buildings, for several years; he loved to look out at the Vltava and the new bridge that arched the river at the foot of the street to the Letna Gardens on the other side. On the banner a ghastly caricature of Kafka's face, a human face turned into a diabolical black and white mask, advertises a play about Kafka at the Black Light Theater: "Every night performances; live music-dance."

This version of Kafka's face, this diabolical caricature, is based

PRAGUE: A banner with a caricature of Franz Kafka, over Pařížská Street, advertising a play about Kafka.

46

on the last photograph of Kafka, a somber picture of a handsome, gaunt man ravaged by the tuberculosis that soon would kill him. In this version, by means of a metamorphosis worthy of the writer himself, Kafka's ears, already sticking out and slightly pointed, have been elongated and pointed even more so that he looks like an elf or a gargoyle or Mr. Spock, the *Star Trek* Vulcan; the gray shadows on his face have become black and much deeper, stretching over the countenance. The hollows around his eyes and beneath his cheekbones have become deep, dark abysses. This is the image that stares out from posters and postcards, from T-shirts and other souvenirs.

In a graffito painted on a wall near Prague's castle, duly photographed and translated into a glossy postcard, the diabolical Kafka caricature is surrounded by three bizarre imaginary faces that look like demons from a fairy tale. "The Four Faces of Franz Kafka," the graffito says. "Franz Kafka's Prague," the postcard is entitled. I can't help noting that the three demon faces surrounding the Kafka-gargoyle all have long, pointy noses and beards—like the caricatures of Jews in anti-Semitic propaganda.

Across the Old Town Square on Celetná Street, another street on which the Kafka family lived for awhile, the new Franz Kafka Theater does a roaring trade with a performance called, simply, *Franz K.* I pick up a handbill, a little surreal in its own right:

> Stranger in his hometown. Vision of life, loves, and death of Franz Kafka. The character, family, loves, anxieties and conflicts of Franz Kafka come to life against the background of his age, so full of dramatic events, revolutionary inventions and cultural movements whose bearers often lived here in Prague. Kafka the man and the writer as a controversial character and as a myth. Czech-German-Jewish Prague as a labyrinth of houses, streets and human interrelationships. All of this accompanied by period musical hits and ditties from Czech and German cabarets. In German language.

I buy a ticket and go to the show. The ticket costs the equivalent of eleven dollars, more than a day's salary for a friend of mine who at that time had a responsible position at a Czech government ministry. All the members of the audience are foreigners, mostly from Austria and Germany. On stage, against a background of pseudo–German-expressionist sets and costumes, there is much shrieking and running around, lots of cawing and flapping of arms like wings to press home the pun: Kafka, sounding like *kavka,* the Czech word for "jackdaw." (Hermann Kafka even used a drawing of the crowlike bird as the logo on his stationery.)

The play is a slapstick biography, a vaudeville presentation of Kafka's life. Through a thick veil of nostalgia, it stresses the coexistence of Czech, German, and Jewish culture in prewar Prague. This subject has become fashionable in the post-Communist environment, partly to make up for the monolithic cultural oppression of the Communist period; partly perhaps as a sop to the German and Austrian tourists; and partly perhaps in guilt (or despair?) over the disappearance of the Jews.

"MY REACTION TO ALL THIS is negative," Mirek Kulstadt, a researcher in history at Charles University (Kafka's alma mater), told me.[17] Kulstadt, a non-Jewish native of Prague who taught a course in Jewish history at a clandestine university in the 1980s, went on: "There is no actual encouragement for people to read Kafka's books. Still, this Kafka commercialization is successful; the Kafka theater is full. But none of it has much influence on people here, on Czechs. If you ask in a bookshop if more people are buying Kafka, well, maybe they did in the first months of the revolution, but not now. They want to read contemporary Czech authors who were banned.

"I think it is terrible that Kafka is becoming part of the scenery of these first steps of a market economy. It's not just a problem of Kafka. Many people feel that Prague, with its atmosphere and scenery, is turning into a tourist theme park—we feel it deeply."

Kulstadt noted, however, that he himself was one of the originators of what has become a staple in Prague: walks through Kafka town.

"Nineteen eighty-three was a big Kafka anniversary, the hundredth anniversary of his birth. We prepared trips for German tourists—literary lectures, walks through Kafka's Prague, etc.," he said. "We did it partly illegally. To do these types of excursions back in 1983 was very nice; there were more possibilities in Prague to present local places with concrete passages in Kafka's books. The streets were half empty—there was a lot of space to make these excursions. Now it's impossible. We lived then, somehow, in 'splendid isolation.'

"I think this whole Kafka thing now is a boom; it's a natural reaction to the repression under the Communists. And if the tourists buy it, why not? I think it will die down, though, in two or three years. Kafka will return to the history of the city, to the history of an ethnic and religious group—not as a monster, but as a writer."[18]

FRANZ KAFKA DIED in June 1924, a month before his forty-first birthday, and is buried in Prague's New Jewish Cemetery, in the same plot and under the same white, crystal-shaped tombstone as his parents, who survived him into the 1930s. He lived with them most of his life, psychologically unable to leave home, and is buried with them for eternity. The epitaph, in Hebrew, gives his Hebrew name, Anschel—the name of the pious provincial rabbi and Talmudic scholar who was his great grandfather—and concludes with the traditional Hebrew abbreviation for verse 29 from 1 Samuel, chapter 25: "May His Soul Be Bound Up in the Bond of Life."

Visitors don't flock to Kafka's tomb as they do to the Old Jewish Cemetery, but some do make the pilgrimage, taking the subway out to the Želivského station, where the New Cemetery entrance is found. There are no caricatures or hokey souvenirs on sale, but a sign just inside the tall iron gates points the way to "Dr. Franz Kafka," as if indicating directions to a consulting room, not a grave. The grave is in the first row, facing the outer cemetery wall, and it is a long, long walk—four hundred meters—from the gates, down a broad, straight path. People stand and gaze at the simple, six-sided stone that marks the tomb of Kafka and his parents; a plaque memorializes his three sisters, who were killed by the Nazis. A small pine sapling springs up alongside.

A bouquet of red roses, wrapped in cellophane, lies on the pristine gravel plot in front of the tombstone. "To Franz Kafka . . . thank you," reads an attached card. Visitors have placed memorial pebbles on the raised concrete ledge enclosing the the gravel; a few have even left kvittleh under the pebbles, just as pilgrims do at the tomb of Rabbi Löw and other revered figures in the Old Cemetery. "In memory of Franz Kafka, whose stories enable us all to partly understand the oppressive nature of totalitarianism everywhere," reads one. Another, a tightly folded square of yellowish graph paper torn out of a notebook and set carefully under a pebble, is blank.

THE NEW CEMETERY, where Kafka is buried, is in Žižkov, an eastern district of the city, near the main Christian cemeteries and a big long-distance bus depot. It was opened in 1890 to accommodate a hundred thousand graves, a projected century of interments, and it is still used today for burials. If the Old Jewish Cemetery is a stone archive of pious medieval and Renaissance Prague Jewry, the New Cemetery is a sculpted history book of a prosperous, upwardly mobile, secularized community whose members wanted even their graves to be monuments to their success. In the monuments and their inscriptions, you can read the progression from shtetl to city to acculturation to Holocaust.

The plain tombstones, black marble obelisks, and sentimental sculpted memorials of the middle class are arranged in sections, rows, and plots, once neatly maintained and separated by paths and tree-lined alleys. Massive sculpted mausoleums and monuments, some designed by leading turn-of-the-century architects, memorialize the wealthy; some list two or three generations of entire families in epitaphs that read like curricula vitae: birth and death dates, birth place (often, for the earlier members of families, a provincial village), occupation, and honors, including knighthoods and other titles and medals bestowed by the state. It's as if these tombs, placed in prime funeral plots like the once-prized pews along the east walls of shtetl synagogues, granted much-sought-after legitimacy to these families striving for acceptance, even—or even more so—in death, where, one imagines, they never thought it could be taken away.

There are lawyers, artists, professors, factory owners, hoteliers, wholesalers, industrialists, salesmen, civil servants, doctors. Dr. Friedrich Elbogen (1875–1934), his tomb states, was vice president of the Bohemian Union Bank; Arnošt Elbogen, listed on the same family tomb, was a pilot. He lived from 1920 to 1944 and "gave his beautiful young life for his country and freedom." Maurus Bloch (1861–1934)

PRAGUE: The tomb of Franz Kafka in the New Jewish Cemetery.

"to his last day [was] a servant of our state." Bohumil Bondy (1832–1907) was a member of the Parliament of the Czech Crown. Jonas Gumperls (1836–1907) was a salesman.

On some tombs, as on Kafka's, memorial plaques or inscriptions list family members who were among the thirty-five thousand Prague Jews who perished in Nazi camps; but only a small minority of Holocaust victims had surviving relatives who could commemorate them in this way.

Most of the stones are lost in the young forest of saplings, shrubs, trees, weeds, and ivy, trailing ivy, that has grown up to envelop tombs and memory over the past five decades. A few plots are cleared, a few graves cared for—islands of survival. But who is left to remember Ludwig Fischer, whose family had his portrait cast in bronze and placed on his massive tomb, now almost completely covered in ivy? Who remembers Valterle—"Little Walter"—a child whose tomb also bears his portrait?

Who remembers the Kubinzky family, whose tomb is said to have been the most expensive among all the grandiose memorials in the New Cemetery, a sumptuous mausoleum situated in a prime position, not far from the cemetery gates and the neo-Renaissance ceremonial hall? The tomb, as big as a small house, is a domed structure, built in 1892 by architect Alfons Wertmüller, who designed it to resemble an ancient temple and embellished it with the opulent decorative elements so beloved by solid citizens of the late nineteenth century: Corinthian columns, niches, false balustrades, pilasters.

"It was a very important family," historian Jiří Kuděla told me. "They were active in the textile industry and public administration, carrying out high functions in Vienna, as well as Prague. It was a typical Jewish family in that there were branches all over the monarchy."

Inside the mausoleum is the tomb of Otto Ritter von Kubinzky, a *"grossindustrieller"* (industrial magnate) who was born on March 6, 1851, and died on August 29, 1894. The term *Ritter* and the use of "von" in the name mean that he had been knighted by the Hapsburgs. Also buried in the mausoleum is Otto's mother, Louise von Kubinzky, 1818–1893, described in the inscribed epitaph as the wife of the *grossindustrieller* Friedrich Ritter von Kubinzky. The grave where Friedrich should lie, next to his wife, is simply a slab—he is not there. An inscription in the tomb says that he is buried "in the old cemetery at Wolschau."

Friedrich Ritter von Kubinzky's absence from the family tomb, the most expensive in the entire cemetery, and his burial across town left me puzzled. Had the couple been divorced? Had Friedrich converted to Christianity and been buried in a Christian cemetery? I created imaginary nineteenth-century family dramas involving an abandoned wife, a son who, despite riches and knighthood, died young only a year after his mother, a roomy, expensive mausoleum put up at great expense so that the family could hold its head high among fellow millionaires despite the scandals. . . .

The truth was far simpler, and it brought to completion for me another of Prague's connecting Jewish circles.

THE "OLD CEMETERY AT WOLSCHAU" refers to what is now known as the old Jewish cemetery in Žižkov, closer in toward the city center. The neigborhood was once a separate community well outside Prague city limits known as Olšany, or Wolschau in German, and the Jewish cemetery was one of several cemeteries founded there in 1680 for victims of a plague, which that year raged through Prague.

"About three thousand people, all plague victims from Jewish Town, were buried in this cemetery in 1680. Then there was a new plague in 1713 and another three thousand three hundred and eighty-eight victims were buried there," Jiří Fiedler, a mild-mannered former children's book editor, told me. Fiedler, who is not Jewish, is one of the pioneers of research on forgotten Jewish relics in the Czech Republic. For more than a dozen years he has traveled to all corners of Bohemia and Moravia, usually alone and often by bicycle or on foot, to seek out ruined synagogues and abandoned cemeteries.

"It's probably my passion to fill in the blank places," Fiedler said. "Christian churches, chapels, castles were listed in books, but not the Jewish monuments." Under the Communists he was more than once hauled in for questioning by the secret police because this type of research—particularly by a non-Jew—was considered "suspicious." He was also denied access to the archives of the Jewish Museum, at that time run by the state. Today, as part of the changes wrought by the revolution, Fiedler works for the Prague Jewish community and has published his years of research as a detailed guidebook to Jewish sites in the republic.[19]

"In 1787 the Old Jewish Cemetery in town was closed, so the Žižkov cemetery became the main Jewish cemetery for all of Prague," Fiedler said. "It was enlarged several times and grew to encompass 7.75 hectares. Between 1787 and 1891, when the last burial took place, probably as many as 31,500 people were buried there, including many, many famous people."

Today, if you want to find this historic Jewish cemetery, look to the heavens, to the skyline of Prague. From virtually everywhere in the city, the silhouette of the modernistic new television transmitting tower dominates the scene, a striking and rather shocking contrast to the ancient monuments in the town beneath. It is like a rocket with a red-and-white-striped tip, standing on three legs and poised to take off; a huge, pointing finger; a science fiction weapon upended on a tripodal base; a dinosaur.

The television tower, built in the late 1980s, grows directly out of what was once the old Jewish cemetery in Wolschau. The three massive legs are rooted in the soil where tens of thousands of Prague Jews were buried.

The main part of the cemetery was destroyed after 1955, Jiří Fiedler told me. The area was turned into a park, named with possibly unintentional irony after the composer Gustav Mahler, a Bohemian Jew who had to convert to Catholicism in order to become the director of the Vienna Court Opera. Only the oldest part of the cemetery, with the addition of some tombstones brought from the razed part, was retained along one edge.

"The park in turn was abolished in 1985 when construction of the television tower began," Fiedler said. "The excavations at that time uncovered hundreds of tombstones, which were probably buried under the park in the 1950s. They were all taken out of Prague, probably as garbage, in the 1980s. I don't know, no one knows, what happened to them."

Tomáš Kraus, secretary of the Czech Jewish community, was bitter when he recalled these episodes. "When the cemetery was destroyed," he told me, "the Jewish community wasn't even asked."

Standing within the cemetery at the foot of the tower, you are almost unaware of it looming high, high above; its three massive white legs, from this vantage point, are just enormous white tree trunks. The gravestones are hemmed in between the backs of apartment buildings and a wall alternating with an iron fence. Here are finely carved baroque and classical tombstones, including that of the renowned eighteenth century Chief Rabbi Ezekiel Landau, who led his community on its first steps out of the closed ghetto and into the modern world after Josef II granted Jews some civil rights in the 1880s.[20]

There are no tourists, no crowds. Straight paths were laid down through the remnant of the cemetery during a restoration project in the 1980s, but the gate to the graveyard is locked. Children from the neighborhood, dogs, a cat or two, sneak in through the bars and play a cowboys-and-Indians-type game among the stones and the shady trees and the season's worth of weeds grown up around the tombs. It's as if the wall between the cemetery and the grounds of the television tower separates two realities.

Only one structure straddles the two spheres: a sort of miniature Greek temple that sticks out from the wall of the cemetery into the park surrounding the base of the television tower. I didn't realize that the little building—a pediment and a shallow peaked roof supported by six Doric columns—was actually the only tomb from the old cemetery left standing outside the perimeter of the wall enclosing the other remnants. Park benches are arranged in the shade inside the little temple, and it's a pleasant place to sit; I was glad to rest for a moment there, to put down my camera bag and notebooks.

And here's where the circles connect, where I feel a little electric thrill as I hear cogs and tumblers click into place.

This little pseudo-Grecian temple, left standing for some unknown reason when the rest of the cemetery was razed, this little temple is the mausoleum of Friedrich Ritter von Kubinzky, the *grossindustrieller* whose wife and son lie in the most expensive tomb of the New Cemetery, where Friedrich's own place is marked by an empty slab and a cryptic notation telling where he is buried.

"*RUHESTAETTE* [Resting Place] of Friedrich Ritter von Kubinzky," says a big marble plaque, in German, on the wall of the little temple. He was, it states, a "*Fabriksbesitzer*" (factory owner) and a "*Ritter des Ordens der eisernen krone III Classe und des Franz Josef Ordens*" (Knight of the Order of the Iron Crown Third Class and of the Order of Franz Josef). Not only that, the plaque states, he was a member of the Imperial Council, the Commercial Court, and the Chamber of Commerce Council. He was a leading member of the Jewish (or Israelite) community, and on the board of the Jewish Hospital in Carlsbad. It

concludes this list with "etc., etc."—too many more honors to spell out.

He lived from December 9, 1814, until October 14, 1888; and this, I see, is why he and his wife and son had separate tombs, both splendid and

PRAGUE: The tomb of Friedrich Ritter von Kubinzky, with the legs of the television tower in the background, at what was the Old Jewish Cemetery in Žižkov/Olšany.

both built like ancient temples. Friedrich died two years before the New Cemetery was opened, when the old Žižkov/Olšany cemetery was the main Jewish burial place. His wife died two years after the old cemetery, where her husband lay in his splendid Resting Place, had closed.

Farther-Out Circles

I often stay in Prague with friends who live in the northern outskirts of the city in a high-rise apartment development so far from the center that to reach it you have to go to the end of a metro line and then ride a bus to its terminal point. I had stayed there many times before I found out that there was a Jewish cemetery—and thus had been a Jewish community—in their very neighborhood, only a five-minute walk from the apartment. No one knew about it. On maps of the city that include such outlying districts, the cemetery is indicated simply as a narrow green strip. When I found out what that strip represented, I made it a priority to see what was there.

To get to the cemetery, I walked south through my friends' development, past concrete high rises so alike that it was easy to lose direction, until I came to a wide, busy street with tram lines running down the middle. Directly across this avenue was a high wall, fronted with thick shrubs. Behind this I could see what looked like a thick forest of tall, unpruned trees—mainly horse chestnuts with wide-spreading branches. I could see the conkers hanging, ready to fall, and the leaves just beginning to turn yellow and crispy brown in the middle of an unusually hot September.

I was sure that this was the place. I paced the length of the wall, looking for an opening or some other indication, but there was nothing until at one point, yes, I just caught a glimpse of the tips of a couple of tall, sculpted tombs peeping over the top.

I looked for an entrance.

At one end of the wall I found the structures that had obviously been the mortuary, or ceremonial hall: two tall buildings with gracefully arched windows flanking an arched, wrought-iron and concrete gate leading into a courtyard. The complex had been turned into a small print shop. I passed this by and turned the corner to follow the length of the wall on the other side. Again, all I could see were the tips of a few monuments. Far down, almost at the end, the featureless brick was broken by a locked gate, but through this I could glimpse only desolation: masses of tall weeds and golden rod, a bird taking flight into the trees.

I decided to try at the print shop; maybe there was a window overlooking the cemetery. There was, it turned out, such a window, but it was hard to reach and in any case was of frosted glass. I pantomimed to a workman, a short, dark man with a cigarette dangling from under a big mustache, that I wanted to look out, and with an incurious shrug he climbed up on a chair and a radiator to remove the pane. Then I climbed up.

What lay before me, framed by the dirty edges of the window, was a secret Jewish garden, a hidden green world of vines and ivy, trees, birds, and a few broken, toppled tombstones almost submerged in the undergrowth. I caught my breath.

This was what remained of the new Jewish cemetery in Libeň, a community where Jews had settled as long ago as the middle of the sixteenth century. This overgrown expanse, and a neoromanesque, mid–nineteenth-century synagogue that stands empty near the district's metro station a mile or so away, are the only remaining traces of what was the earliest of the satellite Jewish communities around Prague. Libeň's old Jewish cemetery, which probably dated back to the sixteenth century, was razed by city authorities in 1964. Libeň remained a separate village, outside Prague's city limits, until 1901,

PRAGUE: "The secret Jewish garden," the new Jewish cemetery at Libeň.

when it was incorporated into the municipality. As a community close to but separate from Prague, it had been a valuable safe haven for Jews when times in the Prague ghetto got bad. Many Prague Jews fled to Libeň during the plague year of 1680, and city authorities even considered transferring Prague's entire Jewish population there. When Empress Maria Theresa expelled all Jews from Prague in the winter of 1745, many found refuge in Libeň.

The new cemetery, this secret Jewish garden, was founded in the 1890s by a middle-class, acculturated congregation—ordinary people in an ordinary neighborhood living ordinary lives. Buried here, and now here forgotten, is one local son who won fame, the writer and humorist Vojtěch Rakous, one of the first Prague Jews to write in Czech rather than German, who died in 1935. His simple, rectangular tomb is against the wall. Rakous, who according to his photographs was a handsome but sad-faced man with soulful eyes and a white walrus mustache, started out as a shoe salesman in Libeň before turning to writing. His popular, comic stories about Bohemian village Jewish life featured Motke, a henpecked husband, and Rezi, his domineering wife: Their names, too, are inscribed on Rakous's tomb.

I sit one evening in the restaurant of the high-rise development across the street from the cemetery. Physically, the establishment is a holdover from Communist days, a typical example of 1960s Socialist style, or lack of style: an unlovely, boxy room with big picture windows, sagging lace curtains, wood trim, and sculptural wall decorations that look like crumpled cellophane. Pots of green plants attempt to soften the atmosphere; light descends from frosted-glass ceiling fixtures and chromium wall installations. At nine P.M., most of the patrons—raw, greasy-haired young people from the high rises wearing jeans decorated with labels reading "Nifty Sportive Taste" and other nonsense slogans—are drinking, not eating. Smoke plumes up from their cigarettes.

I try to connect this group of people, their history, their lifestyle, with the cemetery across the road, but I scarcely succeed. I wonder if they know what's behind that long wall, under those tall trees. I wonder what questions or thoughts they have, these people who live in this drab place and who might have glimpsed the top of a tombstone as they rode the trams that pass alongside that secretive wall. I think about enclosures, walls, neighborhoods, newness, change, population shifts, apathy, neglect, memory, amnesia. The high rises are new, all built within the past twenty or thirty years; only a few prewar houses still stand in the immediate neighborhood. The people who live here are newcomers, too. The secret cemetery remains safe behind its walls, a long, thin strip of green where birds fly, and trees and vines and weeds grow without restraint, and memory, little by little, is covered over.

DIRECTLY ACROSS TOWN, in an affluent neighborhood high up on hills south of the city center, I find memory defaced rather than buried. The Jewish cemetery here is so located that even on a map its position is apparent: It's on a street called U starého židovského hřbitova—Old Jewish Cemetery Street. It is, in fact, the old Jewish cemetery of Smíchov, one of the earliest of Prague's one-time suburbs—it appeared on maps by 1406—and home to an important Jewish community since the eighteenth century.

Smíchov was and is an industrial suburb, and in 1830 the Jewish brothers Moses and Leopold Porges opened its first big mechanized factory to print cotton fabric. The factory became the third largest in Bohemia, and rated a visit from the Emperor in 1833. The Porges brothers, who ran other factories as well, were raised to the nobility in the 1840s, but in June 1844 mechanization and lowered wages at their Smíchov plant were instrumental in sparking a violent wave of strikes by Czech workers against Prague's burgeoning class of wealthy Jewish industrialists.[21] These strikes turned into general anti-Jewish riots and rampages that, supported by sectors of the media, took on overtones of Czech nationalism.

"Textile workers rise up against their bosses, who happen to belong to the Jewish ethnic group, cause damage and destruction to factories, and our dear cultivated and educated Czechs know of nothing better to do than to exhibit openly their own crude and crass Jew-hatred, accusing all Jews, as a single body, of fraud," Jewish writer David Kuh wrote bitterly in the newspaper *Der Orient* in July 1844. "Oh Czechs, you call for freedom and independence at a time when you have dehumanized yourselves, when you have sunk to the level of beasts of prey."[22]

The cemetery on Old Jewish Cemetery Street was founded in the eighteenth century, and the last burial was probably in the 1920s. I had been looking forward to seeing it, as I had been told it had many fine tombstones. A recent Jewish guidebook to Prague[23] described it as well maintained by the Monuments Protection Office. It was described as being surrounded by a wall with a neoclassical ceremonial hall that was also used as a gate, and situated picturesquely on a slope at the edge of a forest.

I made my way to the cemetery on a hot Sunday in September. It was an uphill hike from the Radlická metro station, past a fancy-looking sports club and fancier-looking villas with stupendous views of the city, where sleek Great Danes lounged on well-fenced, manicured lawns. Closer to the cemetery there were neat houses and small apartment complexes with carports: a nice little neighborhood in the inner suburbs.

Old Jewish Cemetery Street runs alongside a wooded area, and here, yes, I found the cemetery. But it was nothing like the guidebook had described. It was a wild island of devastation in the sea of ticky-tacky. This was not the evolution into a forest due to abandonment and neglect that I had seen at the New Cemetery and elsewhere. This was deliberate destruction. The entryway and wall were wrecked; the ceremonial hall was a ruin. Tombstones had been toppled; some had red paint or obscene graffiti scrawled over them—in Italian, no less. On the wall of the ceremonial hall were scrawled a pentagram and the word "Satan." "Satan" was also scrawled on one of the tombstones.

"They say that Satan worshipers hold black masses in old cemeteries," historian Danny Rexa, who accompanied me to the cemetery, told me. We found at least one grave, hidden by an enormous fallen tree, that had been dug up. Maybe whoever did it had been searching for gold, the rumored treasure Jews are supposed to have buried with their dead. "Maybe they were searching for bones, for the black mass," said Danny.

Jiří Fiedler later told me that there had been a big cleanup operation to put the cemetery to rights in 1981–1982. "We worked there to restore the stones, to clean them, to cut back the brush and saplings, and so on," he recalled. "Any tombstones that had fallen or been toppled were set upright, and a class from the masonry school made a new gate, repaired the walls, and so on. The Jewish community newspaper gave a writeup that the cemetery had been restored. Three or four weeks later, someone organized a pogrom against the cemetery. Many stones were toppled, and so forth. From that day, the cemetery has had no care. I think the problem is that the pogrom was probably organized by people who live in the new houses around the cemetery. They want the cemetery liquidated. Or maybe it was students from the masonry school."

Fiedler hit on something that already had disturbed me. How could the people in the surrounding houses bear to live overlooking the devastation of that cemetery? The homes were nice homes; the people obviously repectable. A pleasant-looking man with silver hair was washing his red car under his carport when we visited. Whatever vandalism and black masses had gone on there had to have taken place under the eyes of the neighborhood. And this was Prague, I thought; a city that exalts its Jewish heritage and makes a fetish of it in its tourist-packed old center two miles or so away.

The Smíchov synagogue is empty and abandoned. It is unique for Prague: a modern (or virtually modern) synagogue, a strange and striking example of 1930s functionalist architecture. Actually, it is a striking example of functionalist remodeling. It was built originally in a rather heavy-handed neoromanesque style in 1863 for the wealthy Reform congregation, the local captains of industry. Architect Leopold Ehrmann gave it its new face in 1931; he stripped away all outer decoration, leaving a stark, minimalist building with tall, narrow arched windows and unusual zigzag edging along the flat roof. The building, dusty and covered with grime, stands on a busy corner near an enormous tram factory. There are ambitious long-term plans to close the factory and turn it and the entire neighborhood—including the synagogue—into a sprawling cultural center for the entire capital.

Today, a sausage stand at what was once the synagogue's sheltered entry porch sends up clouds of greasy steam beneath a subtle strip of Hebrew and Czech lettering that still prays, in both languages, for peace and well-being among people near and far.

PRAGUE: Sausage stand at the entryway of the former synagogue in Smíchov. Hebrew and Czech inscriptions appear over the porch.

The Outermost Circle

"Five or six years ago, in the 1980s, we were asked by the former Jewish community leaders to organize a work brigade to help restore the cemetery in Uhříněves," Ondřej Ernyei, a Jewish jazz musician, told me as we had lunch one day in the top-floor cafeteria of a downtown Prague department store. We sat at a table next to the plate-glass windows, looking down at the city, sipping great slopping mugs of beer. It was hot and crowded and not my idea of a pleasant place to eat, but Ondřej was paying that day, and this was one of the few restaurants in the center of the city whose prices were still affordable to the average Czech pocket.

"I went out to Uhříněves twice," Ondřej said. While not a religious Jew, Ondřej had associated himself with Jewish activities during the Communist era as a way of asserting a non-Communist identity.

"We were a group of five or six people. It was no use, though. The place is constantly vandalized. People would come to the old ceremonial hall and, well, use it as a toilet."

Uhříněves, a suburb far to the southeast of town, which was incorporated into Prague's city limits only in the 1970s, is the outermost of Prague's Jewish circles, the furthest limit of the ripples. Yet here there was a Jewish settlement before the year 1685, and here there are still a synagogue dating from 1848 and a large Jewish cemetery whose earliest gravestones date from 1730. Some of these beautifully carved early stones were removed a number of years ago and taken to the New Jewish Cemetery, where they now stand as a decorative memorial near the gates. I was told that more stones than were needed were uprooted for this transfer and that a dozen or so now lie in abandoned heaps near where they had stood.

For me, for my exploration of Prague's Jewish circles, Uhříněves marked the final frontier.

To get there, I took the red metro to the end of the line, Háje, where I emerged into a sterile, futuristic development of prefabricated concrete apartment buildings whose main redeeming feature seemed to be proximity to public transport. Here I got onto the 232 bus, which for at least twenty minutes followed a winding route through countryside, cornfields, and little villages, all now within Prague's borders and all menaced as if in a science fiction movie by encroaching apartment developments in the ever-decreasing distance.

The bus let me off in the middle of Uhříněves. It was like being on a village street: There were the local shops; there was the local church, originally built in the thirteenth century; there was the local pub, a typical old-style tavern full of semidrunks. At a table inside, a group of rough-looking men were singing to the strains of a guitar. I could hardly believe it, but one of the songs sounded like a Czech version of Woody Guthrie's Depression-era lullaby "Go to Sleep, My Weary Hobo." Here beer, served from the tap in half-liter glass mugs, cost half what it did downtown, and simple plates of stewed meat and dumplings were slapped down on the table with slick paper napkins and feather-light aluminum cutlery, just as in the no-frills days under communism.

The synagogue was in the middle of the village not far from the bus stop. Jiří Fiedler had prepared me for what to expect and what to look for. "I visited the synagogue last month," he said. "After the war,

PRAGUE: Washing machines in the former synagogue at Uhříněves, now a laundry.

it was sold legally by the community. Today, it's used as a laundry."

So a laundry is what I found. The manager had frizzy blond hair, bad teeth, and anxious eyes, but she was very pleasant and accommodating. I wondered if she somehow felt guilty about running a laundry in a former shul—but maybe she was just nice. Maybe she didn't even know what the building used to be. I explained to her that I was interested in architecture, and she let me prowl around the steamy interior, taking pictures of the sinks, fluorescent light strips, and solid, industrial washing machines crowded next to each other under the tall arched and vaulted ceiling. Only these arches and their simple stucco decoration, and only the architectural form of the building, which preserves the upper gallery where women once sat, bore witness to its former function.

I headed toward the cemetery. It was hard to find, and I had to ask several people before an old man told me where to turn off the main street near some school playing fields. I followed his instructions but still could not find the cemetery. The playing fields were at the edge of a wooded area, but the path that continued along the woods didn't seem to lead anywhere. A caretaker working in the playing fields told me that, yes, this was the right place. I should just keep following the path. But, he added, "It's kaput, kaput!" And he gestured sharply but eloquently, hands palm down.

I walked down the narrow earthen trail, first alongside and then through the forest. It was extremely lonely, and I kept hearing strange sounds in the woods. I became uneasy, especially when a man came up on the path behind me. Strange, I reflected. If I had been searching for a cemetery isolated like this in the real countryside, I would not have been nervous. But here, within Prague city limits. . . .

I took the initiative and asked the man if this really was the way to the Jewish cemetery, and he confirmed it, yes. He also insisted on walking with me. Where was I from? America? Why was I going to the cemetery? It had been a ruin for thirty years; it was a jungle, terrible. I lied to him. My family came from here, I said. It was the easiest way to explain why someone would want to view desolation. From here? From Uhříněves? What was their name? I pretended not to understand.

There, he finally said. There's the entrance, but I don't think you can go in. And look, there's the wall, but see how ruined it is.

It was hard to tell where the forest ended and the cemetery began. Tall trees continued without a break. Heavy undergrowth made an impenetrable barrier. I could just see a couple of tombstones stuck in there, tightly wedged amid the brush.

The man said good-bye and angled down another path where, farther along, he started knocking walnuts down from a tree. I walked along the perimeter of the cemetery wall, looking for somewhere I might be able to enter. But I didn't look very hard. I didn't really want to go into that cemetery. It was too lonely; the sense of unease I had felt walking down the path grew stronger. The noises in the forest grew suddenly more disturbing. The devastation was too depressing.

I had brought with me a photocopy of the entry on Uhříněves

from a book on Bohemian Jewish communities published in the 1930s. It had a photograph of the synagogue, then neatly maintained and set behind a low picket fence and pruned ornamental trees. It also included photographs of eight worthy members of the Uhříněves Jewish community: Rabbi Daniel Kohn, who died in 1892; Josef Rezek, with a jaunty, upturned mustache; Oskar Rezek, Heřman Poláček, Adolf Freund, Karel Beck, Josef and Vilém Beykovský. Solid, stolid, unsmiling burghers: three of them from neighboring villages that formed part of the Uhříněves community, all of them sober and prosperous looking in dark suits, tight collars, and ties.

I thought of the washing machines where their pews must have been. And I imagined that if I had pushed my way into the forgotten forest cemetery, I might have been able eventually to find their graves.

Or maybe not. "There's been fantastic devastation in this cemetery," Jiří Fiedler told me. "Many modern tombstones were stolen after the war. A new memorial to the Holocaust was demolished, too. It was a monument in the shape of a large, granite stone with a memorial plaque. This plaque was stolen."

❧ 2 ❧

Wine Merchants and Wonder Rabbis
Northeastern Hungary to Southern Poland

❧❧

Boruch ato adonai elohenu melech ha-olom borai peri hagofen.

Blessed art thou O Lord our God, King of the Universe,
who createst the fruit of the vine.

When the rebbe dances
the walls dance with him
the hasidim clap hands
They clap hands when the rebbe dances[1]

 HE TOKAJ REGION of northeastern Hungary, a land of wide meadows and dreamy hills just south of the Carpathian Mountains along the meandering Bodrog and Tisza rivers, has been famous for nearly a thousand years for its unique, semisweet amber wine, the product of volcanic soil, mild climate, late harvest, and special wine-making techniques whose origins are buried in history. King Louis XIV of France proclaimed it "the wine of kings—the king of wines," and other monarchs, popes, artists, and philosophers also sang its praises down through the ages. Composer Franz Schubert did so literally: He wrote a celebrated song about it, "*Lob des Tokayers*"—"In Praise of Tokaj."

Grapes have been cultivated here probably for more than two millennia, but it was in the Middle Ages that the fame of Tokaj wine began to spread. Among the earliest vintners of that era were Italian immigrants brought to the region in the thirteenth century by the Hungarian king following the devastations of the Mongol invasion of 1241–1242. Memories of this long-gone Italian presence linger in the names of wine-making villages such as Tállya, which may have derived its name from "Italia," and Olaszliszka and Bodrogolaszi, from *Olasz,* which in Hungarian means "Italian."

By the sixteenth century, Tokaj and surrounding villages were a mecca for an army of international wine merchants who oversaw the transport of Tokaj wine north, east, and west through what is now Slovakia into Poland, Russia, Germany, and eventually almost all of Europe. Jews were among them, and over the years Jewish merchants and vintners became deeply involved in all facets of local wine production and commerce—out of necessity as well as for profit.

The ritual consecration and consumption of wine is an integral and intimate part of many Jewish ceremonies. The *Kiddush,* or blessing recited over wine, is a symbol of sanctification for holy days, one of the bedrock prayers anchoring the faith that even nonobservant Jews are likely to know by heart. The goblet used to hold wine during the Kiddush—the Kiddush cup—evolved into an important ritual object, essential for family observance, and often a treasured heirloom passed down and cherished from generation to generation. Special goblets are used for *havdalah,* the farewell-to-the-Sabbath ceremony Saturday evening: The havdalah cup should overflow with wine to symbolize hopes for a coming week overflowing with blessings, and the special goblets incorporate saucers to catch the spill. The braided candle used in the havdalah ceremony is then extinguished in this overflow.

Observant Jews—which until a couple of hundred years ago meant all Jews—are expressly forbidden to consume any wine except kosher wine—that is, wine prepared and bottled from start to finish exclusively by Jews, without even the most minimal contact by gentiles. This prohibition became relaxed somewhat for wine used simply as a beverage, but it remained firmly in force for wine used for ritual purposes. A modern kosher winery in the Italian town of Pitigliano stresses this fact in its public relations material even today: "All the operations in the transformation of grapes into bottled wine are carried out by personnel of the Jewish religion," a brochure guarantees.

Wine is such an important Jewish symbol of festivity and celebration that traditional observance even lays down the amount and manner in which it should be drunk on certain occasions. Four cups must be downed at the Passover seder, for example. (*Religious Duties of the Daughters of Israel,* a turn-of-the-century manual for Jewish homemakers, which was presented to my grandmother, my mother's mother, before her wedding in 1919, was extremely precise on this matter: "Each cup contains a quantity of liquid equal to one and one-half eggs at least," it instructed. "At each drink one should take more than half a cup.")

In addition, ten drops of wine are dipped from the wineglass at one part of the seder ceremony, one for each of the ten plagues God sent to smite the Egyptians and thus prepare the Jewish Exodus toward the promised land: Blood. Frogs. Vermin. Beasts. Pestilence. Boils. Hail. Locusts. Darkness. Death of the firstborn. Subtracting thus from a full cup of wine—the symbol of joy—reminds us that our happiness cannot be complete, as the Egyptians, fellow human beings, suffered from these plagues.[2] Another imposing goblet full of wine stands alone in a prominent position on the seder table. This is the cup for the prophet Elijah, herald of the eagerly awaited Messiah, ready for him to drink from if he should enter the home and want to partake of the festive meal.

The need for an ample and ready supply of kosher wine for both religious observance and domestic use meant that Jews became involved in the production and trade of wine many centuries ago. The medieval Pope Innocent III left the following description of Jewish winemakers in a letter dated January 1208:

> At the vintage season the Jew, shod in linen boots, treads the wine; and having extracted the purer wine in accordance with the Jewish rite they retain some for their own pleasure, and the rest, the part which is abominable to them, they leave to the faithful Christians; and with this, now and again, the sacrament of the blood of Christ is performed.[3]

A Jewish presence in the Tokaj wine region is first mentioned in the fifteenth century, and the earliest documents relating to Jewish activity in the wine trade here date to around the beginning of the seventeenth century. Jewish merchants, mindful of the laws regulating kosher wine, bought up the grape production of entire vineyards and then not only harvested and pressed the grapes themselves but also arranged for the storage of the kosher wine.[4] Many of these early Jewish wine producers and merchants came from Poland, a land of many Jews and few vineyards that lay just over the then border from Hungary. Most of the early Jewish population in the southern Polish town of Rymanów were engaged in importing wine from Hungary—to such an extent that around the year 1600 they were granted a special dispensation allowing them to deal in nonkosher wine destined for Christian ceremonies. Polish-Jewish wine merchants eventually dealt extensively in wine for the Christian market.

The thought of this wine trade, and the wine-forged connections back and forth across the Carpathians, excites my imagination. I find it peculiarly fascinating and oddly endearing. Historically, Jews were tremendously important as wide-roving merchants who trafficked in all sorts of goods across the entire span of Europe and into the Near East. And until not very long ago, all merchants, Jewish and non-Jewish alike, faced roads that were treacherous, unsafe, and infested with bandits and highwaymen. Somehow the image of wine, symbol of sanctity as well as of pleasure, adds an extra dimension to my mental picture of the tradesmen's slow caravans; it imparts an atmosphere that approaches the romantic to the daring and danger of this commerce: The centuries-old connections between northeastern Hungary and Poland take on a wine-forged, ruby glow that sets them apart from, say, regions connected solely by more mundane trade in timber or textiles.

These connections become even more fascinating when I consider that the two regions were linked by another factor, too—Hasidism.

Hasidism developed in the Ukraine in the eighteenth century as an anti-intellectual, religious movement based on the teachings of Israel ben Eliezer, known as the Ba'al Shem Tov (Master of the Good Name), a saintly itinerant preacher who lived from about 1700 to 1760. Hasidism stressed piety, joy, and personal love of God as opposed to dry Talmudic teaching and rigid rabbinical scholasticism. Hasidic worship involves singing, dancing, and other outward forms of rejoicing (often well lubricated by wine or schnapps) and was based on a combination of the local *Ashkenazic* (Central European) prayer rite and the *Sephardic* rite, which originated in Spain. Faith revolved around rebbes or *tzaddikim,* charismatic spiritual leaders who, guru-fashion, gathered large personal followings of faithful who believed them to be earthly saints able to work miracles and talk directly to God.

Hasidism spread quickly across Eastern Europe through the movements of the rebbes and their disciples. Sages who studied at the courts of famous Hasidic masters would move on and establish their own courts, either as disciples of their own master or, in some cases, in competition with him for followers. Powerful, sometimes far-flung, Hasidic dynasties were established, with the position of spiritual leader passed on from one rebbe to his son or son-in-law. By the early nineteenth century, Hasidism was the dominant form of Judaism in Eastern Europe.

"The heads of the sect sent regular emissaries everywhere, whose duty it was to preach the new doctrine and win converts," wrote the eighteenth-century Polish-Jewish philosopher Solomon Maimon in his *Autobiography.*

> Now the majority of the Polish Jews consist of scholars, that is, men devoted to an inactive and contemplative life. . . . Moreover, this new doctrine was calculated to make the way to blessedness easier, inasmuch as it declared that fasts and vigils and the constant study of the Talmud are not only useless, but even prejudicial to that cheerfulness of spirit which is essential to genuine piety. It was therefore natural that the adherents of the doctrine quickly multiplied. The rapid spread of this sect and the favor with which a great part of the people regarded it may be very easily explained. The natural inclination to idleness and a life of speculation on the part of the majority, who from birth are destined to study; the dryness and unfruitfulness of rabbinical studies; the great burden of the ceremonial law, which the new doctrine promised to lighten and finally, the tendency to fanaticism and the love of the marvelous, which are nurtured by this doctrine—these are sufficient to make this phenomenon intelligible.[5]

In Hungary, the northeastern corner—which before World War I included Slovakia, Transylvania, and part of Ukraine—was the only part of the country where Hasidism took root and flourished. The region bordered on Galicia (which is now divided between southern Poland and western Ukraine), and the roots of its Jewish communities also lay in that Hasidic heartland. With its ultra-Orthodox observance, anti-intellectualism, outmoded black garb, and blind devotion to mystical, charismatic leaders, Hasidism held little attraction for the more westernized Jews of the rest of Hungary—or, for that matter, for urbanized Jews in larger towns of the northeast. Indeed, Orthodoxy itself held less and less attraction for them: From the 1860s, Jews in Hungary increasingly leaned toward *Neology*, the local brand of Reform Judaism, and many had begun to think of themselves as Hungarians who happened to be Jewish rather than as Jews who lived in Hungary.

I decided to revisit this region of wine merchants and wonder rabbis and to explore the twin connections that for centuries had linked the Jewish people here with their brethren in Poland. In effect, I wanted to follow the route by which wine and religiosity, as well as people, had made their way south to north and north to south through the Carpathians. I wanted to see what, if anything, was left half a century after the Holocaust. I knew I'd be dealing with memory and husks of memory. During earlier visits, I had already seen the lonely, hulking ruins of once-grand synagogues, the tilted, eroding ranks of gravestones, and the protected tombs of the tzaddikim. These seemed to be the only physical evidence that linked the post-Holocaust present with the vital Jewish past: the metaphorical mezuzahs whose wrecked splendor marked the metaphorical Jewish doorposts of this part of the world.

I chose to explore several towns and villages in the Tokaj area that were famous either for their wine or for their tzaddik—or both. From there I moved on, northward, through eastern Slovakia toward Poland, trying to pretend in a way that I was not driving a rented car down the asphalt highways of the 1990s, but that I was a merchant or preacher feeling my way on foot or by horse-drawn cart through tortuous muddy roads across the mountains. I was quite prepared to lose myself, one way or another, for not everyone who attempted the trip made it to the other end—tales of merchants who never reached their destinations are legion. And there is a story, too, about Rabbi Zvi Hirsch from the wine-producing village of Mád, ten miles or so from Tokaj, who in 1809 set off on a trip to Rymanów to visit the great tzaddik Menachem Mendel: Somewhere in the deep, dark forests of the Carpathians he disappeared, and was never heard from again.

THE OFFICIAL TOKAJ WINE REGION includes twenty-nine villages in Hungary's Zemplén County. Jews lived in all of them, and in scores more villages nearby. The region is on one of the main north-south trade routes through Central Europe, and Jews from Poland and elsewhere began settling down here in increasing numbers in the seventeenth century. Records from that period tell of Jewish merchants passing through bearing furs, spices, textiles, tobacco, and many other goods. A few Jews are mentioned as running flour mills. Other early settlers ran village taverns and distilled and sold their own homemade brandy, activities that in later years became traditional Jewish undertakings.[6]

Over time, Jews became more and more immersed in the general, not just kosher, wine trade, carrying out a highly specialized commerce for gentile as well as Jewish customers. A seventeenth-century Pole, Sebastyan Miczyński, accused them of cheating their customers: Jewish wine merchants, he claimed, "buy not only in barrels but entire wine cellars in Hungary, and this is the sole reason why only small barrels arrive in Poland nowadays, and contain wine so diluted as never was the case."[7]

One of the most illuminating and vivid accounts of the wine trade between Hungary and Poland, as well as contemporary conditions in general, is found in the autobiography of the Jewish wine merchant and writer Ber of Bolechów (or Dov Ber Birkenthal), who set down his memoirs several years before his death in 1805. Ber, born in 1723, was both a highly successful merchant and a respected Jewish community leader in Bolechów, a Galician town now in western Ukraine. Often traveling with his father or his brother, Ber made frequent wine-purchasing trips to the Tokaj region, particularly to the village of Tarcal, a few miles from Tokaj, where he eventually became friendly with local Jews and gentiles alike. Most wine was purchased from the cellars of local noblemen or other gentiles; Ber would then arrange for its transport back to Bolechów or L'vov, where he maintained storerooms and would sell the wine, often at great profit, to the local nobility and other customers.

Ber's memoirs are full of meticulous accounts of how he sought out fine wines to buy and drove hard bargains to get the lowest prices for the best quality. He delights in having pulled off especially good deals, particularly if he has managed to get a better bargain than a competitor. He dwells at length, too, on the trials and tedium of this international trade: complicated currency exchanges and customs duties, drunken wagon drivers, icy, unfordable rivers, double-dealing business partners, flea-ridden inns, occasional attacks by roving bandits.

Ber was highly educated—unusually so for the time and place—and spoke Polish, Latin, German, and French as well as Hebrew and Yiddish. In his memoirs, he frequently stresses the importance of knowing foreign languages, particularly for anyone involved in international trade. His fluency in Polish set him apart from most other Jews, even revered community leaders, and on several occasions he won distinction by serving as an interpreter or translator.

Here he describes an incident involving his father and a relative, Saul Wal, a farmer who ran estates in and around the nearby town of Stryi:

> Once Poniatowski [the local count] said to Saul: "I should like to send someone to Hungary to buy me a considerable quantity of good wine. If you know of a fellow-Jew, a trustworthy person who understands the business, I will send him." Saul replied: "I know a Jew who understands the wine business as no one else does; he speaks Hungarian perfectly, and he has been versed from his youth in the Hungarian wine trade." R[eb] Saul sent at once for my father [Judah, born in 1673] and introduced him to Poniatowski, who was favorably impressed. He accordingly decided to send my father for the wine, and handed him 2,000 ducats, that is, 36,000 gulden. He also sent with my father the tutor of his sons, in the capacity of a clerk, in order to register the purchase of the wines and the daily expenses, so that a proper account might be kept. The clerk was named Kostiushko. My father did as he was requested by Poniatowski. He bought 200 casks of Tokay wine of the variety called *máslás*. When they both returned from Hungary and brought the wines to Stryi, Poniatowski was very pleased with the purchase; he gave my father 100 ducats for his trouble, and for keeping the

accounts properly the clerk Kostiushko was promoted to be steward of our native town Bolechów, and he governed our town for many years.[8]

HASIDIC REBBES WANDERED INTO HUNGARY fairly early on. Legend says that the Ba'al Shem Tov himself even got as far as northeastern Hungary, reputedly visiting the town of Szerencs, not far from Tokaj, on a crowded market day in 1746—just about the time when Ber of Bolechów and his father were making their own trips to Hungary to buy wine. The tale is told, too, that Levi Yitzhak of Berdichev, a pioneer Hasidic master renowned for the ecstasy of his prayers, visited the wine-making village of Mád on the festival of Purim in 1783 or 1784. Local people were astonished when he jumped up and danced on the reading desk, so joyful were his prayers, and many in the congregation—including the community's first rabbi, Moshe Wahl—took up the Hasidic way. By the late eighteenth century there were followers of the great tzaddik Menachem Mendel, whose court was in Rymanów, the wine-importing town in southern Poland, in both Mád and nearby Tarcal.[9]

The first Hasidic master to live permanently in Hungary was Isaac Taub, who was born in 1751, some say in Szerencs, the market town said to have been visited just five years earlier by the Ba'al Shem Tov himself. Indeed, Ber of Bolechów writes of having met Isaac Taub in Szerencs, when he unexpectedly spent Passover there in the year 1765 at the home of Isaac's father, Ezekiel. Ezekiel was a brother-in-law of Ber's friend and business connection Ensil Kaz, in Tarcal, where Ber was staying at the time on a wine-buying mission. Ezekiel came to Ensil's home to try to convince Ber to go back to Szerencs with him for the holidays in order that he might also perform the circumcision of Ezekiel's newborn son:

R[eb] Ensil and his wife were very upset that I was not going to stay at their house during the Festival; but they consented, though unwillingly, to my going to perform the ceremony of circumcision on their nephew. . . . R[eb] Ezekiel had no other choice, for when he went to Mád, none of the *Mohels* [performers of circumcision]—although there were many there, because it was a large place—wanted to leave his home and spend the two first nights of the

Festival away. So R[eb] Ezekiel had to come to Tarczal and urge his brother-in-law, R[eb] Ensil, and his wife to let me go. Accordingly I joined R[eb] Ezekiel. We traveled in my carriage, with four horses, and my clerk, Joseph, and the Gentile servant went with me. R[eb] Ezekiel lodged and fed us all, and the horses, for four days; and as soon as we arrived he told my clerk to go into the wine cellar and to choose a cask of a nice wine for my own use. We remained there the two first days of the Passover and the first of the intermediate days. On the second of these days there arrived R[eb] Ezekiel's friends from all the localities and villages in the neighborhood of Szerencs, more than fifty people of consequence. R[eb] Ezekiel arranged the meal, which follows the circumcision, on the third day after the ceremony was performed; I had to attend this ceremonial banquet during the whole day.[10]

It was on this occasion that Ber met Isaac Taub, the future tzaddik, then little more than a child:

When I spent the Passover in his father's house, R[eb] Eisik [Isaac] was a pretty little boy, who played and sang with a pleasant voice. When he grew up his singing made him famous among the Hasidim, as it is said: "Sing unto the Lord a new song and His praise in the congregation of the saints." R[eb] Eisik's first wife was a daughter of R[eb] Ensil, just mentioned, and their mothers were sisters. R[eb] Eisik became famous throughout the country on account of his piety. He was diligent in the study of rabbinical authors, and became a Rabbi and teacher in Israel; to this day he is Chief of the *Beth Din* [rabbinical court] in Nagy Kálló.[11]

From 1781 until his death in 1821 Isaac served as rabbi of Nagykálló, or Kálló, about twenty-five miles southeast of Tokaj. He was a disciple of two great early Hasidic masters, Samuel Shmelke Horowitz of Nikolsburg, Moravia (today Mikulov, the Czech Republic), and Elimelekh of Lizhensk, in Galicia (Leżajsk, Poland). Isaac was renowned for his dreams and mystical interpretation of dreams, and particularly for his songs, some of which have become part of Hungarian folk tradition and some of which were simple herdsmen's songs whose words he changed and embroidered to give them Jewish meaning.

His most famous song, "The Cock Is Always Crowing" ("*Szól A Kakas Már*"), is still sung today by Hasidim and Hungarians alike. It has a haunting, mournful, yet voluptuous melody in a minor key, reminiscent both of Hebrew prayers and Gypsy folk tunes. Isaac's lyrics tranformed a simple peasant love song into a soulful yearning for the days of the Messiah:

> The cock is always crowing.
> It will soon be dawn.
> In the green forest, in the open field,
> A bird is walking.
> But what a bird!
> With yellow legs and wings of blue.
> It is waiting for me there.
> Wait, my rose, wait, always wait.
> If God willed me for you, I shall be yours.
> But when will this come to pass?
> *Yibaneh Ha-Mikdash ir Tziyon temalleh* —When the
> Temple will be rebuilt and Zion will be repopulated![12]

The wonders wrought by the tzaddikim, their sayings, and other occurrences that illustrated their wisdom, insight, and piety were handed down and spread wide in a rich oral tradition of stories, sayings, and song. One of the tales about the Ba'al Shem Tov himself, gathered by the philosopher Martin Buber, touches on the importance of wine in Jewish ritual and joyous fervor in Hasidic life and also recounts a miracle attributed to the Master:

> At the festival of Simhat Torah, the day of rejoicing in the law, the Baal Shem's disciples made merry in his house. They danced and drank and had more and more wine brought up from the cellar. After some hours, the Baal Shem's wife went to his room and said: "If they don't stop drinking, we soon won't have any wine left for the rites of the sabbath, for Kiddush and Havdalah."
>
> He laughed and replied: "You are right. So go and tell them to stop."
>
> When she opened the door to the big room, this is what she saw: The disciples were dancing around in a circle, and around the dancing circle twined a blazing ring of blue fire. Then she herself took a jug in her right hand and a jug in her left hand and— motioning the servant away—went into the cellar. Soon after she returned with the vessels full to the brim.[13]

In his *Autobiography,* Solomon Maimon recounts a somewhat different face of Hasidism. As a young man in eastern Poland he was attracted and fascinated by the new sect and became determined to join it after a Hasidic acquaintance described, among other things, how the tzaddikim "could see into the human heart, and discern all that is concealed in its secret recesses; they could foretell the future, and bring near things remote." Fired by enthusiasm, he traveled to the court of a tzaddik, whom he did not identify by name or place, and was invited to attend the Sabbath meal. This, according to Maimon, is what happened:

> . . . there [I] found a large number of respectable men who had gathered together from various quarters. At length the great man appeared, his awe-inspiring figure clothed in white satin. Even his shoes and snuffbox were white, this being among the Kabbalists the color of grace. He greeted each newcomer with Shalom. We sat down to table and during the meal a solemn silence reigned. After the meal was over, the superior struck up a solemn inspiriting melody, held his hand for some time upon his brow, and then began to call out, "Z . . . . . of H . . . . . , M . . . . . of R . . . . . , S. M. of N . . . . . ," and so on. Each newcomer was thus called by his own name and the name of his residence, which excited no little astonishment. Each as he was called recited some verse of the Holy Scriptures. Thereupon the superior began to deliver a sermon for which the verses recited served as a text, so that although they were disconnected verses taken from different parts of Scripture they were combined with as much skill as if they had formed a single whole. What was still more extraordinary, every one of the newcomers believed that he discovered in that part of the sermon which was founded on his verse something that had special reference to the facts of his own spiritual life. At this we were of course greatly astonished.
>
> It was not long, however, before I began to qualify the high opinion I had formed of this superior and the whole society. I observed that their ingenious exegesis was at bottom false, and, furthermore, limited strictly to their own extravagant principles, such as the doctrine of self-annihilation. Having once learned this doctrine, there was nothing new for a man to hear. The alleged miracles could be very naturally explained. By means of correspondence and spies and a certain knowledge of men, by observing a

man's physiognomy and by skillful questioning, the superiors were able to elicit indirectly the secrets of the heart, so that among these simple men they succeeded in obtaining the reputation of inspired prophets.

The whole society also displeased me not a little by their cynical spirit and the excess of their merriment. A single example may suffice. We had once met at the hour of prayer in the house of the superior. One of the company arrived somewhat late, and the others asked his reason. He replied that he had been detained by his wife having been that evening delivered of a daughter. As soon as they heard this, they began to congratulate him in an uproarious fashion. The superior thereupon came out of his study and asked the cause of the noise. He was told that we were congratulating our friend because his wife had brought a girl into the world. "A girl!" he answered with the greatest indignation. "He ought to be whipped." (A trait of these, as of all uncultivated men, is their contempt for the other sex.) The poor fellow protested. He could not comprehend why he should be made to suffer for his wife having brought a girl into the world. But this was of no avail: he was seized, thrown down on the floor, and whipped unmercifully. All except the victim fell into an hilarious mood over the affair, upon which the superior called them to prayer in the following words, "Now, brethren, serve the Lord with gladness!"

I would not stay in the place any longer. I sought the superior's blessing, took my departure from the society, resolved to abandon it forever, and returned home.[14]

In the spring of 1944, on the orders of Adolf Eichmann, virtually all the hundreds of thousands of Jews in the Hungarian provinces were rounded up and within three short months deported to Auschwitz and other Nazi death camps. Few survived, and most of those who did left the country, either right after World War II or following the abortive Hungarian revolution against the Communists in 1956. Several surviving Hungarian Hasidic tzaddikim relocated to New York, where they have carried on a traditional shtetl-style life surrounded by their followers in a few Brooklyn neighborhoods.

Although Reform Judaism and more mainstream Orthodoxy eventually had become dominant in Hungary, Hasidism remained a potent force in the northeastern part of the country, as in Poland, eastern Slovakia, northern Transylvania, and the Ukraine, until the

Holocaust. Indeed, followers of the early tzaddikim and other more recent Hasidic rebbes still come by the dozens from Israel and the United States to pay their respects at the tombs of their masters.

Tokaj

Tokaj, the historic heart of the wine region on the southeastern edge of Zemplén County, was the first stop on my journey, in the brilliant late October of 1992. Before the breakup of the Austro-Hungarian Empire after World War I, Zemplén County stretched northward through what is now the eastern tip of Slovakia, all the way to the Polish border. The frontiers drawn when Czechoslovakia was established in 1918 split it in the middle. Before the Holocaust, about sixteen thousand Jews lived in the Hungarian part of Zemplén County; perhaps twenty individual Jews live there today.

The first time I visited the Tokaj region, two years earlier, I had no idea that any Jews still lived in the area. I saw cemeteries and empty synagogues; some of the cemeteries were well protected and cared for, but I thought it was all done by American or Israeli Hasidim preserving the *obels,* or protected tombs, of their beloved rebbes. In Tokaj itself, I recall, the massive synagogue—its size and grandeur testifying to the prosperity of the prewar Jewish community—was hidden by scaffolding and undergoing renovation; nobody could tell me for what. A small, squat building with a Jewish star on its entryway stood next door, but it was locked and closed up tight. It was a miserable, rainy day; I quickly noted the well-maintained cemetery rising rather dramatically into the distance behind a locked gate on the road out of town but didn't take time even to ask how one would visit the other Tokaj cemetery, situated on an island in the middle of the Bodrog River. It was far too wet, far too muddy.

This time I was determined to visit that island cemetery; the very thought of it intrigued me: Jews burying their dead on an island in the middle of a river.

Tokaj, a small town of six thousand people, lies at the point where the Bodrog River runs into the Tisza; it's not much more than a large village sandwiched between the rivers and a fifteen-hundred-foot hill that's partly wooded, partly meadowland, and partly planted in vineyards. When Jews lived there, I was told, the vineyards went all the way up to the summit.

The old section of town has a few streets lined by neat, pastel-colored buildings and plastered with signs advertising private rooms for rent and privately made wine for sale. There's a little town square with two tall, steepled churches, a glass-windowed department store, a couple of smoky cafés serving wine from glass pitchers set on the bar, and an uproarious statue of a drunken male nude, right in front of the main church.

Along the riverbank at one end of town is an incredibly ugly modern hotel whose stark white front decorated with red balls and other space-age trim looks totally out of place in the otherwise fairly idyllic setting. At the other end of town, a new disco advertises top-less women dancers. Around the corner stands the synagogue, one of the largest buildings in the village, supposedly one of the ten largest synagogues in Hungary. The scaffolding had been removed since my first visit; the outer walls had been restored and painted bright yel-low, but the inside still was unfinished, the windows empty and shielded with plastic sheeting.

There is no bridge across to the Bodrog island, but it wasn't hard to find what looked like a ferry. No one was on it or around it. I was traveling that day with a friend, Edward Serotta, an American photog-rapher who has spent years documenting Jewish life in Central Europe. He sat in the car, listening to tapes of Hungarian folk songs and looking across the rippling water to the green, brown, and gold woods on the island, while I, with my marginal command of Hungar-ian and my overwhelming determination to see the old cemetery, went in search of someone to run the ferry. The someone turned out to be a middle-aged woman with a missing tooth, a red head scarf, blue trousers, a long blue coat, and black rubber galoshes. When I told her where we wanted to go, she was skeptical about taking us across.

"*Sár!*" she said, repeating a word I had got to know quite well during my travels in search of Jewish relics in rural Hungary. "Mud!"

"It's OK! Boots!" I replied, pointing to my then still fairly chic black leather Italian numbers. She looked down at them, dubiously cocking her head, looked up at my encouraging smile, looked down at my boots again, calculating, finally agreeing that maybe it would

TOKAJ: Boatwoman being photographed as she rows us across the Bodrog River to the island where the old Jewish cemetery is located.

be OK, if I said so. Maybe. (Crazy foreigners.) But we couldn't take the car. No, no, she said. Too much *sár*.

She punted us across the river in a pale blue rowboat that rocked pleasantly. As we stepped ashore, she warned us again about the mud, pantomimed directions to the tip of the island, where the cemetery was, then told us to holler across the water when we were ready to go back. She pushed off, leaving us alone on the island.

It was a perfect fall day, a sunny respite from a week of rain and fog. The colors glowed; the mud was rich, deep black; the trees were beginning to turn color; autumn wildflowers flamed golden; grass and leaves brazenly exhibited at least four shades of green. It was very lonely, and I was glad I was not there by myself. We walked in utter muddy silence for what must have been half a mile, losing ourselves amid other muddy lanes at one point, finding a lone farmstead at the water's edge, realizing that people actually lived on the island and that we weren't as isolated as we felt.

The cemetery was at the back of the farm. The brick-red iron gate, with a Star of David in the middle, was smashed down and lying flat in the grass at the top of crumbling stone steps, but that was the only sign of deliberate damage or lack of care. Otherwise the scene was calm and peaceful—dreamy, like so much of the landscape around Tokaj, slightly unreal. Wild plum trees thrust lean black trunks above the hundred or so tombs, their leaves making a shimmering greenish canopy, diffusing the sun. Fat purple plums hung like precious ornaments or, fallen, glowed like giant jewels in the grass. We shook some down and tried to eat them, but spat them right out: They were overripe and mushy, far too sweet, almost fermented natural plum brandy.

This was the burial place for historic Tokaj Jewry, the men and women who saw their small number become consolidated into a prosperous community. Most of the tombstones are so weathered and eroded that neither date nor epitaph can be deciphered; the oldest tomb whose date can be determined is 1825. The last burial was in 1878, nearly two dozen years before the big synagogue was constructed to replace the first prayer house, which was destroyed along with much of the town in a great fire in 1890.

An epitaph on a tombstone shaped like a pointed gothic window reads:

Here is buried
a righteous woman
whose work was pure
who followed the words of her teachers
and left a good name
Mrs. Ziporah Rechil
daughter of Mr. Me'iri Asher
died on the eve of New Year's
in the year [5]629 [1869]
May Her Soul Be Bound Up in the Bond of Life.[15]

We wandered among the stones, taking photographs. Most of the tombstones were upright *mazzevahs,* typical of the gravestones of Ashkenazic Jews, Jews—like almost all of those in Central and Eastern Europe—originally of German origin. Two of the tombs, though, were marked by the coffinlike monuments typical of Sephardic Jews, Jews of Spanish origin. I noticed that all the

TOKAJ: The Old Jewish Cemetery.

tombstones, of whatever type, bore hand-painted numbers on the side or back.

Jews settled permanently in Tokaj in the eighteenth century. Most of them, as in other nearby villages, were immigrants from Poland and Galicia to the north. Only two Jewish families lived in the town in the 1720s; by 1746 the community had at least twenty-nine souls. According to prewar local Jewish historian Henrik Lefkovics, the Tokaj community reached about twenty families in the 1750s. At that time, or possibly somewhat later, they built their first synagogue, a simple building near the riverbank, consisting of a sanctuary with the bimah in the center of the hall and an upper gallery for women that was entered from the outside. The town's first rabbi, Nathan Spiro, also took up his post, and the community established a *Chevra Kaddisha*, or burial society, in the mid-eighteenth century.

The cemetery would have been established some time after that; I was told that it had to be sited on the island due to a discriminatory edict issued by Empress Maria Theresa, who ruled from 1740 to 1780. One of the horizontal, Sephardic-style tombs, which bears no date, appears to mark the resting place of the man who put up the money for the synagogue:

> This is David who built the big house
> And it is a synagogue in which prayer and praises are raised
> His way was holy, a shelter to the poor and [he] pitied the
> unfortunate.[16]

Most of the early Jews in Tokaj cultivated vineyards or produced and sold wine, little by little taking the place of the Greek wine merchants who had controlled the trade up until then. Many became very wealthy. As time went on, Jewish numbers swelled with the arrival of more settlers from Poland. They became farmers, peddlers, shopkeepers, small businessmen, artisans, doctors, lawyers, teachers, musicians, brandy distillers, tavern keepers, beggars.

By 1860, there were about four hundred Jews in Tokaj, most of them Hasidic. According to local legend, Hasidism was brought to Tokaj—as to nearby Mád—in the 1780s by the famous tzaddik Levi Yitzhak of Berdichev. Tokaj's Hasidim have been described as being very religious indeed. In his memory book commemorating the Jews of Zemplén County, Meir Sas recounts that at one point in the nineteenth century a Tokaj Hasid discovered that the supposedly silk buttons on his capote were actually made from the ritually impure mixture of wool and linen. The panic-stricken Hasidic community immediately drew up plans to open a bone-button factory of their own to meet what they expected to be a sudden, huge demand for ritually clean fasteners. Tokaj Jews did start factories in the latter part of the nineteenth century: a match factory, an ice factory, a brandy factory, and a factory making tartaric acid.

Ed and I made our muddy way back to the landing place opposite the ferry station. We had to holler and whistle long and loud before the kerchiefed boatwoman took heed and came across to fetch us. She spoke to us nonstop in Hungarian, but it was easy to catch her drift. She was, in fact, directing us to the man who was to become my guide to the Tokaj region.

"You're interested in Jewish things?" she asked. "Go see Lajos Lőwy."

LAJOS LŐWY TURNED OUT TO BE a stocky, forty-three-year-old son of Holocaust survivors, one of the last four adult Jewish men in Tokaj. A lonely man despite having many friends, Lajos is obsessed by a private mission to preserve the memory of local Jews. "I can't sleep at night sometimes," he told me at one point. "I keep seeing them, thinking of them: the cemeteries, the synagogues. . . . Day and night, I think only of how to save these places."

It was he who had painted the numbers on the tombstones in the old cemetery on the Bodrog island. One of his projects is an attempt to photograph and number each tombstone in each Jewish cemetery in Zemplén County—if possible before neglect and erosion obliterate the inscriptions—so that the epitaphs and, thus, the memory of the people buried will be preserved. So far, he has been able to find funds to document fully only four cemeteries: the two in Tokaj, one in Mád, and one in Olaszliszka. In Zemplén County there are another sixty or so cemeteries to go, most of them abandoned and crumbling into dust. He's running, he knows, a race against time.

"I number each tombstone and I number each photograph so that the numbers on the pictures and the tombstones match up,"

Lajos explained. "From the Hebrew texts we can learn who is buried there, so that if relatives or descen-

TOKAJ: Lajos Lőwy outside his dry-goods shop.

dants come and try to find the graves of their ancestors or family members, they will be able to do so. Now I'm trying also to dig up the birth and death certificates of these people; they are available as of 1820. The birth certificates are so detailed that you can find out a lot of things: who performed the bris—the circumcision—of a boy baby, for instance. Or who was the godfather."

Lajos also collects old photographs of local Jews and tries to find out about their lives, matching up dusty clippings and grainy photos with the graves and keeping a sort of posthumous archive of the community.

"When someone comes here looking for traces of his family, and if by chance I can show them a picture of a relative, they start to cry, because during the war everything was destroyed," he said. "Before 1944, when the Jews were deported, each person had his own place in the synagogue. I'm trying to find out which place was whose." He also makes lists and notes from old municipal employment rolls, town ledgers, and other archival sources.

"It bothers me," he said, "that I have to ask this information from gentiles."

A widower—his wife died of cancer at only thirty-four—Lajos runs a narrow, overcrowded dry-goods shop on Tokaj's main street, Rákóczi út. It's the same shop, selling much the same goods—envelopes, pins, pens, notebooks, wrapping paper, clothing, tape, string—that his father and his grandfather, who founded the store, sold before him. Like them, like countless other Jewish shopkeepers in towns large and small through the centuries, he lives in the apartment upstairs. He fully expects his twelve-year-old son, Peter, to take over the store after he is gone. "Before the war," he said with a sweep of his arm, gesturing at Rákóczi út, "all these shops were owned by Jews."

Lajos was born in 1949. Both his parents were survivors of the Nazi camps; his mother originally was from Miskolc, thirty miles to the west, his father from Tokaj. "They didn't want to leave after the war, and they didn't want to leave in 1956," Lajos said. "They were afraid of everything after coming back from the deportation. I didn't want to leave, either. My father was very, very religious; he could read the Torah, blow the shofar, and chant the prayers. Once he was invited to Munich to lead services, but he didn't go even though he could have earned three thousand Deutsche marks in three days."

One of Lajos's main concerns is to make sure that the restoration of the great synagogue is completed, and that when it is, the building will be used for a dignified purpose and contain at least a corner dedicated to the memory of the lost Jewish community of Zemplén County: "I don't want to see the synagogue turned into a restaurant or wine museum. There should at least be space for an exhibition in memory of the original function of the building, an exhibition about the history of Jews in Zemplén County, with documents and ritual objects, maybe a Jewish archive. And I want a memorial plaque placed on the wall of the synagogue for every town and village around here, listing the names of all those fifteen thousand Jewish martyrs who were taken away and never came back."

The synagogue was built in the 1890s to replace the first shul, which had been destroyed in the devastating fire that swept the town in 1890. It's a grand building, one of the most imposing structures in the entire town, set back from the road in a big fenced-in yard and built in an eclectic, slightly Moorish style with tall arched windows and a curving mansard roof. It could seat one thousand people and has been described as having been the "jewel box" of the town.

In the yard surrounding the synagogue remain other buildings that still belong to the Jewish community: a former matzo bakery; a former mikvah, or ritual bath, which is now rented out as a ceramics workshop; the squat little one-story brick prayer house, built as a Hasidic *shtibl*—prayer room—in the 1930s by the wealthy local iron-monger Mór Seiler and used as the only prayer house after the war. There's been no minyan since Lajos's father, who led the services, died more than a decade ago, but the tiny sanctuary looks as if people had just got up from their prayers. Ancient, battered prayer books lie on pews and tables; half-burned candles stand in front of the Ark; cabinets contain moth-eaten prayer shawls, moldering books; even the four wooden poles of a wedding canopy—a *chuppah*—stand in one corner. Gypsies now live in the sagging houses behind the synagogue; they stared at me impassively as I walked around back to take pictures.

The great synagogue was declared a historic monument in 1952, but it was scarcely usable. German Nazis and Hungarian fascists had wrecked it during the war, smashing the stained-glass windows, shredding prayer books, trashing the sanctuary. In the early 1960s, it was sold by the fast-dwindling Jewish community to a cooperative that intended to restore it and use it as a furniture store. Instead, it was used as a warehouse and was later sold to another cooperative that wanted to transform it into a factory making wine bottles. The roof was taken off and the windows and doors were removed in preparation for this reconstruction work. Unfortunately, the firm ran out of money. For years, as Lajos put it, "this ruined building stood in the middle of a busy one-way street in a world-famous town like a symbol of the Jews' tragedy."

"I remember well how the great synagogue was before the war," said Júliana Hadassy, a sixty-one-year-old gentile woman who has lived in Tokaj all her life. "When I was a child, I remember that I wanted to go inside it very, very much, but it was not allowed. We children used to stand at the door and look in—once one of our Jewish friends took us right into the doorway, not inside but right at the door so we could look around—and it was a wonderful sight, and on the outside it was beautiful, too. I always think about that when I walk by there now."

I sat talking with Mrs. Hadassy, a plump, comfortable grandmother who works for the local old-age charity and thinks stocky Lajos, whom she has known all his life, is too thin. We sat in the toasty-warm living room of her home near the main town square. She had many memories of the way things used to be, in the years before the deportations, when some fourteen hundred Jews lived in Tokaj—twenty percent of the town's population.

"I remember the Lőwys, Lajos's father's family, very well," she said. "They had a dry-goods store before the war, and Lajos's father started it up again when he returned from Auschwitz. That whole street was full of Jewish shops; all the stores on this main street were owned by Jewish merchants. Little shops, tailors, textile merchants. There were a lot more shops here in town then. The Lőwys's shop was just the same, before and after the war. They were very talented salesmen. If someone went into their shop, he couldn't leave without buying something.

"Before the war, when the Jews owned the vineyards, there was a good possibility of getting jobs in there," she said. "A lot of people worked there, not just people from Tokaj, but from the surrounding area, too. Now there's a lot of unemployment here. There was a lot more religious life, too, before the war. The Jews were very religious, but so were the Christians.

"I remember on Friday nights," she said, "it was very quiet in town, because there were so many Jews living here. The only thing they did on the Sabbath was go to synagogue. Before the Sabbath came, the women would make *sólet* [*cholent*], I remember that too," she said, referring to the traditional dish of beans, barley, and meat sealed into an oven before sundown on Friday to cook overnight by the remaining heat in order to be ready for Saturday lunch. "Everything was made ready on Friday evening, then they did nothing. In every home, candles were lit. There was a little table, and candles were put on that."

She described a town in which the Jewish men wore white shirts and black coats, in which most of the men had *payis* (sidelocks), and many had ritual fringes hanging out from under their jackets. Some of the women wore wigs; all of them wore head scarves. Mrs. Hadassy's grandmother was the "Shabbos goy" for a Jewish tavern keeper; every Sabbath she would light the fires and do other tasks Jews were prohibited from doing. Mrs. Hadassy, too, as a girl, she said, used to light Sabbath fires for elderly people.

"Jews never invited Christians to their holidays," Mrs. Hadassy recalled, "but they used to give us cakes and matzos. I remember everything from that time, all the names of the specialties. On my way home from school, I always went by the house where an old Jewish woman lived. When she had fresh bread or something, she would beckon me with her finger like this to come in and have a treat, goose liver or fresh bread."

Christians, she said, were allowed to take part in Jewish funeral processions. "But during a funeral procession, if a Christian church bell started to ring, then the whole procession stopped and they waited for silence to go on again."

As we talked and sipped strong coffee from tiny cups, another woman, seventy-year-old Borbala Nagy, came to join us. She, too, had fond memories of prewar times and had had close relations with her Jewish neighbors. "I can only think back with love," she said. "These people were very kind, intelligent, helpful. . . . Life was completely different. Everyone was religious; because of this, they didn't fight each other. They lived in peace. Everyone wanted to work. Now, there are so many people who don't want to work. It was really very nice back then. People accepted what they had—they didn't want anything exaggerated. They lived really in peace."

Their memories are colored, of course, by the nostalgia of age and time. Certain things they mentioned, though, indicated that there may have been less love between the Jewish and gentile communities than they recalled. The small, nondescript town of Tiszaeszlár lies less than ten miles south of Tokaj. It was here in 1882 that local Jews were accused of murdering a Christian girl (who probably actually had committed suicide) and using her blood for ritual purposes. This notorious blood libel touched off a wave of anti-Semitic violence and political activities that lasted for years, even though the Jews were all acquitted of the charge when the case went to trial.

At some point in her childhood, said Mrs. Hadassy, stories about that blood libel of more than half a century before began to circulate in Tokaj. "A lot of people were afraid of Jews, then. They said that if they went into a Jewish house to light the candles, they'd be killed and their blood would be used to make matzos. But I never believed this. I was never afraid of Jews. Some of this still lingers; before I went to Israel not long ago, some people asked me if I wasn't afraid. But, actually, that was probably because of the Middle East situation."

The memories of Tokaj on the eve of war tally with those Elie Wiesel has recounted in his writings. Almost the same age as Mrs. Hadassy, Wiesel remembers life in a largely Hasidic village in Hungarian-ruled Transylvania not all that far from Tokaj, where normality reigned until the very moment when the Jews were rounded up and deported in the spring of 1944.

That spring, Wiesel wrote in his early memoirs, *Night,* "The trees were in blossom. This was a year like any other, with its springtime, its betrothals, its weddings and births."[17]

No one had an inkling of what was about to happen, despite the war going on, despite anti-Jewish regulations. Both women in Mrs. Hadassy's toasty Tokaj living room recalled the sudden round-up and deportation of Jews within a few short days in April 1944 as a major trauma for the gentile community as well as for the Jews who were being sent to their deaths.

"It was horrible," recalled Mrs. Hadassy, who was a teenager at the time. "No one could believe that it was true. We heard what was going on, but we couldn't believe that it was happening. Everyone was crying. It happened so suddenly; it was unbelievable. The Jews were put into the prayer house. It was awful hearing the crying of the children. One woman had a one-year-old baby. She asked someone to take the little child, but no one could do it because everything just happened so quickly. It was horrible when the Jews were rounded up and the deportation started. Almost everyone in Tokaj was standing there on the road, watching what was happening, how they were being taken away in horse carts. One Jewish woman said to me, 'You are crying as you watch what is happening to us. At least we have someone to watch us and cry for us, but there won't be anyone to cry for you when the time comes.'

"She was right. Later, when the Russians came, many people from Tokaj were deported. It was the same scene as with the Jews. They were collected in a house, then taken away by the Russians. My own mother was rounded up, but she wasn't deported.

"We felt terrible sympathy for the Jews when they were taken away—we wept; we felt so sad. But we couldn't do anything. If we tried to give something to the Jews, we were beaten by the police. We were kept away; we couldn't even speak to them, either.

"My mother took milk to them, bread, whatever she could," said Mrs. Nagy. "Me, too. Once I was caught by the police and taken home. The police said that if I did that one more time, I too would be deported."

Only a few Jews came back; about one-tenth of the prewar community survived. "Those who returned were very, very closed," recalled Mrs. Nagy. "They didn't want to speak. They turned inward into themselves."

TOKAJ TODAY IS A "TWIN CITY" with Binyamina, in Israel—the two towns are linked by civic, social, and cultural exchanges—but Lajos Löwy is the only one of Tokaj's four remaining Jewish men who takes an interest in preserving the past. All those people who died before he was born are still alive for him; they speak to him somehow through the stones he is trying to save.

Lajos had to speak most of the time with me through a translator, Flory, a bright and handsome student of twenty-four who was born and brought up in Tokaj but knew nothing, or almost nothing, about Jews, Judaism, Jewish history in general, or even the Jewish history of his home town. Our visits to Jewish cemeteries and ruined synagogues, our chats with elderly residents of several wine-country villages opened up a new world for him.

"You have to know something of history," I told him at one point.

"But what history?" he countered. He told me that the only book about Israel and Judaism he had read had been given to him in Germany by an American. When he described it, it was clear that it was a crude anti-Semitic tract, the kind that equated Ashkenazic Jews with Nazism because of the "-nazi" in the spelling.

"How was I to know it wasn't true?" he asked. "I had read nothing else. That's why I don't want to know about history, because how do you know what's true?"

Sátoraljaújhely

Sátoraljaújhely is a sleepy border town on the Hungarian side of the frontier with Slovakia. We visit on an early Friday afternoon in October: *Erev Shabbos*—the eve of the Sabbath—in the home of Rózsika Róth. Tall silver candlesticks gleam on the round dining table in a stuffy dim sitting room crammed with dark furniture. A prayer book lies beside the candlesticks, ready for sundown. Four round, braided *challahs* are baking in the oven; slices of fresh carp fill a basin in the kitchen, ready to be prepared for the traditional Sabbath meal.

We sit, four of us, in the sitting room crowded with furniture, all staring at, or possibly beyond, a small black plastic box on the table: a tape recorder. Mrs. Róth, one of seven Jews left in Sátoraljaújhely; Lajos, one of four Jews left in Tokaj; myself; Flory, the young, jeans-clad Hungarian translator to whom Judaism and the Jewish world here were long before his time, little more than myth or legend.

The tape machine, a cheap cassette recorder I use for interviews, is playing a scratchy tape that Lajos had brought along. It is the voice of his father, József, who died eleven years before. An Auschwitz survivor, he served as the cantor for the postwar remnants of Tokaj's Jewish community, leading services in the small, squat prayer house across the yard from the ruined main synagogue until his death. On the tape he chants Rosh Hashanah prayers in a high, untrained, rather rough voice. The recording is far from expert. There is a slight echo, and his voice wavers from time to time as if he moved farther and then closer to the microphone. Mrs. Róth and Lajos are transfixed; Flory looks on.

"It makes me shiver to hear this," says Lajos, writhing his shoulders and back and head for a moment as if to shake something off. His face is screwed up; he's trying not to cry at the voice reaching him over the years. He rubs his eyes, then opens his wallet to show a picture of his father—a bland, ordinary, rather forgettable head shot of a middle-aged man with slightly pointy features. "He never would let anyone take a picture of him," Lajos says. "This was for his ID card."

There is a click on the tape, and the voice abruptly changes to a rich bass with all the cantorial flourishes.

"Listen," Lajos says to Mrs. Róth, lifting his chin at her.

SÁTORALJAÚJHELY: Rózsika Róth outside her home.

The voice, that of the one-time *shochet,* or ritual slaughterer, in Miskolc, an old man now crippled and unable to carry out his trade, sings sentimental Yiddish songs. "My yiddishe mamma," he sings. And then his voice catches as he sings about Belz, "*mein shtetele Belz*"; about children and family and a whole lost world. "*Oy, Belz, mein shtetele Belz, mein heimele*"—"my little home." (A man of Mrs. Róth's age, who came from a village not all that far from this northeast corner of Hungary, once told me, "In the town where my uncle the lawyer lived, they always had to find a shochet who also sang. I always wondered: How could someone who could sing like that, how could he be the same person who killed animals?")

Mrs. Róth sits there, tears trickling from her eyes, staring beyond the tape recorder into the past, into that lost world she still feels part of, as she waits for the challahs to bake and waits for sundown.

I FIRST VISITED SÁTORALJAÚJHELY in November 1990.

"*Újhely*" means "new place" in Hungarian. "*Sátor,*" "tent," is the name of the low mountain that rises up over the town, so Sátoraljaújhely—which even Hungarians abbreviate simply to "Újhely," pronounced *OOeehay,* means "new place at the foot of tent mountain." To Jews, Újhely was also known as Ohel—the Hebrew word for "tent," which also refers to the protective building constructed around the tombs of many tzaddikim and rabbis.

Újhely was, and still is, the most important town in Zemplén County. The county was split up when borders were redrawn in 1918, and part of Újhely itself was left in Slovakia. This Slovak part retained the same name, but in the Slovak language: It is called *Slovenské Nové Mesto,* "Slovak New Place."

Before the Holocaust, Újhely was a bustling town with more than four thousand Jews. The Jewish school, founded in 1838, was famous. The town was also the historic seat of Moses (Moshe) Teitelbaum, the Hasidic tzaddik who settled there in the early nineteenth century and became the founder of a famous dynasty of rebbes, whose influence spread through surrounding areas. His son, grandsons, and later descendants established their own Hasidic courts in towns and villages in northern Hungary, Galicia, and what is now northwestern Romania: Sighet, for example, where Elie Wiesel was born, and Satu Mare—Szatmár—whose last resident rebbe, Joel Teitelbaum, Moses's great great grandson, narrowly escaped deportation to Auschwitz in 1944 and ended up in New York's Williamsburg section of Brooklyn, where he wielded tremendous influence over his large community of followers.

Moses Teitelbaum was born in 1759 in Przemyśl, now in the very southeast corner of Poland, and was believed to be a descendant of the great sixteenth-century rabbi of Cracow, Moses Isserles, known as REMUH. He studied with the great Hasidic master Jacob Isaac Horowitz ha-Hozeh, the charismatic sage with strange, intense eyes, who was known as the Holy Seer of Lublin. Teitelbaum moved south to Sátoraljaújhely in 1808, becoming—along with his contemporary, Isaac Taub of Kálló, one of the first Hasidic masters to settle in Hungary. Oddly enough, his wife's father had been a wine merchant who made frequent purchasing trips to Hungary.

Many stories are told about Teitelbaum, who, though he became one of the most influential tzaddikim of his time, began his career as an opponent of Hasidism. He was greatly influenced by his vivid, spiritually symbolic dreams, which he analyzed carefully, seeking in their interpretations guidance for a wide variety of problems. He was famous also for his firm conviction that the Messiah was on his way—some say Teitelbaum used to climb Sátor Mountain, peering this way and that for his coming. In his old age Teitelbaum even felt as if he had been tricked by God because the Messiah had not arrived:

> Rabbi Moshe Teitelbaum was always waiting for the coming of the Messiah.
>
> Whenever he heard a noise in the street, he asked in trembling tones: "Has the messenger come?"
>
> Before going to sleep he would lay out his sabbath clothes near the bed and lean his pilgrim's staff against them. A watchman had orders to wake the rabbi at the very first sign he saw.
>
> Once someone wanted to sell Rabbi Moshe a fine house right next to the House of Prayer. "What would I do with it?" he cried. "Soon the Messiah will come and I shall go to Jerusalem." . . . Even when he was very old, it never occurred to him that he could possibly die before the coming of the Messiah. . . .

When he was eighty-two, he prayed on the eve of the Day of Atonement before "All Vows" [Kol Nidre]: "Lord of the world, you know that I am a wicked sinner, but you also know that I intend to speak the truth. I do not lie and so I shall say only what is so. Had I, Moshe, the son of Hannah, known that my hair would turn gray before the Messiah came, I would very probably not have stood it. But you, Lord of the world, have made a fool of me day after day, until I turned gray. By my life, it is indeed a great trick for the Almighty to make a fool of an old fool! I implore you, Lord of the world, let it come now! Not for our sake, but for your own, that your Name may be sanctified amongst the many![18]

Teitelbaum gained a reputation as a great mystical healer, and Jews and non-Jews alike sought charms and amulets from him and asked him to pray for their health. Legend has it that Lajos Kossuth, the future Hungarian revolutionary leader, was brought to Teitelbaum at the age of nine by his despairing parents in hopes that the rebbe could cure him of a severe illness. The Kossuth family was not Jewish, but a blessing from Teitelbaum, the story goes, was enough to ensure the boy's recovery (or so it was believed).

Teitelbaum, who was extremely rigorous in obeying all Jewish commandments and following all Jewish ritual, was head of the Jewish community in Újhely for more than thirty years and wielded great influence among Hungarian Jews, particularly through his descendants and disciples. In Újhely itself, however, Hasidism was on the wane even toward the latter years of Teitelbaum's life. His grandson succeeded him as head of the Jewish community, but opposition from the more Reform-oriented majority forced him out after six years. His eventual replacement, Rabbi Jeremiah Lőw, was a staunch *mitnagged,* or opponent of Hasidism.

Moses Teitelbaum died in 1841, and an ohel was erected over his tomb in the old Jewish cemetery within a year. Each year on the anniversary of his death, hundreds of Jews from all over Eastern Europe came in increasing numbers to pray and to leave kvittleh, the prayers and requests for blessing and intercession that were written on small slips of paper. Admission was charged to get into the ohel.

Meir Sas recalled the busy scene at the cemetery in his memory book about Zemplén:

During the twenties of this century, the border with Czechoslovakia, at the city's eastern boundary, was opened so that Jews could cross over without transit documents. . . . The cemetery was opened from the early morning hours, and a market of holy books and religious calendars was conducted on the narrow approach street. Admission fees were collected at the gate, and the tickets were given to the guards at the entrance to the ohel. A scribe, seated at a table at the entrance, wrote out the supplications for those who could not write in the holy tongue [Hebrew]. Others brought their entreaties, and those of others, with them, already written out. Still others wrote their requests on the wall, where they remained until they faded with time.[19]

THE OLD JEWISH CEMETERY is on the main road on your left as you drive into town from the south, and it was this cemetery and monument that led me to Mrs. Róth.

I knew nothing about Teitelbaum when I made my first visit to Sátoraljaújhely. I was not planning to stop there at all: I intended, rather, to go straight through town and cross the border into Slovenské Nové Mesto to look for the former synagogue building there, which, I had been told, had been turned into a Catholic church.

The day was gray and rainy, and I drove slowly as I entered Sátoraljaújhely. Just before the downtown district, I noticed a fenced-in area along the left side of the main road, with some lumpy stones, like the stumps of worn teeth, set in a barren pebble base. At the end of a sort of driveway alongside the fence was a cement wall behind which stood a modern-looking, gray-domed structure, like a miniature planetarium, with Hebrew writing above the gate. All was surrounded by concrete apartment buildings, weedy waste ground, and buildings under construction.

I pulled into the driveway to take a look and saw that this was a Jewish cemetery of sorts. On the locked gate, which was decorated with an ironwork menorah, a hand-lettered sign gave the address of a Mrs. Rosenberg, where the key could be obtained.

I turned away. I wasn't really sure if I wanted to take the time to visit this odd-looking, rather grim cemetery memorial. It was so ugly; it was such a gray, ugly day. The dome obviously marked the tomb of a Hasidic rebbe, but, I thought, I wasn't really interested in seeing it.

As it turned out, my indecision before getting back into the car and driving on determined my course. A workman at the building site next door dropped his tools, rushed over, and began talking to me incomprehensibly but with some urgency in Hungarian, apparently offering to help me find the address and the person noted on the sign. He gestured. He got into my car, continuing to speak in words I couldn't understand. He pointed where I should go. From his breast pocket he pulled out pictures of a wrecked automobile—apparently his own, totaled—and seemed to be recounting a miraculous escape. He kissed his hand to the car I was driving: a tiny, rented Volkswagen Polo, which indeed had been serving me well. He guided me to a tall green gate on Árpád Street, number 39, not far from the cemetery memorial—and asked for money.

The green gate opened into a long, narrow yard in which stood a one-story orange house with an overhanging roof. Doors all the way down the house led to individual apartments. At the first door, a brown wooden mezuzah, shaped like a ruler and at least six inches long, was fixed to the frame.

This was the home of Jenőné Róth—Mrs. Roth, the wife (or in this case widow) of Jenő Róth. Her own first name, I found out much later, was Rózsika, Rosie. The Mrs. Rosenberg listed on the sign at the cemetery had died, and Mrs. Róth, an old Jewish woman with a shawl wrapped around her, false teeth, and a slightly sagging lower lip, was now the keeper of the key. A vision from the past, she addressed me in Yiddish, which I tried to counterpoint in my broken German.

"Are you married?" was the first thing she asked me, ever the Jewish mamma, although her husband and her children and all her family, she told me, had been wiped out in the Holocaust. "Do you keep *Yiddishkeit*? Do you go to shul?"

I felt a little uncomfortable; in my bag was a decidedly unkosher salami and cheese sandwich left over from breakfast. I could scarcely remember the last time I had attended a synagogue service. Since leaving my parents' home, I had never put up a mezuzah.

"No," I replied. "I'm not married."

Mrs. Róth ushered me into the house. She gestured at my muddy boots and called in an old man from the courtyard, ordering him to clean them as I stood in the kitchen, booted foot hiked up on a chair, then ordering me to pay him exactly what she deemed appropriate— in dollars. Two dollars, if I recall correctly.

The house was rambling and ramshackle, stuffy and dim; the air was a distilled essence of prewar times, soured by age, poverty, solitude, and memory. "Before the war there were six thousand Jews in Újhely," Mrs. Róth told me. "Today there are eleven." Prayer books and silver candlesticks stood prominently on a shelf; on the frame of every door hung a mezuzah. The refrigerator was full of kosher meat brought twice a month by the shochet from Miskolc, fifty miles away.

Mrs. Róth led me into her bedroom, where on her dresser was a shrine to all the local tzaddikim, their pictures lined up neatly against her mirror along with mementos from her vanished family and vanished times: handsome Moses Teitelbaum with his enveloping tallis, long white beard, and bulging forehead, on which sat an oversized skullcap, which could not prevent a curly, almost rakish, white lock from escaping from above his hidden ear; slightly sour-looking Saje Steiner, the rebbe from Bodrogkeresztúr (where earlier in the day I had got stuck in the mud trying to reach his tomb), with his lowered gaze and long earlocks dangling from beneath the broad brim of his hat; Isaac Taub from Nagykálló; and Zvi Hirsch Friedman from Olaszliszka.

Mrs. Róth flung open chests and opened drawers to reveal heaps of hand embroidery: tablecloths and placemats, napkins and doilies— blue and red, orange and green and white. She spread her wares, and I bought—more because she wanted me to than because I wanted to.

It was dusk, and still raining. Mrs. Róth rolled stockings up over her swollen legs, showing me with a helpless lift of her hands the varicose veins—"What can you do!" She stuffed her swollen feet into battered shoes, took the key, and stepped outside, kissing the mezuzah on the outer doorpost over and over again. Now we would go to, as she put it, "the tzaddik."

But at the cemetery, in the wet and cold and falling darkness, the key would not turn in the lock. She tried, I tried, the workman with the wrecked car, who had come back to the cemetery with us, tried. The key would not turn.

In the morning we tried again, and the lock opened easily. I looked at the tomb; I wandered a little amid the eroded remains of the cemetery; I moved on. "Next time," Mrs. Róth told me, "you must stay at my house, not the hotel."

TWO YEARS LATER, revisiting Sátoraljaújhely and Mrs. Róth was like revisiting a dreamscape, like stepping into a strange film loop or watching a movie I'd seen before, except some of the colors were faded, the timing a little slower. Or maybe I was simply stepping into a ritual she repeated whenever she had a Jewish guest, the luxury of questions, conversation, and gestures of Jewish intimacy she was denied with most of the people with whom she came in contact.

It was October, a sunny Friday noon. Cats were playing in the paved area that runs along the face of the faded orange house. Clothes flapped from a line.

We arrive unannounced and find Mrs. Róth at home. We—myself, Lajos, Flory—enter directly into the kitchen, where four round, braided challahs are rising on a baking tray and about to be popped into the oven. On the kitchen table stands a small open bottle of schnapps. There is a general feel of disarray or disorder.

Mrs. Róth has aged. Her gray hair is straggly, caught under a red and blue scarf; she wears a red and blue print housedress, fastened with a safety pin in front—like Italian peasant women in fortress hilltop villages who wear safety pins on their breasts as protective talismans.

Her pale eyes seem glazed—myopic? unfocused? Her mouth sags a little. Flesh hangs in folds from her heavy arms, reminding me of my grandmother, Becky, my father's mother, who died nearly twenty years ago and who had the same solid, aged body, the same heavy, fleshy arms.

She ushers us into the sitting room. Lajos has brought a yarmulke with him; he puts it on and gives me a conspiratorial grin. "For Frau Róth," he had said when he showed it to me earlier, back in Tokaj: She wouldn't let him in the house without one. The ritual begins.

Mrs. Róth does not remember me or my visit of two years before. She speaks to me, acts with me, as if everything is new. Much of it *is* new; after all, there is Lajos, and there is Flory to translate, and conversation is somewhat broader. But the ritual is there, the luxury of Jewish intimacy. Even if I hadn't asked, she would tell me certain things, show me certain things, ask me certain things.

"There were six thousand Jews here before the war," she says. "Now there are seven." Her face dissolves in tears. On the table, the prayer book and tall silver candlesticks stand ready, waiting for sundown, as I knew they would be. The challahs are baking in the oven.

"I'll make you a piece of fish," she says, bringing in the basin of carp and then setting slices in a pan to simmer.

"We were six brothers and sisters, and we had eighteen children among us," she says. "All were deported to Auschwitz. All were killed. Why did I stay here when I got out of the camp? When I came back, I thought I'd be the happiest person in the world just to have a room to live in, just to live in Hungary. Maybe that's why. Now, I'm totally alone. I have a few cousins in the United States and in London. Otherwise, I'm alone. It's terrible to be alone. . . . When someone [and by someone she means a Jew] comes to visit you," she tells Lajos, "send them on to me."

The house is much as before, rambling and ramshackle and stuffy and dim, and not very clean. Mrs. Róth doesn't see well anymore; she doesn't move well. Surfaces are heavy with oily dirt; gray laundry in gray water soaks in the grimy bath. When she serves us the carp—plump sections of fish swimming in pale gravy—I almost can't eat because the silverware is so encrusted. I try to touch each bite with as little of the fork as possible; I use the fresh-baked challah she sets before us as knife and spoon. Lajos digs in; Flory, the gentile, eats only bread.

"Are you married?" she asks me.

"No," I reply, "I'm not married."

"Ah. But you are so nice, so sympathetic." I see her dart a quick glance at Lajos, the widower. Centuries of Jewish tradition are coursing through her veins; they pep up her imagination. "So nice, so sympathetic. You must come back more often."

"Come," she gestures. She leads the way into her bedroom, and there they are—the pictures of the rebbes lined up on her dresser along with mementos of her vanished family. She takes them down, one by one, to show us: handsome Moses Teitelbaum, with his enormous draped tallis and oversized yarmulke, his bulging forehead and long white beard; Saje Steiner glancing up from under the wide brim of his hat, his straggly earlocks dangling; Isaac Taub from Kálló; Zvi Hirsch Friedman. There's a picture of herself, too, a strong-faced young woman with a bright smile and thick, dark hair beautifully coiffed in a 1940s pompadour.

"Don't you want to buy something?" She opens drawers and pulls out her embroidery. "How about this—twelve hundred forints [about sixteen dollars]." She shows a crocheted antimacassar. I tell her I recall other, colorful embroidered pieces, and she rummages to find them: blue and red, orange and green and white. Lajos is making furtive motions: "Buy something, buy something!"

Of course I buy something, and throughout the rest of the visit she makes pointed side remarks in Hungarian, which Flory translates, to make sure I don't forget to pay.

I ask her about keeping the traditions.

"I've never worked on Saturdays," she says, and points to a big gray metal box in the corner. "See? I bought that electric storage heater so that I wouldn't have to light a stove on the Sabbath." She still gets her meat twice a month from the shochet making his rounds from Miskolc. The Sabbath prayer book accidentally gets knocked to the floor; she kisses it as she picks it up. Flory, the translator, has never seen anything like this. "These people are so *weird*," he breathes.

Lajos says, "I take my hat off to her as a woman who's stayed so faithful, so religious, so kosher. My father never ate anything that wasn't kosher, either."

Every so often Mrs. Róth is called to the kitchen by the voice of a man or, less often, a woman. She talks with them. Some beg for money; some ask for drink; some sound already drunk. It becomes clear after awhile: In the long tradition of Jews in this part of the world, Mrs. Róth sells liquor, small measures of rotgut schnapps served in thick, greasy glasses. This pious old woman runs a makeshift kitchen tavern.

Sátoraljaújhely was once full of Mrs. Róths.

"Ninety percent of the economic life in this town was carried out by Jews," she says. "And there were a lot of doctors and professors and artists and scientists. We Jews lived very well together with the

Christians. Oh, there was some anti-Semitism, but most of the Christians were very good people. We had rich Jews and poor Jews, but the rich ones helped the poor."

It's time to leave.

"You're so nice, so sympathetic," she says to me, looking meaningfully again at Lajos as I stifle a sputter of laughter. She presses a warm, fragrant challah on me, and we go outside to take some farewell pictures.

She straightens her hair under her head scarf and takes off her sweater to look nicer for the camera. On one heavy forearm the tattooed number from Auschwitz is clearly visible. It is faded though; forty-eight-year-old pale blue tracery on her seventy-three-year-old skin.

Satoraljaujhely's Jews, and thousands more Jews from the rest of Zemplén County, were forced into a ghetto right here in this neighborhood around Árpád Sreet and deported to Nazi death camps in the spring of 1944. Mrs. Róth would have been twenty-six.

How beautiful is my love
with her everyday clothes
and a comb in her hair.
Nobody knew she was so beautiful.

Maidens of Auschwitz,
Dachau maidens,
Have you not seen my love?

We saw her on a distant journey,
she no longer had her clothes
or a comb in her hair.

How beautiful is my love,
pampered by her mother,
and her brother's kisses.
Nobody knew she was so beautiful.

Maidens of Mauthausen,
Maidens of Belsen,
Have you not seen my love?

We saw her on the frozen square
with a number on her white hand
with a yellow star on her heart.[20]

A man passes in the background, staggering a little as he goes into his own doorway—had he bought his liquor from Mrs. Róth's kitchen tavern?—just as I line up Mrs. Róth in my lens.

"If you get me in that picture, I'll kill you," he rumbles. Flory translates; a look of shock appears in his eyes, as if he can't believe the words coming out of his mouth.

Mád

If one can fall in love with a building, I fell in love with the synagogue in Mád long before I ever saw it.

I came across pictures of it in a big full-color book on Hungarian synagogues: a scallop-sided baroque facade rising from a hill, looming over a jumble of red tile roofs in the village below, soaring over the surroundings. The elegantly simple flat face gleamed pale ice blue and white, as if it had just been painted; it seemed to reflect the cobalt of the sky. Four pairs of false pilasters, flat, stylized Ionic columns, divided the lower part of the building into thirds beneath the upper curved triangle, which was topped by a sculpted vase like a decorative crest or an impudent tuft of hair.

The synagogue was built around 1795. It is one of the oldest existing synagogues in northeastern Hungary and one of the oldest in all Hungary. The Jews of Mád had moved there from Polish Galicia in the early eighteenth century, and the synagogue was constructed around the typical massive Polish-style four-pillared bimah.

The building was now empty, abandoned. But the pictures in the synagogue book showed that inside much of the former splendid decoration had survived: rampant sculpted lions and griffins rearing proudly above the Ark, flanking boldly rendered reliefs of the Ten Commandments and invocations to the Lord. The pillars of the bimah appeared painted a rich but faded blue, and their strong vertical lines flowed upward into the curves of the vaulted ceiling, which still bore traces of ornate fresco decoration. The arched windows gaped empty, letting in shafts of sunshine. From outside they looked like deep black Jewish eyes in the flat white facade, one on either side of a false window positioned like a saucy snub nose between them. In

MÁD: The front of the baroque synagogue, built in 1795.

one photograph taken from below, the window eyes look up toward heaven; the building is pensive, a little coquettish, too, basking in the sun against a background of blue. In another photo, they peep slyly over the red roofs of the village: "Hey, here I am despite everything," they seem to say. It was easy to anthropomorphize. The building definitely had a strong personality.

Some years later I stood with a friend at the massive rusting door, which is crowned by sculpted garlands draped over the gentle arch of its lintel. "I love this building," I said.

"What's there not to love?" he replied.

What indeed.

The synagogue in Mád stands at the top of a steep, muddy lane that dwindles into a footpath and continues up toward vineyards and open country beyond. It is a graceful, simple building—from the outside, little more than a rectangular white structure with a red-tiled peaked roof—whose elegant false-front gables and elevated position on the hill make it look much more impressive than it really is.

Today, the opaque glass in most of the arched windows has been broken by vandals, and the stucco work on the exterior walls is flaking away in great chunks. It is empty and neglected and almost but not quite forgotten, and I'm still in love.

"Not a week goes by without someone coming to visit the synagogue," says Irene, the woman who lives in the house at the bottom of the lane and who keeps the key—a massive, heavy instrument like a miniature barbell that took both my hands to turn in the lock. "What I want now is a guest book, so that the visitors can all sign their names."

Irene is a middle-aged woman, round and comfortable looking, with a soft voice and sweet face; her hair is done up in a huge bun, making her head and face look almost too big. Her eyes are big and round like her face, and slightly slanted; her mouth is tiny, a little too soft to be called pursed. It's late afternoon on a Friday in October, and the sun is beginning to cast long shadows.

Irene has been caring for the key for only a year. Before, it was kept by a man who lived in what used to be the rabbi's house next to the synagogue, an L-shaped building with arched loggias on two floors. That building, unique in Hungary, is now owned by the town council, and poor families are assigned to live there. An old man, bony and almost toothless, cackles to himself as he struggles from a side shed with a load of firewood in his arms. Laundry flaps from lines strung beneath the arches of the loggia. What looks like an outhouse is built up against one wall.

Irene is just old enough to remember Mád before the war, when, she says, "Every second house was a Jewish house or shop: wine shops, butcher shops, all kinds of shops, bakeries." Many more shops than there are today.

The synagogue, she says, "was very, very nice. I feel so bad about it, that it is falling into disrepair. It is such a valuable building," she says. "It means a lot to me—that's why I arranged to take charge of the key."

As we stand on the sidewalk talking in the golden light, she nods to an old, gnarled woman dressed in black making her way along the street with the aid of two canes. She is small and twisted and very wrinkled; her eyes are distorted by thick-lensed glasses with thick black frames, and her head is enveloped by a scarf.

"You should talk with Mrs. Terko over there," Irene says. "She is the only Jew left living here in Mád."

Her maiden name was Terko Deutsch; she is, or was, Mrs. Lajos Klein—or Kis. *Kis* in Hungarian and *klein* in German both mean "small." Even Orthodox Jews in Hungary were so immersed in mainstream Hungarian life that they often changed German or Yiddish names into Hungarian counterparts.

"I was born here and lived here, and I'm eighty years old," she declares. "My great grandfather lived here, too."

Frau Klein would love to stand and talk there at the bottom of the muddy lane leading up to the synagogue, at the corner where she has passed most of her life, but she can't, she simply can't.

"I have to get home, you know," she insists, "it's nearly sundown. Shabbos!—I must get home and light the candles. Really!"

Shabbos. The Sabbath. The sweet Jewish Bride. The one day of the week when every Jew used to feel like a king or queen, when candles were lighted, when families, even poor families, sat down to golden chicken broth swimming with coin-sized circles of fat, to roast meat, to fish, to sweet wine and honey cake. At this time of day on a Friday when Mrs. Klein was young, this muddy street would have been full of men in black rushing up the hill to the synagogue; and later on, rushing home to the festive Sabbath dinner.

Mád was a Hasidic town, almost from the time that its Jewish community was established in the eighteenth century. Most Jews were involved in wine production and trade, and links were strong between the local people and the rebbes of Rymanów, the wine-importing village in Poland to the north. "The community constantly battled against assimilation and any foreign influences," wrote Meir Sas in his memory book. He relates that in the early nineteenth century local Jewish vintners and brandy distillers met in the synagogue after prayers to fix the prices of their products. Jews who violated these prices ran the risk of ostracism in the community.[21]

MRS. KLEIN MAKES AS IF to leave, to walk the few slow steps to her house, where, alone in the silence of her home, she will stand in front of the two white candles and close her eyes as she recites the ancient blessing over their flames: "Blessed art Thou, O Lord our God, King of the universe, who has sanctified us by Thy command-ments and instructed us to kindle the Sabbath lights." It is the house-wife's prayer, one of the few blessings specifically recited by women. The lighting of the candles is a function so basic to the identity of the Jewish woman that carvings of candlesticks, and sometimes hands raised before them in blessing, are a traditional way of marking the graves of Jewish women. But no, she stays a minute and talks a little bit more.

"I've seen a lot of changes here, a lot of changes in the world in my day, but I've never seen anything like it was in Auschwitz," she says. She leans forward for emphasis and raises her voice. "Seven hundred and sixty-six Jews from Mád were deported. I left my hus-band and son in the camps. And now I'm alone."

Inside the empty synagogue of Mád, under the faded, flaking frescoes that still decorate the sweeping arches of the vaults, affixed to the bare stone wall next to the still-proud Ark with its damaged lions and griffins, is a marble plaque on which all the names of the martyred are listed. It is here, in the synagogue, that they were rounded up in the spring of 1944 before being shipped by rail to the ghetto in Újhely. The name of Lajos Klein, Mrs. Klein's husband, is among them, and there is a long list of Deutsches, Mrs. Klein's own family: Elkán, Irén, Ernő, Ernőné, Géza, Gézane, Ferenc, Lajosne, Sándor, Tibor. . . .

Mrs. Klein still keeps the holidays, all by herself; she buys her meat from the kosher butcher who comes from Miskolc; she makes sure that the old Jewish cemetery at the edge of town, which was fenced in by followers of the rebbes buried in two ohels near the ruined, battlemented mortuary near the gate, is well tended by the warty-faced peasant woman who lives nearby and keeps the key.

The cemetery is on a steep, grassy slope; the stones are weathered, and some are illegible. They are slipping and tipping over from age and gravity. Many bear traces of bright red and blue paint. One fine set of black marble obelisks marks the resting place of the wealthy Weinhandler family. The name means "wine merchant."

"Really, usually, I invite everyone home as a guest—but I can't now, you understand, Shabbos is coming," Mrs. Klein repeats. She looks piercingly up at us through her glasses, a shrewd, birdlike creature. She glances anxiously over her shoulder toward home; she taps her canes. The shadows are lengthening fast. The gold of the afternoon is beginning to dim. There is no question any more of lingering for another moment of conversation.

"Shabbos is coming," Mrs. Klein says again. "I must get home— but come another day, please; you'll find me here."

We watch her make her slow way down the street. Up on the hill, at the top of the muddy lane, the white walls of the synagogue catch the lingering light of the late sun, and shine. Irene steps out of her house with a tray of coffee. We drink; it's getting chilly, so we leave.

"You know, I think it was fate that brought us here, that led us to meet that woman at the foot of the road to the synagogue, right here," says Lajos, as we walk to the car, looking back. Mrs. Klein had asked him why he cared so much about preserving local Jewish memories and places, what he was getting out of it. "It's my faith," he replied. "Ah, Lajos, you are very good," she told him. "Do your best."

A FEW DAYS LATER, we return. It's another late afternoon, chilly and wet. The dampness brings out the burning colors of the seasons on the hills around: smoky, dark greens and browns highlighted by brilliant yellow and deep red foliage, and glistening touches of emerald green.

We pass vineyards full of harvesters; their cars are parked along the country roads. Here in the Tokaj region, the grapes are left on the vine late, until the end of October. The leaves and vines are already brown; the grapes themselves are extra sweet and beginning to shrivel. We pass vast vineyards, too, that have been abandoned, a casualty of the collapse of communism. Once they were worked by the state-run wine-making cooperative, which produced huge amounts of wine, mainly destined for the Soviet Union. The Soviet market has dried up, however, and the cooperative has run out of money. The grapevines are not even pruned; the grapes are simply left to rot. This never happened, I am told, when the Jews were here.

Mrs. Klein is not home; her house is locked up tight. There is a small grocery shop across the street, and we go there to ask if the proprietor knows where she is.

"Of course," he replies. "She's off doing the grape harvest."

I can't believe it—that bent, frail octogenarian who needed two canes to walk and wore glasses as thick as Coke bottles. A grape harvest! Two stout women approach us down the street, dressed in head scarves and blue overalls and carrying baskets full of grapes strapped to their backs.

Yes, they know where Mrs. Klein is—why sure, she's in the vineyard up the hill behind the synagogue, that one, you know, on a little dirt road. We drive up there to try to find her. Flory and I sit in the car, waiting as Lajos squelches up a path into a patch of vines. I can see the whole village spread out below, beyond the synagogue, the autumn hills floating in the distance. Once again, I reflect on how much I love this synagogue, how I love the sweeping curves of the front and back gables, the sculpted tuftlike urns at their highest points. From above like this I can look down on the red tiled roof, so deceptively like all the other red tiled roofs in the village.

Lajos comes back with a companion, an exceptionally handsome young man bundled up in work clothes and a sheepskin hat who strides toward me through the mud in his big rubber boots like some god of the great Hungarian outdoors.

"You speak English?" he asks, speaking the language perfectly himself. "Hello—I'm the rabbi of Debrecen [a city fifty miles to the south]; I just took up the post four weeks ago after living ten years in New York. I was born in this village," he goes on, unmindful of my surprise, puffs of steam coming from his mouth, "and this is the family vineyard. The old lady you want to see is my aunt, and I've come here with her sister, my other aunt Rózsika, who lives in Miskolc, so we can do the harvest."

The rabbi's name is László—Leslie in English—Deutsch. He is

apologetic; he does not think his aunt will have time to talk with us that afternoon. He won't be able to chat, either.

"We have to finish here, and then go back to her house and get everything unloaded and settled, which will take at least an hour. And then, well, I have to leave right away to drive Rózsika back to Miskolc and then drive on directly back to Debrecen—it's Rosh Chodesh, you know." He pronounces it with a Yiddish accent, *Rosh Choydesh*—the first of the Jewish month, the New Moon, a minor holiday that calls for a blessing.

"But maybe, if you want to wait . . . ?"

We wait. In the gathering darkness of the early evening, a villager walks by and sees the young rabbi. "Ah, Ládek!" he calls, smiling. "You're back, eh? How are you?"

Gnarled, bent, short, stooped, Terko Deutsch Klein eventually makes her way down the muddy path from the vineyard toward the truck. She can hardly walk even with the help of her canes, and it is difficult to imagine that she and her equally elderly sister had been harvesting grapes all afternoon. The rabbi helps her and her sister into the cab of the truck. "I can't talk to you today," she calls, closing her eyes behind their thick lenses and motioning us to go away. "I'm too tired. Too tired."

Bodrogkeresztúr

The first time I tried to reach the tomb of the tzaddik Saje Steiner I got stuck in the mud. It was in November, a rainy November, and I got lost on the dirt roads leading up above Bodrogkeresztúr to the cemetery—which, according to a legend I would strongly tend to discount, also is said to have a grave containing the remains of the Ba'al Shem Tov himself.

I had seen the cemetery from below, even through the curtain of rain; it was easily visible on the hilltop behind the village. But I simply couldn't find it. I asked people, several people, and I thought I was following their directions, but I never found the Jewish cemetery. I found a Christian cemetery, but no apparent way beyond it; the one road through the soggy hilltop fields that might have taken me to where I wanted was axle deep in mud. And that's where I got stuck.

It was lonely on the hilltop, and wet. I could go neither forward nor back. I half hoped someone would come along to help—but half hoped not, too. I didn't know if I wanted to meet someone in those lonely, wet circumstances, surrounded by graves and empty fields. So I maneuvered and maneuvered and after maybe half an hour, managed to slither out. The car was muddy, and I too was covered with mud; my boots were soaked, and huge clumps of sticky brown glop clung to the soles.

One of Lajos Lőwy's pet projects is to collect enough money from pilgrims to pave the road up to Steiner's tomb.

"I have a Jewish friend in America who's from Bodrogkeresztúr," Lajos told me. "I call him once a month to ask him for help. A road would only cost twenty-five thousand dollars—that's nothing for a millionaire in America."

Saje Steiner, born in 1851, came to Bodrogkeresztúr at the end of the nineteenth century from nearby Olaszliszka, where he had been a pupil of the famous rebbe Zvi Hirsch Friedman, who in turn had been a pupil of the great Moses Teitelbaum in Sátoraljaújhely. Jews settled in the village, a few miles from Tokaj, around 1700. By the middle of the nineteenth century the community numbered about four hundred people—about one-fifth of the village population. It had become a stronghold of Hasidism in the early part of the century, largely due to its then rabbi, Zvi Hirsch Glanc, who was a grandson of Moses Teitelbaum.

Steiner—known by the diminutive Reb Shajele—was believed, particularly by local women, to have supernatural powers. He lived in a typical village house on one of Bodrogkeresztúr's main streets, Kossuth utca. Today the house is owned by the city council and still has no inside plumbing or running water. Another of Lajos Lőwy's pet projects is to turn part of the building into a little Hasidic museum and guest house for pilgrims visiting the grave.

"People come all the time," said the woman who now lives in the house. She was middle aged and tough looking, with dark painted eyebrows and missing bottom teeth. "A lot of people come. Sometimes they arrive at eleven or twelve o'clock at night! We have to wake up, and go out, and then they take photographs and sometimes they track thick mud into the house. We're tenants of the city and have been living here for about ten years. Before we moved in, we didn't know that this had been the rabbi's house. Then I met Lajos and he told me the story. It's only in the last three years or so that people have really started coming—before, I think they were afraid. Or maybe the whole thing started in '87 or '88. One day back then, I saw a group of four or five Jews standing outside and praying in front of the window! I told them to come in and they were very surprised. 'Oh! We can come in?!' I think this group told a lot of people in America that this was a famous house, and so many others started to come."

With Lajos's help she had set up some facilities for the guests. A table in the corner displays Steiner's picture, along with a sign asking for donations to fix the road and establish the museum and guest house. There is also a big guest book for visitors to sign—most of the signatures are in Hebrew.

"This year, people have come throughout the entire year," the woman said. "On the anniversary of Moses Teitelbaum's death, in Sátoraljaújhely, three big coaches arrived here! There were a lot of people, all Hasids with sidelocks, sometimes a few women. Lots of children, even little ones, five years old. They all walk up to the cemetery on foot. The day before yesterday there were four of them. They walked up in mud that was calf deep. It was nine-thirty P.M. already when they arrived, dark; and they walked up there at night, using flashlights. Then they came here. I asked them to donate something to help pave the road. They could see how much mud there was, they were swimming in mud. But it didn't matter. They didn't give anything."

Said Lajos, "I should go to America to get this money. I would knock right on windows and doors. And if they didn't let me in, I'd go through the chimney!"

We sat and drank coffee made from water drawn from a well in the yard and talked about the Hasidim and their ways, the Jews and their ways.

"Some *Lubavitchers* came to my shop once, a few years ago," recounted Lajos. "They didn't let me close the door, but they put on their tefillin and tallises and started praying, right there. They frightened the customers! There were three of them—two Jews and an interpreter. They said they wanted me to pray. One was a rabbi from Morocco, and one was from the U.S. They made me put on tefillin.

My jacket was hanging on the wall. I told them, wait, I have to get my jacket. I asked them, please, let me close the door; two customers were outside. They looked in and were very surprised to see me with a tallis and tefillin on. Then these rabbis checked my mezuzahs. I have a mezuzah on every door in my apartment above the shop. They wanted to know if they were kosher. They found out the address of every Jew in Tokaj and visited all of them and checked whether they could pray. They gave out presents, too, books and chocolate—they wanted to win these Jews for their sect. At that time, there was a rock concert going on in the square. The rabbis wanted to have a mineral water, but I didn't let them go up to the café on the square to get it, as I was afraid they would be hassled by the crowd there. I tried to explain to them about the condition of the synagogues and cemeteries, but they didn't care about that. They just kissed me and took a picture, and then left."

Our hostess mentioned several times that her grandfather was Jewish.

"He was a Jewish lawyer, Mór Goldberg," she said. "He was very well known in the region. I grew up in this village, but I never heard about Steiner. I heard his name when I was about fourteen, but just as a name."

Her remark puzzled me: She herself was obviously not Jewish. The big living room, with its wooden beams and stenciled wall decorations and scattered family photographs, had the little shrine to Steiner in one corner, but a primitive-style glass painting of Jesus in shades of deep blue hung on the wall above the big sideboard.

I asked Lajos what the story was.

"Later," he told me through Flory, "I'll tell you in the car." But after a moment, in another gesture of conspiratorial Jewish intimacy that he obviously couldn't resist, he leaned toward me behind Flory's back, raised his eyebrows, and, nodding, whispered, *"Momzer!"*—the Yiddish word for "bastard."

"She was the illegitimate daughter of the son of the Jewish lawyer and the maid," he explained later, as promised, in the car. "They settled it with money—the son didn't want to know about it."

Lajos said it had been common for young Jewish men from good families to have sex with the servants.

"My own father and uncle also played around with their family's Christian maid," he revealed. "Yes! It was the tradition. When my father came back from Auschwitz, he even lived with the maid for awhile. Then he married my mother."

There were no momzers in his family, though. "They were careful," he said.

Tarcal

Tarcal, a little village a few miles west of Tokaj, was the place where the eighteenth-century wine merchant Ber of Bolechów did much of his business, particularly in the 1760s. Only a few Jews lived in Tarcal in Ber's time, but most of them apparently were involved in the wine trade. Ber was particularly friendly with the wine merchant Ensil Kaz, whom he described as a German Jew and who was both the uncle and the father-in-law of the celebrated tzaddik Isaac Taub of Kálló. Ber also dealt, however, with a Greek wine merchant whose shop and home were on the main street of Tarcal, as well as with other gentile dealers and producers.

Ber's accounts of trade in Tarcal give a feel for some of the hard bargaining and cutthroat business practices of the time. In 1761, for example, Ensil Kaz and two associates took advantage of another of Ber's friends—a Bolechów Jewish community official who was inexperienced in the wine trade—and sold him poor-quality wine ("grape juice," Ber called it) at the exorbitant price of eight ducats a cask. The next year, Ber bought what he smugly described as much better quality wine for half that price, from the same three people, who by then had formed a wine-dealing partnership. So friendly did Ber become with Ensil Kaz and his partners that on one trip he agreed to spend nearly a week going through their complicated accounts and putting their books in order. He also, in 1765, brought Ensil and the Jews of Tarcal a collection of beautiful ritual objects from Poland:

> In that year . . . I ordered from the silversmiths and goldsmiths at Lemberg [L'vov], who were renowned for their skilful craftsmanship, some sacred vessels made of pure silver for a Scroll of the Law belonging to R[eb] Ensil Kaz of Tarczal. I ordered a large

breastplate for the Scroll, made of solid silver . . . beautifully orna-
mented, well plated with gold and set with precious stones, worth
80 Hungarian gulden; further, two silver rollers, nicely chased and
also plated with gold, valued at 50 ducats; also a silvern pointer,
very finely worked, worth 12 ducats. Many experts agreed that their
like was not to be found throughout all Poland. The aged R[eb]
Leibush Malish, a learned and famous Jewish leader, when he saw
these ornaments together with the other Elders of the community,
remarked: "Even in the time of King Solomon, peace be with him,
these ornaments would have been fit for the Temple." He was at
that time a great expert in all crafts.

In the month of Marchesvan [Cheshvan], [5]526 (October 16–
November 14, 1765) I arrived at Tarczal and handed to R[eb] Ensil
Kaz all these sacred vessels. He was very pleased when he saw
them and paid all the expenses I had incurred in obtaining them.
He desired to present me with a cask of wine for my trouble, but I
said: "I do not wish for any reward for the trouble I have taken in
honor of the Torah."[22]

If this Torah, with all its exquisite silver, gold, and jeweled ornamentation, was still in the possession of the community when Tarcal's
little baroque synagogue was built, it certainly would have taken
pride of place in the Ark built into the sanctuary's eastern wall. The
synagogue is believed to have been built in the 1790s, at about the
same time as the baroque synagogue in nearby Mád, and would have
been a beautifully proportioned structure with its arched windows
and high, rounded facade. Péter Wirth, a Budapest architect and
expert on Hungarian synagogue architecture, told me that an inscription on the walls referred to the year 1792 or 1794. "The Tarcal synagogue was a brother to the synagogue in Mád," Wirth said. "I am
convinced that it was built by the same architect."

Perhaps because of Ensil Kaz's family relations with the tzaddik
Isaac of Kálló, Hasidism gained an early foothold in Tarcal. This trend
was strengthened and solidified when Rabbi Ezekiel ben Joseph
Panet, a devoted follower of Isaac of Kálló, Menachem Mendel of
Rymanów, and other Hasidic masters, served as rabbi of Tarcal from
1813 to 1823.

Today the synagogue in which Panet prayed is a ruined hulk,

crumbling by the year, the month, the week, the day: I myself noted considerable deterioration since my first visit two years before.

TARCAL: The ruined baroque synagogue, built around the 1790s and a "brother" to the one in Mád.

The building stands in a fenced, weed-choked yard at the side of a narrow lane behind a new shopping center just off the main road through the village. The rounded upper tip of the facade has vanished—as if a giant hand had reached down and snapped it off, like snapping off the edge of a cookie. A Star of David, twisted out of place, leans atop the covered stairs leading up to the women's gallery. The windows gape black and empty, and the smooth stucco surface is peeled and worn and blasted away from the stone.

Carved into the delicately curved lintel above the entrance is a Hebrew inscription from Psalm 118: "This is the gate of the Lord; let the righteous enter thereby." Few are the righteous who have entered here for many years. The sanctuary is gutted; chunks of plaster and rubbish litter the floor. At the east wall, half a dozen steps lead up to what was once the Ark, where Ber of Bolechów's Torah may have been kept: a raw, rectangular hole in the stone. Shadows of frescoes surround and surmount it. Above, two faded lions flank the shadow of the tablets of the Ten Commandments under the shadow of a crown. Shadowy painted curtains, once blue, white, and gold, are still visible at the sides.

In the middle of the room the bimah, where the reader read the Torah, is simply a raised, battered platform: All structure and decoration have disappeared. Only the ceiling retains color: A geometrical motif of squares and stars in still bright blue and russet sags over the sanctuary, and a brilliant azure field hangs above the women's gallery.

In his office in Budapest, Péter Wirth showed me a thick set of plans he had drawn up, years before, for the restoration of the synagogue. Drawing after detailed drawing showed how he envisaged transforming the building, whose congregants had been immersed in the wine trade, into a museum about the history of that commerce in the Tokaj region, and, at least in part, of the Jews and other merchants who were involved in that trade. In the project, all Jewish details and decoration had been retained and enhanced; even the door had been envisioned as reconstructed with a network of Stars of David as a design.

"Local people are, or were, rather interested in the project," Wirth told me. "The synagogue is owned by a wine cooperative in Tarcal, and there is no more money. Privatization means the vineyards are going back into private hands; the big Soviet market has dried up. There is no more money. No one who sowed the seed for this project could be sure that they would harvest it."

TARCAL'S OLD JEWISH CEMETERY is an unfenced field at the side of a road. A handful of eroded tombstones stand tilted, nearly lost in tall grass. Some lie fallen on the ground. The stones are so badly worn that some of the inscriptions literally crumble into dust when I touch them. On one tombstone, the only remaining decoration is a carved bunch of grapes.

TARCAL: On a heavily eroded tombstone in this wine-producing village, the only thing still visible is the carving of a bunch of grapes.

Through Slovakia

The merchants in bygone centuries loaded their carts and horses with heavy casks of wine and slowly trudged off along the dirt trail that led through the mountains to Poland. From Tokaj, they might have followed the valley of the Hernád or the Bodrog River, heading north into what is now the easternmost extremity of Slovakia. They would have walked through a landscape of low, wooded mountains interspersed with meadows and farmland. Even today this is a remote region; it is even lonelier, perhaps, and more isolated—at least for Jews—than in the past, when Jewish settlement here was thick, and most towns and villages along the way would have offered kosher hospitality to religious travelers.

This far eastern tip of eastern Slovakia is on the western edge of what was once called Sub-Carpathian Ruthenia, one of my favorite geographical designations. Today a part of Ukraine, Sub-Carpathian Ruthenia was a long tail of territory that before World War I belonged to Hungary, between the wars became part of Czechoslovakia, and after World War II became part of the Soviet Union. Here were great centers of Hasidism and Jewish Orthodoxy, and great pockets, too, of impoverished shtetl societies. Reform Jews—Hungarian Neologs— also lived here but were in the minority.

Josef Klánský, a writer in his seventies now living in Prague, told me about his family's history in this region. "My mother's home was in Michalovce, a little town now in Slovakia about thirty miles north of Sátoraljaújhely. My grandfather there was a well-to-do man with a mill and an electricity works. He was *Rosh ha Kahal,* head of the Jewish community. When I was a child, I was always told what a good family we were: In World War I, when the Cossacks invaded Galicia and the Jews all fled, the famous Hasidic Rabbi of Belz was a guest in my grandfather's house. Whoever told this story always used to emphasize that the rabbi also ate the food cooked by my grand- mother. This proved how kosher she was, though the family, while Orthodox, was not Hasidic!"

Klánský said that probably one-third of the population of Michalovce was Jewish. "The town looked like a big village, and the synagogue had a more central place than the Catholic church. There was no division in housing; Jews lived all over in the town—most of the shops on the main street were Jewish owned," he said. "My grandfather there built his steam mill in Michalovce, and he built the electric works to make sure that the mill worked at night, too. He practically introduced light bulbs into the town!"

Klánský himself was born in another little town, Kosino, which today is in Ukraine. "My father was a landowner; he had vineyards and agricultural land. There was quite a big Jewish community; part of the Jews were engaged in vineyards and agriculture like my father. There was also a Hasidic community, a Hasidic rebbe and his son-in- law, and Hasidic *bochers* [young men, students] who danced in the street. The two Jewish communities emphasized their differences. When the Hasids had the occasion to dance in the streets, my family, and the other landowners, etc., stayed on the sidelines. . . . In our home they used to comment, yes, these are religious people and should be supported—but why on earth don't they work? In my eyes as a child, most of the Hasidim I met were beggars."

Gertrude Birnbaum, who was born the daughter of a cantor in the nearby town of Humenné in 1914 and emigrated to the United States with her family in 1924, remembered similar conflict and fascination with local Hasidim.

"On Simchas Torah, we went to the Hasidim," she recalled.[23] "We sat at a long table and we had a flag, an apple, and a candle. And they danced and drank. All the kids used to go there. Over there was the fun. They really went crazy."

The Hasidim, she said, "were very religious . . . there was a fight over my father's singing. They said their way was better." The Hasidic rabbi quarreled with her father because he would not wear a *shtreimel,* the big fur hat that was part of the customary garb for Hasidic men. Things got so tense, she said, that "once the Hasidim came over to argue with my mother. My father wasn't there. My mother picked up the chamberpot with my younger brother's shit and threw it at the Hasidim!"

As a teenager, Josef Klánský had had another experience with Hasidim, an experience of quite a different sort. Klánský's Uncle Samuel was a lawyer who lived in the little town of Sabinov, about fifty miles northwest of Michalovce. This uncle, Klánský recounted, had begun to shed his Jewish Orthodoxy. "The household was kosher, but my uncle shaved his beard and did not wear a hat outside. He went to synagogue only on the High Holy Days—Rosh Hashanah and Yom Kippur."

There was no Hasidic community, Klánský said, in Sabinov. "But north of Sabinov, in the village of Čirč [right on today's border with Poland], there was a 'Wonder Rabbi.' My aunt—the wife of the lawyer—sent him money so that he should pray. When already Hitler had come to power in Germany in the thirties, my uncle took me—I was about fourteen years old—and we went to the Čirč rabbi, who gave me his blessing. We were received; we talked. The rabbi started to talk about Hitler, saying that it was God's punishment on the German Jews for not being religious enough. Everyone in the rabbi's house was wearing a black caftan. Afterward, my uncle said to me, 'For him, it's quite easy to have an explanation for everything.'"

Uncle Samuel died in Auschwitz. In Michalovce, where Klánský's grandfather had introduced light bulbs, the imposing synagogue, which used to have a more central place than the Catholic church, was pulled down years ago. First a parking area was built on the spot, then the headquarters of the Communist party. As for himself, Klánský told me, "I think I completely lost faith during the war. You cannot coordinate the existence of God with the existence of the Holocaust."[24]

IN TOKAJ, I LOADED MY SUITCASE into the back of a rented car and drove north at fifty miles an hour along a two-lane asphalt highway. The roads were good and there was not much traffic; there was not even much of a line at the border crossing into Slovakia. I reflected that if I didn't make any stops, I could reach Poland in the space of a few hours. A few hours! Two hundred years ago, it would have taken Ber of Bolechów and his wine-laden caravan many weeks.

If he had traveled by this route, Ber surely would have made a stop in Bardejov, whose Jews were also heavily involved in the wine trade. Bardejov has been described as the best-preserved medieval town complex in Slovakia. Situated amid the forested, rather wild Carpathian hills just south of the Polish border—wolves can be heard in these hills howling in the winter—it is encircled by ancient fortified walls. The large, cobbled market square at the center of the medieval core is lined with steep-roofed gothic and Renaissance houses and is set amid an extensive historical district that includes many other centuries-old buildings. One of these, dating back to the fourteenth century, is known to have been used as a wine tavern as early as medieval times. The town of Bardejov owned its own vineyards in the Tokaj region, and wine from there was stored in the tavern's cellars.

It was not far from this old wine tavern that I met Meyer Spira, who with his sister and brother-in-law are Bardejov's only remaining Jews. On earlier trips I had not found Spira at home, but this time I called ahead. He told me he would wait for me on the sidewalk in front of the old synagogue. I'd heard a lot about Spira and was curious to meet him face to face. When I had first visited this part of eastern Slovakia two years before, he had been described to me as a shochet, a ritual slaughterer, who provided for the kosher needs of tiny scattered Jewish communities all over Slovakia, including the kosher lunchroom run by the Jewish community in Košice, the biggest city in eastern Slovakia, where as many as a thousand Jews still lived.

Since that trip, a rabbi had taken up office in Košice—a rabbi, fifty-three-year-old Lazar Kleinman, who was born in Transylvania and educated in Israel, who was an Australian citizen, and whose last rabbinical post had been in Finland. He had come to Košice about two months earlier, at the end of the summer in 1992. I spoke with Kleinman in his office on my way to Bardejov, and he was candid about having already alienated many of the older members of the congregation by essentially cutting them out of his plans to revitalize the community.

"Thanks to God, the leadership of the Jewish community here is not in the hands of old people," he told me. "The board of the community is made up of young people. I am not listening to the old generation here. The old people think that they know Judaism, but they are backward by fifty years."

He told me that one of his areas of conflict with the older generation was in the handling and supply of kosher meat, until recently a task carried out by Spira.

"As soon as I arrived I changed the situation," Kleinman said. From now on, he told me, he himself would supervise both the slaughtering and the koshering of meat. Also, he told me, he wanted to establish a modern, hygienic kosher meat supply system, in which meat would be sold to community members slaughtered, soaked, and salted, wrapped in plastic, and frozen, just as in supermarkets in the West. "This has provoked problems with some of the older people," he admitted. And indeed, as I waited for him in his office, I witnessed a heated shouting match between Kleinman and an elderly woman about the meat situation. "She's complaining because she wants the feet of the chicken she buys," Kleinman shrugged. "But you can't freeze feet. They're dirty. But she wants the feet. People have to get used to good things, too."

Meyer Spira was one of the older local Jews alienated by Kleinman over the kosher meat issue—and possibly over other issues, too. I never did quite get the real story: One man told me that Kleinman didn't like Spira's slaughtering methods; another told me that it was Spira who thought Kleinman's way of slaughtering was not ritually pure. "He says the knife isn't sharp enough," one eighty-year-old man explained. Not only that, the same people who two years before had described Spira to me as a shochet this time said, no, he was simply a butcher. Others gave the impression that he was a difficult man to deal with generally and not much liked by other Jews in the area. "I don't like him because he is not a good man," one man told me succinctly, without offering further details.

I pulled my car up to the curb outside the complex of semi-ruined buildings that once had been the heart of Bardejov's intense Jewish world, and there he was, a stocky, seventy-year-old man with thick glasses and a gold tooth. He was bundled up against the chilly autumn weather, sheltering near a wall where only a few months earlier a Holocaust memorial plaque had been put up commemorating thirty-seven hundred local Jews deported to death camps in the years 1942 to 1945.

Bardejov's crumbling old synagogue and the huge old Jewish bathhouse and school that stand crumbling alongside it are among the oldest and most important Jewish relics in Slovakia. I'd heard a rumor that an American Jew originally from Bardejov had put up a big sum of money for restoration work; but if he had, nothing had been done with it. The scene was as I remembered it from my previous visits: Still owned by the remnants of the Jewish community, the buildings were leased to a plumbing supply company that used them as warehouses. Spira had set the time of our meeting early, before the workday was over, so that we would be able to enter and take our time looking around.

He led me inside, down steps into the immense, ravaged sanctuary whose floor was beneath ground level. "This synagogue," he said, "is two hundred and seventy-six years old." Ber of Bolechów may well have prayed here.

The structure was built in the Polish style, with a massive bimah in the center, whose four thick, square pillars rose up to form graceful supports for the vaulted ceiling arching over the pipes, tubing, radiators, and toilets that were stacked up on the floor. Bright traces of red and blue frescoes featuring Stars of David and geometric patterns still clung to the ceiling vaults.

"A few Jewish families came down from Polish Galicia to settle here in about 1680 to 1720," Spira said. "About fifty to sixty percent of Jews here were of Polish origin, even in the twentieth century, when a lot of young people from there came."

He walked me around the ruined hall, pointing out the places where scenes of joy and prayer, study and social snobbery had taken place.

"Here on the bimah, on Shabbos, they read the Torah. . . . Right here, this was where my grandfather, my father, and my uncle sat, right here by the bimah near the steps. . . . Over here, there were two great big desks, where the young children from the *cheder* studied; they learned how to pray. . . . . Over here, where it's empty, this is where the Ark, the Aron ha Kodesh, was. After the war it was gone; we couldn't find it. I was here one week before Rosh Hashanah in 1942, and the Aron was still in place then, but there were very few Jews left. Right here, next to the Ark, at the east wall, is where the most honored men, the president of the community, and so on, sat. Each one had a little niche in the wall for his tallis and prayer book.

"Now it's a warehouse," he said. "But the synagogue belongs to the Jewish community of Bardejov. It should be made into a museum or something. But, unfortunately, there are no Jews here. It's a warehouse, but for me it is always a synagogue."

We stepped back outside, and Spira pointed out the ruins—and the memories—of other Jewish buildings in the complex.

"About thirty-five hundred Jews lived here before the war," he said. "Everyone, or mostly everyone, was very Orthodox; we had a Polish rabbi. On Rosh Hashanah, this whole courtyard by the synagogue was filled with men—you had to bring your own chair from home if you wanted a place to sit. Daily morning and evening services were held in a big *Bet ha Midrash*—study house—next to the synagogue. Every evening after work the young, unmarried men came here together to study. And next to the sanctuary there was another cheder for older kids."

A memory book of Bardejov's Jews, which Spira showed me later, had page after page of pictures of these young men and others in the town. They were presented simply as squares on the page—no captions, no names, simply face after face of solemn men with sidelocks, beards, black hats, and burning eyes. The women in the pictures looked a little more modern, but only one page had pictures of men who had shed their Orthodoxy to the extent of shaving off their beards.

"Up until the deportations, Jews made up more than fifty percent of the town," Spira said. "There were six thousand people altogether, and thirty-five hundred of them were Jews. The whole town was Jewish houses; in the market square only four or five were not Jewish."

He pointed to the empty area in which the ruined synagogue complex stood, fenced in by a barrier of rusting corrugated iron topped by barbed wire. Across the wide street was a modern theater in a broad paved plaza; to one side was a small modern factory or workshop of some sort. Behind were a muddy lane and vacant lots.

"All around here used to be little houses," Spira recalled. "There was an open stream, too, which has been covered.

"The young people who live here now don't know what a Jew is," he said. "But when an American Jew with a beard and black suit came here once, they said, 'That's a rabbi.'"

We got in my car and drove the few hundred yards to Kláštorská Street, not far from the market square, where there was another synagogue, much smaller, much less historic, much different from the old ruin. I had seen this synagogue from the outside already. It looked like an ordinary house, but it had two tall, gothic-arched windows and a Hebrew phrase traced above them under the roof line. We entered; Spira led the way down a dark corridor, through an inner door. We stepped into a small, chilly room. Every surface seemed piled with vegetables—squash, cabbage, cauliflower. But it was a little study house, a Bet ha Midrash. There was a little wooden Ark; piles of tattered books, decaying Talmuds. Spira motioned me through another door, and we walked, in a sense, into the past.

We were in a compact, fully furnished little sanctuary, with wooden pews, a wooden bimah in the center, a women's gallery above. It was a time capsule.

"People used to pray here every evening," Spira said. "They were mainly businessmen, tailors, craftsmen; those were the people who prayed here. . . . People prayed here until May 5, 1944; it was always full." He pointed to the Ark, a simple but elegant wooden cabinet standing between the two tall, arched windows. Its curved upper section was marked by the shadows—the memories—of two lions flanking the tablets of the Ten Commandments; the shapes were unmistakable. "It was very beautiful once; it had golden lions," Spira said. "But they were stolen three years ago. Simply, I came here one day, and they were gone."

Spira told me there had been a minyan, the quorum of ten men needed to conduct a Jewish service, in Bardejov until 1970, and they had prayed here in this little synagogue. Nowadays, he said, he still came here—alone—every Friday evening and Saturday, to pray by himself, to continue to use the synagogue as a house of Jewish worship. "It was originally just a house," he told me. "And then the community bought it—in 1929—to make it into a shul. There were ten small prayer houses like this in Bardejov. This is one of the few synagogues in the country that is original, that wasn't destroyed by the Nazis or the Slovaks. It was saved because from the front, from outside, it doesn't look like a synagogue. During the war, a Christian woman lived in the little study room, which I now use to store vegetables. . . . After the war, other religious groups wanted this place to take over for their own church. But as long as I am here, I will not permit it. Also, some Jews in Los Angeles want to remove this and take this shul to the United States. But I will not allow it. I will not give this away."

Spira excused himself for a few minutes; he wanted to pray. He stepped back and immersed himself in a prayer book, allowing me to look around at the little sanctuary on my own. The walls, stained by damp, were decorated with faded painting—salmon-colored vertical stripes on the lower portion and trompe l'oeil red curtains seemingly drawn back from the nearly floor-to-ceiling windows. High above, the flat ceiling was painted with bands of paisley-like floral designs in red and deep blue, framing a pale blue sky sprinkled with stars. The women's gallery encircled the room on three sides. But wait, one of the galleries, too, was actually just a wall; it was painted with another example of trompe l'oeil decoration to simulate a gallery all the way around. On a little reading desk in front of the Ark lay a pair of folded eyeglasses.

SPIRA INVITED ME back to his apartment for a cup of tea. He lived in a high-rise concrete apartment block outside the town center. A widower, he lived alone, but the walls were hung with embroidered pictures worked by his wife. His two sons had gone to the United States; one was in New York, and the other somewhere in the Middle West.

He showed me their pictures; the one in the Midwest was a kosher butcher in a supermarket that sold cuts of meat hygienically packaged in a way the new rabbi in Košice would have approved.

Spira puttered about the apartment; he made some tea and brought out cookies and homemade preserves. "Here, eat something," he said. He took down books to show me: photograph albums; the memory book of Bardejov, with its pages full of unnamed pictures of Jews with black clothes and burning eyes. I asked Spira if the Jewish and gentile communities had got on well before the war. "There wasn't any anti-Semitism then," he replied. "Now there is, though they don't let it out publicly. Most of the people who live here now are newcomers to the town; there are very few people from old Bardejov. It was built up here under the Communists; there's industry here now. Before the war we were friends with the Christians, but now—I don't like it. . . . I have no good friends here; no friends here. I do nothing, I don't go out. I don't go to the movies or to the theater."

He brought another cup of tea and another book.

"This book is interesting," he said. It was a small, well-worn book in Hebrew or Yiddish—I couldn't tell from my quick glance—stained and fragile from years of use. "This book," he told me, "lists all the *yahrzeits*—all the anniversaries of the deaths—of all the Hasidic rebbes."

It was, in a sense, Spira's guide. As a boy, in Jewish Bardejov, Spira had been a Hasid. Now, in his old age, in his solitude, he journeyed through the year to the tombs of Hasidic masters to pay his respects on the anniversaries of their deaths. The relaxation of border-crossing procedures and visa requirements since the collapse of communism made these trips a lot easier. "I was in Rymanów," he told me, referring to the town to the northeast, on the other side of the Polish border, which had been the seat of the great tzaddik Menachem Mendel, who died in 1815. "I was in Leżajsk"—a town north of Rymanów where the famous eighteenth-century tzaddik Elimelech lived.

Spira was a particular devotee of the Halbersztam dynasty of tzaddikim. The founder of the dynasty, Hayyim ben Leibush, had established his court in the southern Polish town of Nowy Sącz, and his descendants had been rabbis in Bardejov. In the Jewish cemetery in Bardejov, there was an ohel to one of these rabbis. "I go every year to Nowy Sącz to Hayyim's tomb," Spira told me. "And I go to Bodrogkereztúr every year, too, to Saje Steiner's tomb, and to Sátoraljaújhely, to that of Moses Teitelbaum. It's not a bad trip these days—from here, by car, it's just an hour and ten minutes to Újhely."

Poland

I had wanted to go from Bardejov directly on into Poland, but there was a complication with the rental car insurance and I wasn't permitted to take the car across the border. It was some months later, then, in late spring, that I finally drove through the Dukla Pass toward Rymanów, the town in southern Poland whose Jews had been so active in the importation of Hungarian wine, and whose Hasidic masters, among the most famous in Eastern Europe, had had such devoted followers in the wine villages near Tokaj.

The Dukla Pass is the lowest and easiest north-south route through the western Carpathians, and by the sixteenth century it was already a well-established artery for trade, including the wine trade. The town of Dukla itself prospered as a major center for the import of Hungarian wine, although Ber of Bolechów recounted that the Jewish wine traders from there were not always quite honest. He told the story of a certain Reb Hayyim of Dukla, who made a large purchase of wine in the Hungarian town of Miskolc at the same time that Ber's brother and two other associates were there. Unfortunately, Reb Hayyim paid the Hungarian suppliers with counterfeit money—golden ducats that turned out to be gold-plated copper—and Ber's brother and a friend were arrested along with Hayyim, even though it was acknowledged that they had not held any of the bad coins.

The three were kept in jail for a year, until, after much nerve-wracking investigation, the origin of the bad coins was traced to a monastery, which in turn had received them from local noblemen, who made a practice of circulating debased coinage at that time. Ber's brother was released from prison and was even paid a considerable sum in compensation for wrongful arrest, Ber wrote. But the affair had taken a toll: The stress and tension had caused Ber to break out in spots.

During World War II the Dukla Pass was the scene of bitterly fought battles between combined Czechoslovak and Soviet armies and the Germans. The bloody mountain fighting in the autumn of 1944 destroyed the German defenses and left a hundred thousand soldiers dead. The towns of Dukla, to the north of the pass, and Svidník in Slovakia, to the south, were almost totally razed. I passed numerous memorials to this fighting as I drove along the gentle curves through the wooded hills. Monuments had been erected to the fallen, and ruined tanks, artillery pieces, and airplanes had been left in place where they had been at the close of the conflict, rusting memorials to the battle.

Dukla itself was a small town clustered around a stage-set market square with a white market hall at its center. Nearby, I found the synagogue. It had been built around the middle of the eighteenth century, and the wily Reb Hayyim may well have worshipped there. Now it was a ruin. It had been destroyed during the wartime battles and had simply been left as it was, four massive stone walls and little else, looming in a small hollow. At the edge of town, a few graves still stood in the Jewish cemetery, surrounded by a brilliant carpet of wild spring flowers.

FROM DUKLA, I DROVE ON to Rymanów, my final destination, ten or twelve miles away. I was a little apprehensive. The first time I had visited Rymanów, three years before, the desolation of the ruined synagogue had hit me with particular force.

It was a hulking ruin at the edge of a nondescript little town, a massive pile of stone and brick that spoke eloquently of a lost civilization. The raw power of the ruin, crouched just below the crest of a little hill, made a statement so strong that it shouted. It looked as if it had fought—and fought hard—against its destruction, its oblivion; but it had lost. The ruin was a vast cube of stone, pierced by deep, arched windows. Most of the stuccowork had fallen off the outer walls. The roof was gone, and from the crumbly upper surface grew a tangle of shrubs and vines, tossing in the breeze like bushy, green hair.

I had been able to get the key to the chain-link fence that surrounded the synagogue and go inside. The roof was a crisscross of beams through which I could see the sky, and birds flying, calling. The four tall pillars of the central bimah reached up toward nothingness. On the walls were still fragments of polychrome frescoes—a lion, a tiger (or leopard), an eagle, recalling the Talmudic exhortation to be "as strong as a leopard, light as an eagle, fleet as a stag, and brave as a lion to perform the will of thy father who is in heaven." Clear blue sky and stars had been painted around the Ark. And there was also a vivid fresco depicting Jerusalem and the Wailing Wall; it had seemed fitting above the ruined portal of the ruined shul.

Rymanów was founded in the fourteenth century, and Jews settled there not long afterward. Almost from their earliest presence in the town, they were active as wine merchants, importing wine from Hungary. A synagogue—probably a wooden synagogue—existed in the town by the year 1593. It was replaced, probably in the late eighteenth century, by the once splendid building that is now a hulking wreck. In 1765, more or less at the time the synagogue was built,

RYMANÓW: The ruined synagogue.

135

more than a thousand Jews lived in Rymanów and made up nearly forty-three percent of the town's population. About this time, too, or a little later, the town began to develop as a major Hasidic center, thanks to the tzaddik Menachem Mendel, who made it his seat. His house, it was said, and the synagogue were the most magnificent buildings in town.

Menachem Mendel was known, among other things, for his austerity, his ascetisicm, and his belief that the Napoleonic Wars that raged in the early part of the nineteenth century were the battle of Gog and Magog, which, according to legend, would precede the coming of the Messiah. Indeed, along with his friends and fellow tzaddikim the Seer of Lublin and the Maggid of Kozienice, Menachem Mendel prayed for Napoleon's victory, which, they believed, would hasten the Messiah's coming. Napoleon himself is said to have always seen a vision of a red-haired Jew praying for him during battles in which he was victorious—but he failed to see this vision as he went into his last battle, the crushing defeat at Waterloo in 1815. The red-haired Menachem Mendel and his two friends all died that year.

> The first ruling Rabbi Mendel had made in Rymanov was that the daughters of Israel should not parade up and down the streets in gay-colored, lavishly trimmed dresses. From then on the Jewish girls and women of Rymanov faithfully followed the tzaddik's orders. But the daughter-in-law of the wealthiest man in town, the wife he had just fetched for his son from the capital of the district, refused to let her finery turn yellow in her chest with none to admire it.
>
> When Rabbi Mendel saw her strutting up and down the main street, dressed in her best, he sent for the most mischievous gutter-snipes and gave them permission to call after the woman whatever went through their heads. The rich man, who was one of the pillars of the community, came to the rabbi in a rage and tried to make clear to him that his ruling was contrary to the Torah, for Ezra the Scribe had included in his ordinances permission for traders to travel from place to place so that the daughters of Israel might adorn themselves.
>
> "Do you think," asked Rabbi Mendel, "that Ezra meant them to parade up and down the streets? Do you think he did not know that a woman can receive the honors due her nowhere save in her home?"[25]

I stood in front of the ruined synagogue in attire of which Menachem Mendel certainly would not have approved: a cotton knit summer tunic, short leggings, and espadrilles. The ruin was as I had remembered it, but Rymanów had changed with the explosion of private enterprise since the ouster of the Communists. The empty slope above the synagogue had become the site of a bustling little marketplace where trucks, stands, and newly built stalls of corrugated iron displayed a colorful variety of food, clothing, housewares, and kitsch. Someone had planted a vegetable garden up there, too. Few of the people going about their business glanced at the ruined synagogue; it was part of the landscape. It belonged to another world, the past. That was then. This was now.

I drove the short distance out of town to the Jewish cemetery, where Menachem Mendel and his main disciple, Zvi Hirsch, are buried and where their followers still come, as they have for nearly two hundred years, to honor their memory. I had to park the car some distance away and walk down a narrow, grassy path that

RYMANÓW: The shadow of the author's hand on a fallen tombstone in the ruined Jewish cemetery.

skirted lush farm fields and gardens. People were digging there, weeding their vegetables; wheat waved; green, gentle hills stretched into the distance, calm and beautiful. The cemetery, spreading out wide over a rounded hilltop, was a ruin—like the synagogue, a scene of devastation. The tombs of the tzaddikim were protected in a locked ohel, erected by modern followers, but few other tombstones remained standing; they reminded me of broken teeth.

I didn't want to stay. I didn't want to look. I didn't want to pick my way through the nettles to examine the toppled stones.

I had written down somewhere the name of a man in Rymanów who kept a collection of Judaica. Also, I had heard that an American Peace Corps volunteer teaching English in the town had been trying to gather support for getting the synagogue restored. They might have been interesting to talk to. I was sure, too, that the older people I had asked for directions and who had pointed out the road to the graveyard could have told me stories about the way things were before the war.

But I really didn't want to inquire. I didn't want to talk to anybody. That was then, and this was now. I found myself quoting Jerome Rothenberg's poem. "Were there once Jews here?"

Yes, once upon a time.

~ 3 ~

Synagogues Seeking Heaven

Looking for Lipót Baumhorn

Lord, thou has been our dwelling place.
—Psalms 90:1

And I will bring your sanctuaries into desolation.
—Leviticus 26:31

UDAPEST'S MAIN JEWISH CEMETERY is a vast, walled expanse on Kozma utca—Kozma Street—near Ferihegyi Airport on the far eastern edge of the sprawling metropolis. To reach it you drive away from the Danube, out through the broad avenues of the gracious if crumbling turn-of-the-century heart of the city, out further through a grimy, open landscape of smog-shrouded industry, smokestacks, and, eventually, massive, belching breweries and occasional flower stalls and tombstone manufactories. You maneuver your car sharply across a tram line through a gate and pull up in the parking lot in front of the towering, turreted ceremonial hall, where a big notice board lists the hours of the day's funeral services.

It seemed a mild winter morning when I set out from the city center in a rented Russian-built Lada whose squeaking steering wheel gave a running commentary on the drive. The sky was pale blue under only a thin veil of clouds, the air was still, and there was even a hint of the sun. By the time I reached Kozma utca, the clouds had grown thick and threatening; the sky was gray; the air was much colder, and a bone-chilling wind eddied about the open spaces.

In its enormity and neglected grandeur, Kozma utca Cemetery represents an almost overpowering monument to the size, wealth, and promise of Budapest's prewar Jewish community. Well over two hundred thousand Jews lived in Budapest, making up nearly one quarter of the city's population. Hundreds of thousands of people are buried here, perhaps more than three hundred thousand, according to one cemetery attendant—some people say twice that number. They lie in mainly abandoned, overgrown tombs laid out in scores of mapped and numbered sections. There are the simple gravestones of simple folk and the more monumental markers of the middle and upper middle classes who made up most of Budapest's Jewish population. Many stones bear cloyingly sentimental epitaphs and inscriptions; others are simple black marble slabs whose size and expensive material alone pay tribute to the dignified social status of the dead.

Along the outer walls, massive mausoleums and memorials of wealthy families—of which there were many—form a bizarre, eclectic perimeter. Rich Budapest Jews hired the top architects of the day—many of whom were Jewish themselves—to immortalize them with monuments that in many cases are mini-masterpieces of design. The 1903 family crypt for Sándor Schmidl, designed by Ödön Lechner and Béla Lajta, two of the era's most famous architects, is a paradoxically joyful, even sensuous, art nouveau gem incorporating bright turquoise stone and sinuous floral mosaics. The Grósz family tomb by Zoltán Bálint and Lajos Jámbor looks like a slightly sinister fairy-tale fortress, and tombs for the Halmos family and Zsigmond Fayer by István Sárkány vaguely resemble immense stone African sculptures. Lined up next to each other, the perimeter tombs, hundreds of them, all face inward, backed up against the cemetery wall and the living world outside. Many have gates or doorways that are rusted, gaping open; ivy chokes the crevices and claws at the stonework; young trees block the entryways. Sculptural elements have crashed to the ground and broken.

One entire section of the cemetery has been transformed into a

Holocaust memorial. On row after row of huge, upright panels, the names of thousands of Budapest Jews who were killed by the Nazis or Hungarian Fascists are listed, one by one. Friends and family members have used pencil and ink to fill in the names of loved ones who inadvertently were left out.

I came here on this winter morning to look for the tomb of an all but forgotten man whose lifework, or, rather, its scattered fragments, is, like the cemetery, a testimony to the ultimately misplaced optimism of Hungary's turn-of-the-century Jews. I was looking for the grave of Lipót Baumhorn, a Budapest-based architect who lived from 1860 to 1932 and who, I had recently learned, was buried here at Kozma utca. Baumhorn was not a great architect, particularly when compared to contemporaries like Ödön Lechner, or Lajta, or Dezső Jakab and Marcell Komor, who were trail-blazing pioneers of Hungary's distinctive art nouveau and folk-inspired national style. What set Baumhorn apart was that, while he designed everything from banks to schools to private houses, he dedicated a major part of his forty-year career to the design and construction of synagogues. He designed about two dozen between 1888 and 1931—more synagogues, according to architectural historian Carol Herselle Krinsky, than were designed by any other known architect in Europe.[1] Most were large, highly ornate, and sumptuously decorated buildings in provincial towns, where ostentation sometimes strongly won out over what many would consider good taste. They were synagogues constructed to be the pride not just of their Jewish congregations but of the towns in which these congregations lived, and their size and splendor demonstrated that the local Jews who commissioned them had the money, power, and social aspirations to pay for the costliest of craftsmanship.

In her valuable study *Synagogues of Europe*, Krinsky related the work of Baumhorn and other synagogue designers in Hungary to the new Jewish freedoms of the time, freedoms that were coupled with a growing sense of Hungarian—*Magyar*—identity among largely assimilated Reform Jews and religiously Orthodox Jews alike. Indeed, from the latter part of the nineteenth century, Hungarian Jews, particularly in Budapest and other urban centers, increasingly considered themselves "Hungarians of the Jewish persuasion" or "Hungarians of the

Mosaic faith": Hungarians who happened to be Jewish rather than Jews living in Hungary. Increasingly they belonged to Neolog congregations—the Hungarian brand of Reform Judaism—and spoke Hungarian, not Yiddish. More than 340 Jews or converted Jews were raised to the Hungarian nobility; most were bankers and businessmen, but their number also included the chairman of Budapest's main Neolog congregation. Despite the fact that Zionist pioneer Theodore Herzl was born in Budapest, *Zionism* gained little hold on Hungarian Jews: Their place, they felt, was in Hungary. There was even something of a mass movement among Jews to replace their Jewish or German-sounding names with Hungarian names, sometimes translating them directly (*Klein,* meaning "small" in German, becoming *Kis,* meaning "small" in Hungarian, for example), sometimes simply keeping the same first letter or sound, sometimes making a complete change: The architect Béla Lajta began life as Béla Leitersdorfer.

Krinsky put it this way:

After 1896, when Judaism was placed legally on a par with Christianity in Hungary, and when Jewish optimism and Magyarization increased as well, there was an efflorescence of lavish, wildly eclectic synagogue designs. The work of Lipót Baumhorn is central to this trend. Ten years after his rather sober striped oblong synagogue . . . at Esztergom, his Szeged synagogue of 1900–1903 was a surprising contrast; it had a central cupola rising high over a Greek-cross plan, mixed Gothic, Moorish, and Romanesque ornament, busy surfaces, and a pinnacled skyline. Competition drawings by other architects for this project were almost as opulent. Synagogues by Baumhorn and others at Braşov, Szolnok, Tîrgu Mureş, Salgótarján, and Subotica were built in the same mode. Perhaps they were meant to celebrate the differences between these provinces of the [Austro-Hungarian] empire and Vienna itself. Perhaps the designers hoped that by combining stylistic features from many countries and all ages they could produce something Jewish—international, appearing in all periods of European and Middle Eastern history, and not conventionally Christian. In their eclecticism and joyous abundance, the synagogues are related to such secular buildings as theaters and apartment houses, but not to churches; in this respect, their style may have satisfied Christians who wanted Jews kept at arm's length as well as Jews who did not want to imitate church architecture.[2]

BY JANUARY 1993, WHEN I PULLED INTO the parking lot at Kozma utca cemetery, I had been following Baumhorn's trail, rather vaguely and on and off, to be sure, for more than three years. My search had begun in early September 1989 when I joined hundreds of other people in Szeged, on the Tisza River in southeastern Hungary, for a gala ceremony rededicating the Great Synagogue there following a full-scale restoration that had been funded by a former Szeged Jew, Péter Varadi, in honor of his family members killed by the Nazis.

The Szeged synagogue is considered Baumhorn's masterpiece. It was my introduction to his work, and I found it all that Krinsky had described—and more: an eclectic extravaganza of baroque, Moorish, romanesque, and even art nouveau styles bristling with cupolas, turrets, arches, tracery, mosaics, gilding, stained glass, and frescoes—all under and around a massive 158½-foot dome surmounted by a Star of David. It sat in the middle of a fenced-in, tree-

SZEGED: Exterior of the synagogue.

shaded yard, almost an entire city block in size, and dwarfed the simple, neoclassical synagogue next door that it had been built to replace. "Let them argue," Jewish Telegraphic Agency correspondent Susan Birnbaum had written in an article handed out as part of press background materials: "The synagogue in Szeged is perhaps the most beautiful in the world." I had certainly never seen a Jewish building quite like it, so totally dazzling, with so many intricate elements that it made the head swim and breathing tight—out of wonder or, perhaps, just vertigo.

Seven busloads of people had driven the 120 miles from Budapest for the dedication ceremony, which was advertised by posters all over Szeged. Parts of the service were broadcast on nationwide television. Well over one thousand people filled the pews of the mighty building, including the town's deputy mayor, government representatives from Budapest, Hungarian Jewish community leaders, the Israeli representative in Hungary (at the time the two countries had not yet resumed full diplomatic relations), and officials from the American Joint Distribution Committee, the New York–based Jewish charitable and relief organization that had administered Varadi's donated funds.

"This will be a most memorable day for me and for everyone who was here," Ralph Goldman, the JOINT's honorary executive vice president, declared. "We all take back with us the beauty and the dignity of the service for the dedication of the synagogue. Beyond these memories, it is a historic day—for the Jews of Szeged, for the Jews of Hungary, and for world Jewry as a whole."

To the sounds of the powerful organ whose 1,276 pipes form the backdrop of the immense and opulent bimah and Ark facade at the eastern wall, men carrying Torah scrolls staged a solemn procession around the glittering sanctuary. Cameras snapped away as children's, teenage, and adult choirs from the Jewish community in Budapest lifted their voices in prayers and Jewish songs. And, dramatic in his black beard, tall black hat, and flowing black robes, cantor Joseph Malovany of New York's Fifth Avenue Synagogue performed an emotional concert of liturgical and secular Jewish music from the elevated main pulpit. "If I forget Thee, O Jerusalem, let my right hand lose its cunning," he chanted, intoning the elemental Jewish vow from Psalm 137 before leading the choirs and congregation in the joyful *Shehechiyanu* prayer and a rousing *Hallelujah*. The shofar was blown, in another expression of solemnity and celebration: The Bible tells us that in ancient times the raucous, eerie notes of the shofar were sounded to proclaim "freedom throughout the land." Overhead, the huge, highly decorated arch that soars triumphally above the bimah framed the scene. Across its span, in distinctive gold letters against a powder blue background, run the words, in Hebrew and Hungarian: "Love thy neighbor as thyself."

To me, and I imagine to most people attending, the ceremony was profoundly symbolic. The dedication took place at an optimistic moment for both Hungary and Hungary's hundred thousand Jews, ninety percent of whom live in Budapest: The country was just shedding its Communist regime and embarking on its difficult attempt to forge a new democracy. Less than two weeks after the Szeged gala, Hungary and Israel restored diplomatic relations that Hungary, like most other Communist states, had broken in 1967 after the Six Day War.

At the turn of the century some six thousand Jews lived in Szeged; Hungary's borders stretched far to the east and south, and the town, one of the homes of Hungary's paprika industry, was a booming commercial center, many of whose leading businessmen were Jewish. The town had replanned and rebuilt in great style after a disastrous flood in 1879 washed much of the center away. (A marker on the wall of the old synagogue denotes how high the water came even here, six blocks or so from the river bank.) Much of the rebuilding was made possible by international aid grants, and cities that had helped with reconstruction were immortalized in the names given sections of the new ring boulevard girding the center: London, Paris, Moscow. The new synagogue in all its glory had symbolized the optimism of Szeged's prosperous Neolog Jews—and indeed, Hungarian Jews in general. The terms and timing of its rededication nearly ninety years later symbolized the optimism of the current moment. Under a landmark agreement, the restored synagogue, far too big for the few hundred Jews who now lived in Szeged, was to remain a synagogue, but its maintenance and upkeep would be carried out by the Hungarian government and local city authorities. In exchange, the sanctuary would also be used for secular concerts and cultural events.

"This is the first synagogue in the world to carry on under such an agreement," Ralph Goldman, courtly with his white hair and bowtie, said as he toasted the dignitaries gathered for a gala banquet at long tables in the ornate community hall—also designed by Lipót Baumhorn. The walls of the hall displayed large, framed portraits of community worthies dating back to the nineteenth century. Most prominent among them were Szeged's three most influential rabbis: Lipót Lőw, his son Immánuel Lőw, and József Schindler.

These three men, all dead years ago, had been instrumental in bringing us to that moment. The Lőws, father and son, had dominated Szeged's Jewish life for nearly a century and had had a major impact on Jewish spiritual and scholarly development nationwide. Schindler, a survivor of the Holocaust, had helped pick up the ragged pieces after the war and had led the remnants of the Szeged community during the difficult early days of communism. About five thousand Szeged Jews were deported by the Nazis in 1944: Some were sent to Auschwitz, some to labor camps in Austria. About half survived, but most of them left Szeged for elsewhere. The names of those who perished are inscribed on the walls of the entryway into the synagogue.

Schindler's portrait is in the middle of the group, between those of the Lőws; he is a modern-looking, youngish man with glasses and a little mustache, a slightly jarring contrast to the venerable, bearded sages at either side.

"He was the most important rabbi in Hungary after World War II," Rabbi Tamás Raj asserted when we met in early 1993 over coffee and pretzels in Hungary's grandiose Hall of Parliament on the bank of the Danube in Budapest. Raj, who served as rabbi in Szeged in the 1960s, had lived through years of conflict with official, state-linked Jewish community authorities under communism. As a result of "suspect" activities such as supporting Zionism, teaching Judaism to young people, and protesting the cheap sale of Jewish property to the state, he was removed from the rabbinate in 1970 and was not reinstated until fifteen years later. A deceptively mild-mannered man with dark skin and a black beard, he was elected to Parliament as a deputy of the Free Democrats Party after the fall of communism. His ever-present yarmulke set him apart even from other Jewish MPs, of which there were several. Raj, born in 1940 and a survivor of the

Budapest ghetto, had been Schindler's student at the Budapest Rabbinical Seminary and was serving as his assistant rabbi in Szeged when Schindler died in 1962 at age forty-four—the result of heart disease brought on by his suffering at Bergen-Belsen concentration camp.

"On his tomb it is written that he lived, dreamt, and felt for his people," Raj told me. "He was a declared Zionist. This was not an easy thing—he had to endure many attacks; he was strongly attacked by the very Jewish community leadership in Budapest. . . . I inherited these attacks myself."

Schindler is buried in Szeged's sprawling Jewish cemetery beyond the edge of town. His rather simple tomb is near the grand, Grecian temple–like mausoleum of Lipót Lőw, who died in 1875, and the more austere monument to Immánuel Lőw, a 1944 victim of the Holocaust at the age of ninety.

Lipót Lőw, a barrel-chested man with the burning eyes, full beard, and flowing hair of an Old Testament prophet, was a passionate Hungarian patriot as well as a charismatic Jewish leader. Born in 1811 in Moravia, he was a descendant of the revered Rabbi Judah ben Bezalel Löw of Prague, the legendary creator of the golem. Lipót Lőw is generally regarded as the first Reform rabbi in Hungary; beginning in 1844, he was the first to deliver sermons in Hungarian. He fought for Jewish emancipation and Jewish civil rights, but also for the Hungarian cause. His fiery sermons and uncompromising stand when he served as chaplain to Hungarian revolutionaries during the abortive insurrection against Austria in 1848–1849 led to his arrest and imprisonment for three months.

After a troubled four years as rabbi in the western Hungarian town of Pápa (where Orthodox enemies of his Reform views spread rumors that he did not properly observe Jewish ritual), Lőw in 1850 took up the post of rabbi in Szeged. Here he settled in to what became his lifework: the promotion of the reform of the Jewish community from within, particularly through improvement and modernization of education. One of his many projects was a Jewish newspaper, *Ben Chananja,* which he edited from 1858 to 1867. He had high ambitions for the paper. Initially it was a scholarly and religious journal, but it was expanded to include topical articles, commentary, political and Jewish community news, and articles advocating Jewish advancement and emancipation. Lőw wanted to make it the broadest possible forum for Jewish information and even had foreign correspondents based in New York, Jerusalem, and Berlin.

A young, shaggy-haired blond caretaker led me down a long, damp path through acres of neglected gravestones to reach the tombs of the Lőws and Schindler. Bushes and wild shrubs grew on both sides of the path in such abundance that at some points they nearly met overhead, making a living tunnel over the leaf-strewn cobbled way. In an open area to one side a strangely proportioned ceremonial hall, also designed by Lipót Baumhorn, loomed like a tall, yellow brick mushroom without a cap.

The three rabbis' tombs were in an irregular clearing surrounded by trees and leafy, dark green shrubs. Lipót Lőw lies in a noble sarcophagus on a raised platform covered by a Grecian-style roof atop six fluted Doric columns. On the top and sides of the sarcophagus, inscriptions in Hebrew and Hungarian cite his career and achievements. It is a simple and dignified tomb—inspirational, if you will, rather than melancholy—very impressive against the leafy green background. I pressed into the shrubbery to take pictures, and the young caretaker suddenly appeared struck by a twinge of conscience. "Wait, wait!" he pantomimed, and ran off to get a broom to sweep away the small shower of dead leaves from the steps up to the platform. Ostentatiously he kept sweeping as I photographed, first Lipót Lőw's tomb, then Immánuel Lőw's simple headstone a few feet away. It was like sweeping sand from a beach: The entire cemetery around this clearing was a mass of rampant brush and weeds, but the steps up to Lipót Lőw's tomb were now swept clean for the American visitor's camera.

Lipót Lőw died in 1875, and his son took over as Szeged's chief rabbi a couple of years later. Immánuel Lőw led the community for more than six decades, through its most prosperous years all the way to its destruction; indeed, they died together.

"He was deported in 1944 when he was ninety years old and half blind," Tamás Raj recalled. "In Budapest, he was taken from the deportation train, but he died in the Budapest ghetto hospital."

(Facing page)
SZEGED: Ceremonial hall, like a mushroom without a cap, designed by Lipót Baumhorn.

SZEGED: A young attendant sweeps leaves from around the tomb of Rabbi Lipót Lőw in the Jewish cemetery.

Portraits show the younger Lőw as an ascetic, scholarly man, with a thin, intellectual face, black clothes, and a long-tailed white clerical collar; he could be an old-fashioned Protestant minister. He was, indeed, a scholar—a noted etymologist, folklorist, botanist, and natural historian who spent years researching the plants and flowers mentioned in the Bible and other ancient Jewish texts. He published his findings in the monumental *Die Flora der Juden* and other works. It was his knowledge and interest in botany and Jewish symbolism that put the stamp on the lavish decoration of Baumhorn's Great Synagogue.

Lőw was a great proponent of Hungarian Reform Judaism, Neology, and a leader of Jews who considered themselves Hungarians of the Mosaic faith. The English Zionist official and journalist Israel Cohen, writing about his travels in Hungary to investigate a flare-up of anti-Jewish persecution just after World War I, was scathing about this type of Jew—and about Löw himself. Cohen detailed widespread violence—a so-called White Terror—directed against Jews by Hungarian soldiers and nationalists, allegedly in retaliation for the short-lived Communist regime led by a Jew, Béla Kun, who seized power for a few months in 1919:

Jews were dragged out of their homes, abused, flogged, robbed, tortured, and driven or deported to some other town or to Budapest itself. They were compelled to sign fictitious confessions of penal offenses, and if they refused at first they were flogged until they submitted. They were accused of illicit trading, of war-profiteering, of unemployment—of anything that could serve as a pretext: the real accusation was that they were Jews. The tortures that were inflicted upon imprisoned Jews in both the provinces and the capital read like a chapter from the Inquisition. They were flogged naked until they became unconscious; they were then besprinkled with water and asked what was the matter. If the victim was wise enough to say that he had a fall, or something similar, he was allowed to go, though not without a parting warning that if he divulged what had happened to him he would meet with a sorrier fate next time. Some of the worst tortures were practiced in the Komarom fortress, where men had to drink blood from their own wounds; others were buried neck deep in the earth, and others had to hold a mouse in their mouth or to eat the hair pulled off their chin. . . .

But despite the pall of oppression, the leading Jews of Hungary stirred not a finger to defend themselves, or to repel worse disaster that might be lurking. Hungarian Jewry had always prided itself on its ultra-patriotic Magyarism, and it remained true to this policy down to the end. The leaders were afraid that the Hungarian escutcheon might be sullied if they proclaimed their woes to the world, so they were dumb. Nay, they even denied that there were any grievances worth speaking of. . . . Such was the pride of the Hungarian Jews that a Rabbi once wrote a learned thesis to prove that they were descended from the Hungarian hero, Arpad, and that they had only religion in common with the other Jews of the world. The Chief Rabbi of Szegedin [Szeged], Dr. Immanuel Loew, always wore the Magyar national costume and oozed forth with ultra-patriotic exhortations. And yet he had been in the Szegedin gaol on the false charge of anti-patriotic sentiments. There had, indeed, been a veritable stampede to the baptismal font, some

30,000 Jews in Budapest alone having deserted their faith in the preceding nine months. In some places almost entire communities had gone over to Christianity. And in the face of all these perils the Liberal Jews, or "Neologen" (as they were called), still held aloof from the Orthodox, and both denounced Zionists as traitors to the fatherland.[3]

TEN HUNGARIAN ARCHITECTS VIED FOR THE JOB of designing the new Szeged synagogue, in a design competition held in 1899 whose prize was not only the synagogue contract but also the hefty sum of three thousand crowns.[4] Design competitions for public buildings were held frequently around the turn of the century and drew the top architects of the day; it was prestigious simply to have one's design among the runners-up. All the designs submitted for the Szeged project were grandiose, and four were given prizes by a jury composed of architects from Budapest, Vienna, and Szeged itself. That of Gyula Ullmann, second runner-up, was a rather somber, solemn design resembling a vaguely eastern fortress. It featured a tall central section with a big, elongated dome, flanked by much lower side parts with more rounded domed tops. The outer walls were smooth, simple, and somewhat cold. The first runner-up, a design by Marcell Komor and Dezső Jakab, was totally different: Bright and fanciful, it incorporated sumptuously full-bodied art nouveau curves and colorful decoration based on Hungarian folk embroidery.

Rabbi Immánuel Lőw worked closely with Baumhorn on all details of the decoration of the new synagogue. Every painted panel, every pane of stained glass, every inscription, every carving was imbued with a symbolic meaning that Lőw explained at length in detailed published accounts.

The tall bronze menorahs flanking the Ark, gilded and decorated with semiprecious stones, derived their form both from biblical descriptions and from the menorah looted from the Temple in Jerusalem, as depicted on the triumphal Arch of Titus in Rome. The massive dome is supported by twenty-four columns representing the twenty-four hours of the day. The stained-glass interior of the dome, created by Miksa Róth, the most sought-after contemporary stained-

glass artist, depicts the heavens, with the sun's rays spreading from a Star of David in the middle. Stained-glass windows on the ground floor employ ritual symbols and accurately detailed representations of plants and flowers

SZEGED: Interior of the synagogue, considered his masterpiece, designed by Lipót Baumhorn and inaugurated in 1903. Shown are the Ark and the bimah.

to symbolize Jewish holidays. Even the trees planted in the garden outside—yews and pyramid oaks—were selected by Rabbi Lőw to best set off the soaring lines and pale yellow brick of the exterior.

I REVISITED SZEGED A BIT MORE THAN THREE YEARS after the gala rededication and saw the synagogue empty this time, in dim light, and in, as it were, its everyday clothes. Leaking water, I noticed, had already seeped through and stained the ceiling high above the pews. Workmen were putting out poison to rid the building of a plague of pigeons.

Imre Gráf, president of the Jewish community, told me that the agreement with local authorities for the use and maintenance of the synagogue was working well. "We have good connections with the town hall, and I have good personal relations with the mayor," he smiled, adding that the city had recently decided to contribute a large sum of money toward the cleanup and maintenance of the Jewish cemetery, too. "We only have services in the big synagogue on the eve of Yom Kippur, for Kol Nidre, and on the anniversary of the Nazi deportations," he told me. "But there are concerts quite often. Tourists come, too. About twelve thousand to fourteen thousand come to see the synagogue during the tourist season. They buy a ticket for twenty forints [at the time, twenty-five cents], which helps pay for the electricity." On the wall of Gráf's office was a big poster of the synagogue put out by the local tourist board, which described Hungary as a land of heritage.

Márton Klein, the community's cantor, unlocked the synagogue for me and let me wander around. He pointed out a stack of paper yarmulkes at the entry for the use of tourists and people attending concerts. Klein was eighty or so, and, I was told, in bad health. On the wall of Gráf's office, a black and white photograph from years back, captioned "Chief Cantor of Szeged," showed him vigorous in flowing robes posing in full throat in the main elevated pulpit. Tamás Raj told me that it had been he who hired Klein as a *shammas*, or sexton, for the community in the 1960s. "We invited him to come to Szeged from Makó, not far away, because he knew how to wash the dead, and we needed someone like that," Raj said. "He was a nice, honest type of person and became cantor when the previous cantor died, after I left Szeged."

For years now, in the absence of a rabbi, Klein has led the community's prayers. Not too many people come to services regularly; many in the congregation are from the twenty or thirty Israeli students studying at the local university or the local pharmacy school.

"May I sing something for you?" he asked, as we prepared to leave the sanctuary. "You choose—I'll sing whatever prayer you like."

I chose two—the most familiar and the most fundamental—the Kiddush, or blessing over wine, and the Shema, the profession of faith in one God.

Klein stood in front of the bimah, a short, sweet, elderly little man in fedora hat and sheepskin coat, and opened his mouth. The prayers soared up, up toward the dome, somewhere curved dimly there high over our heads.

IN THE THREE OR FOUR DAYS FOLLOWING the rededication ceremony in Szeged in 1989, I traveled around in a rented car looking for synagogues and former synagogue buildings in half a dozen towns. I was accompanying my brother Sam, who had recently been named director of the Jewish Heritage Council of the World Monuments Fund. The fund is a private, nonprofit organization that sponsors on-site preservation and related research, training, and advocacy. The newly formed Jewish Heritage Council was to concentrate on these issues as they relate to Jewish sites. A coffee-table book on Hungarian synagogues had just been published[5]—we had picked up a copy in Budapest—and unable to read Hungarian, we used the pictures and maps to find the buildings.

Most of our little tour was in Hungary, but we made sure to cross the frontier into Yugoslavia to see the synagogue at Subotica. It was slow going at the border point: The Soviet Union had relaxed travel restrictions, and scores of Russians, on what was probably their first venture outside their country, were lined up at the frontier. They reminded me of pictures and films I'd seen of the Okies during the Great Depression: tanned, leathery folk with sad eyes and gold teeth, driving clapped-out Moskvitches, Volgas, and Trabants—small, old, junky cars—filled with children, bags, and elderly grannies. More bags and suitcases—and inevitably bald tires—were strapped to the roofs. Those going south into Yugoslavia, I knew, were headed to the great flea markets just over the border to try to trade all sorts of goods. They looked dirt poor, and compared to the westernized Hungarians and Yugoslavs alongside them, they were. But I knew that even to have a car and to be able to afford such a trip they must be better off than most Soviets.

Subotica, called Szabadka in Hungarian, is in Serbia's Vojvodina province, which formed part of Hungary until the breakup of the Austro-Hungarian Empire after World War I. Here, buildings by Budapest architects Komor and Jakab—whose synagogue design for Szeged had come in second after Baumhorn's—and others created something of an art nouveau theme park of the town center. Among these buildings was, indeed, the synagogue, designed by Komor and Jakab in a plan that was almost identical to their Szeged competition entry. "The design was too radical for the people in Szeged, but in Subotica they liked it," Gábor Demeter, from Subotica's monuments preservation office, told us. The building had been sold years ago by the remnants of the Jewish community and was used as a theater. Demeter was involved in slow, sporadic restoration efforts, but he was seriously hampered by lack of funds. He took us all over the building, pointing out everything from the spooky, pigeon-infested interior of the cupolas to the specially molded terra cotta tiles that were set off against the cream stucco of the outer walls. The interior of the dome glowed anew with the reds, blues, and gold of the detailed stained glass and fresco work that looked like the embroidered place mats and peasant blouses found in every souvenir shop in Budapest. Otherwise, everything was sad and shabby, covered in dust.

One of the most remarkable-looking synagogues pictured in the book on Hungarian synagogues was that in the town of Gyöngyös, about fifty miles northeast of Budapest. When the photograph was taken, the building had obviously been empty and in a state of considerable disrepair, but it still looked like a miniature Taj Mahal—or, perhaps better, a movie theater in Miami or Hollywood in the 1930s based on the Taj Majal. The picture alone made us want to go see it, but the fact that it had been designed by Lipót Baumhorn, working in collaboration with his son-in-law György Somogyi in 1929–1931, gave it an added allure.

The picture in the book showed a monumental, cream-colored building in a bare yard, with a big central dome surrounded by more than half a dozen lower-domed elements. The windows and doors, particularly the massive main entrance, were shaped like Indian-style pointed arches, and the walls and various roof levels were decorated with false crenellations and other details recalling Indian or Eastern architecture. What we found was something quite different. The building was under reconstruction, rather than restoration, and most of the decorative outer detail—and from what we could see the interior detail as well—had been removed. It was painted a depressing canned-pea green, but the Star of David was still atop the main dome.

I think it was the contrast between the Szeged synagogue and the one in Gyöngyös that consolidated my interest in Baumhorn. I learned that he had designed about two dozen synagogues at least, and I wanted to know where they were and what had become of them. Baumhorn had been the most prolific synagogue architect of his day, but existing lists of his work were only fragmentary. This made it only more enticing to try to find out just what synagogues he had designed and whether they were still standing. Could they all be as grand as the ones in Szeged and Gyöngyös? As I returned again and again to Central Europe, I made a point of looking for Baumhorn's synagogues and visiting them if I could. In my search—far from systematic—I discovered Baumhorn synagogues in various parts of Hungary as well as in the territories that before World War I used to be Hungary—Slovakia, Vojvodina, and even Transylvania. I began fleshing out my own list of his synagogues and gathering bits and pieces of information about his life and work.

∽ In Esztergom, perched above the Danube River bend north of Budapest, I found Baumhorn's first synagogue, built in 1888 when the architect was only twenty-eight. It was quite different from anything else of his I saw—a distinctive, ornate building, yes, but without the idiosyncratic character so apparent at Szeged that I learned to recognize in the other Baumhorn synagogues I discovered, too. In *Synagogues of Europe,* Carol Herselle Krinsky pointed out the dramatic development of style between the Esztergom synagogue and Szeged, and I could appreciate the conceptual leap. Something—other than just maturity—had to have happened to Baumhorn in the meantime. The Esztergom building gave the impression of being a typical, late-nineteenth-century, Moorish-style synagogue. It was unusual for its oblong shape, but it contained what I had learned to see as "normal" Moorish-style design elements—orange and blue horizontal stripes, fretted Oriental horseshoe archways, decorative bulbous cupolas at the top edges of the facade. The building had been converted into the offices of a technical institute in 1964, but it was well maintained and boasted a plaque giving its history. Out front, too, was a small Holocaust memorial, a stark sculpture of an anguished human figure.

∽ In Szolnok, a bustling town on the bank of the Tisza River southeast of Budapest, I found a synagogue built by Baumhorn in 1898–1899, ten years after the one at Esztergom. Already the style was radically different and approached the design of the Szeged synagogue, but on a much smaller scale. Situated picturesquely on the river bank, it was very ornate, with neoromanesque and gothic elements and a tall, ribbed dome. Vaguely churchlike, it had big rose windows set in arched facades over arched portals. It had been turned into an art gallery and was well maintained, although the interior, including the inside of the dome, had been painted completely white, obscuring any fancy details. A brochure in four languages—Hungarian, German, English, and Russian—was available at the gallery. The English translation (and I assume the German and Russian) was slightly mangled but understandable:

The Gallery of Szolnok

By one of the three churches characterizing the view of Tisza-bank at Szolnok, a marble plaque was placed on the 20. August 1899 and still there is in the porch behind the wrought-iron gates representing the main entrance of the former synagogue by having triple openings. The following is written on the plaque:

1898–1899
It was built by master builder Antal Vaskovits
by the drawings of architect Lipót Baumhorn
from the generosity of the congregation
with the help of Szolnok city.

Lipót Baumhorn was a famous expert in building synagogues, his name is associated with the designing of the synagogue in city Szeged.

The synagogue which was built in eclectic style is remarkable both in mass-effect and its details. The dome and trussing have metal-framed structure and carry the stamps of moorish-style.

The building became a characteristic element at the Tisza-bank end of the Ságvári boulevard by the historical reconstruction work. In addition to its history: the building which was broken-down by the damages during the II. World War and the following neglect and disuse, was bought by the city council from the religious community at the end of the sixties and after the renovation it was given to the Damjanich Muzeum for the purpose of exhibition hall.

It was opened in the spring of 1972 under the name of Szolnok Gallery by the show of the best work of the Szolnok Colony of

Artists. From that time it was a place of numerous national and international exhibitions as well.

The synagogue serving originally as a place of religious ceremonials—after the historical reconstruction work keeping the original characteristics of the building—is still serving under the name of the Szolnok Gallery the mankind, the culture, the art for the pleasure of many.

I cannot remember—nor did I record in my notebook—what was on exhibit the day I visited.

꼬 In Cegléd, a small market town near Szolnok, an hour's drive southeast of Budapest, I found a square, boxy synagogue, looking dull and dingy on a dull, dingy November day. Its outer decorative elements were incorporated into the structure and included what I eventually learned were typical Baumhorn touches—windows cut and shaped to fit into arches; pale yellow brick walls with structural lines and ribbing delineated in decorative fashion by different-colored brick; a tall, rounded arch over the main entrance. Old pictures show the synagogue, built in 1905, dwarfing the men in bowler hats and the women in sweeping skirts who are taking a breather outside during a break in services. Today, the building is used as a gymnasium.

꼬 In Novi Sad, the capital of Vojvodina, I found a monumental synagogue with vast arches, two massive cupola-topped towers, and a big central dome with a stunning stained-glass interior. The exterior edges and archways of this synagogue were emphasized by bold bands of reddish brick that vigorously combined structure and ornament. The synagogue was built in 1906–1909, when Novi Sad was the Hungarian Danube-side city known as Újvidék. When I saw it in the spring of 1991, it was in the process of being transformed into a concert hall. The two large buildings on either side of the synagogue harmonized perfectly; they had been built by Baumhorn at the same time as a Jewish school and a community center, making up a complex of Jewish buildings that took up a whole block of a major downtown artery. The office of the Jewish community, which numbered under three hundred members, still occupied a room in the building on the right.

ᔗ On the main square of Kecskemét, a market town halfway between Budapest and Szeged whose downtown complex of art nouveau buildings rivals that of Subotica (and indeed, was designed by many of the same architects), I found a dazzling, white, Moorish-romanesque–style synagogue with a tall steeple topped by a curious lotus-bud–shaped dome. The synagogue had been converted into a conference center/gallery complex: The upstairs exhibition hall was devoted to full-sized reproductions of statues by Michelangelo. The synagogue had been built in 1864 to 1871 by architect János Zitterbarth, but Baumhorn remodeled it and designed the exotic new main dome (and the matching, much smaller, side domes) after the original round dome was knocked off the tower by an earthquake in 1911.

ᔗ In Lučenec, Slovakia (formerly the Hungarian town of Losonc), I found a ruin. "It was the most beautiful synagogue in Central Europe," Mr. Novak, a Holocaust survivor from Lučenec and now secretary of the Jewish community in Košice (in eastern Slovakia), told me. An old picture shows a dense crowd of people filling the street and pressing close outside the sleek, new facade (with its typically Baumhorn arch and window combinations) at its dedication in 1926. There are men and women, some with hands clutched behind their backs, apparently straining to hear a speech by a local dignitary. Back in the crowd, three chuppahs with Stars of David glinting at the top of the upright poles are being held aloft. In the foreground, a young girl with bobbed hair and a short, pale dress stands apart from the crowd and looks away from the synagogue, clutching her coat, as if she had lost her parents in the crush behind her and didn't know where to turn. The shadows are long; it must have been late in the afternoon.

I visited the synagogue twice, both times in the driving rain. The huge hulk, with a massive central dome and two cupola-topped towers flanking the entrance, loomed dramatically, in lonely incongruity, outside the town center next to a seedy and inhospitable modern hotel that was surrounded by row after row of concrete apartment blocks under construction. A prefab snack bar selling sausage, beer, schnapps, and weak, lukewarm coffee occupied the muddy lot next door, almost flush with the synagogue walls. Dusk was just approaching when I visited the synagogue the first time. The sight of the ruined building was shocking; I felt real pain as I strained my eyes to take in every corner. I pushed my way through a broken, rusty fence and scrubby weeds to enter what had been the sanctuary. Here I found total, overwhelming devastation. The vast size accentuated everything—the gutted fixtures; sagging, broken planks; crumbling walls. I was scarcely able to make out the inner curve of the dome in the gloom. "It's like postnuclear Hiroshima," I scrawled in my notebook. "It could be the scene of some nightmare or some horror movie. . . . You must compare this with Szeged or Szolnok. Here is the death of a magnificent community—and wealthy: Who else would erect this type of synagogue?"

Some twenty-two hundred Jews made up about fifteen percent of the population of Lučenec when the synagogue was built; there had been nothing really special about them. I fantasized, though, about the congregation leadership getting together at some point after World War I—after the new borderline was drawn a few miles away,

LUČENEC: The ruined synagogue, designed in 1926 by
Lipót Baumhorn.

placing Lučenec in the newly formed Czechoslovak Republic—and deciding to build a new synagogue. I fantasized about them contacting Lipót Baumhorn, already in his sixties and famous for his many synagogues, and discussing money and size and location and all the other details. I fantasized Baumhorn in his office, puffing on a cigar, perhaps, as he drew up the plans; then, perhaps, overseeing the construction. There was sure to have been a plaque inside the synagogue entryway honoring him for his design (and the leaders of the congregation for having hired him). I fantasized a lot in Lučenec, which both times I visited struck me as otherwise empty of fantasy. "Potentially pretty but rundown and awful," I wrote in my notebook. The town, according to a capsule history in one guidebook,

> was founded at least in the thirteenth century, overrun two centuries later by the Hussite wars, swept by Turkish invasions between the sixteenth and seventeenth centuries, decimated by the plague of 1719, and today is fundamentally a railway junction with some textile industry; a good part of the population is composed of Hungarians and Gypsies. At one end of the main square, the former Calvinist church has become an exhibition hall . . . ; beyond the other end of the square, there is a grand synagogue, in ruins.[6]

འ When I revisited Gyöngyös, three years after first seeing the synagogue there, I found the reconstruction complete. The Star of David still topped the big central dome, and the building was still canned-pea green. It had been turned into the "Fönix" housewares department store. Displays of cheap plastic goods and home textiles filled new glass showcases built out in front.

Next door, on the former neoclassical synagogue, which Baumhorn's synagogue had been built to replace, a plaque noted that the synagogue was a "Monument, designed by Károly Rabl in 1816–1820," but it did not mention the type of monument it was or what the building used to be. Since my earlier visit this synagogue had been converted into a billiard hall and video game salon, with a bar and pinball machines in the front room. A fattish youth who looked like a fish asked me something I couldn't understand as I photographed the "Monument" plaque next to the door. I followed him inside, where pinball bells were ding, ding, dinging and video games were making bloopy computer noises. Conversation was virtually impossible, so I just smiled, papering over a sudden torrent of anger with studied amiability. After all, what did these people know? The fat youth stopped me from entering: My boots, he indicated, were too muddy; would I please wipe them outside? Ah, yes, oh, of course. I smiled and smiled.

IN JANUARY 1993, I WENT TO BUDAPEST to try to piece together into a more coherent form the fragments I had been collecting about Baumhorn. I had followed his trail for more than three years and for many hundreds of miles. He and his work had become something of a constant in my travels. Since there didn't seem to be any definitive list of what he had designed, I kept expecting to run into his synagogues whenever I ventured into what had been Hungary before World War I. Baumhorn's work, and what became of it, had become for me a commentary on or even a metaphor for the Jewish experience in this part of Central Europe over the past century: splendor, isolation, destruction, transformation, oblivion.

And I felt fear, or at least concern, for the future a little, too: Three years after the ouster of the Communists, little more than three years after that joyous rededication of the renovated synagogue in Szeged, anti-Semitism was becoming an increasingly open political platform of Hungary's nationalist right wing. The very week I was in Budapest that January, supporters of the right-wing populist leader István Csurka, who had issued heavy-handed anti-Semitic diatribes and had repeatedly blamed Hungary's woes on Jews, liberals, Western financiers, and the press, increased their presence on the presidium of the country's ruling Democratic Forum Party. Rabbi Tamás Raj and other prominent Jews regularly received hate mail. And just a few days after I left the city, a Jewish schoolgirl, the granddaughter of an Auschwitz survivor, was stabbed—injured but not killed—in front of her home by neo-Nazi skinheads who called her a "damned Jew."

In Budapest, I finally sought out the synagogues Baumhorn had designed here, in the capital, the city that had been (and still was) the spiritual and population center for Hungarian Jewry. Despite the fact that as many as ninety thousand or more Jews still lived in Budapest, I found the same pattern of splendor and oblivion I found in the provinces.

There was a large, squarish synagogue with steep gables, for example, built in 1908 on heavily trafficked Dózsa György Boulevard. "I had my bar mitzvah there," Andras, a tour guide in his late fifties or early sixties, told me—but he professed to forget what the synagogue had looked like back then, before the war. "It was so long ago," he said, shaking his head, and I didn't press the point. Like the synagogue in Cegléd, this synagogue had been sold years before and turned into a sports hall. The sweeping lines of the outer decorative ribbing around the gables and windows were painted a dirty turquoise, and the panels where the Ten Commandments would have been affixed under the rounded peaks of the gables above the rose windows were blank. Inside, various levels housed sports facilities, including basketball and handball courts and—high up, on an open deck under the central dome—fencing courts. A constant sound of

BUDAPEST: The exterior of the synagogue on Dózsa György Boulevard, designed by Lipót Baumhorn in 1908.

thumping balls, athletic shouts, and heavily running feet echoed through the building.

A children's fencing class was under way when I visited. No one minded that I made notes and took pictures. Vaguely sinister-looking

BUDAPEST: The interior of Baumhorn's synagogue on Dózsa György Boulevard—now used as a sports hall. A fencing class is in progress underneath the painted dome.

masked instructors in gym shorts or sweatsuits coached lunging, masked, and padded pupils tethered by elastic cords, oblivious to the great dome that blossomed overhead. The busy blue floral and geometric frescoes that covered the inner cupola and the swooping vaults and arches appeared to have been recently restored, and the stained-glass heart of the dome still glowed.

In Budapest, too, I found a large synagogue designed by Baumhorn in 1923, in a courtyard on Páva utca. Its exterior, rather plain and simple, reminded me of the Baumhorn synagogue in Nyíregyháza, in northeastern Hungary, which was built the same year and which I had seen in my earlier travels. Both featured outer walls whose main decorative elements were almost identical window arrangements of panes and panels cut and fitted into an arched form that approached the grand Indian-style Taj Mahal arches I had seen at Gyöngyös. The over-the-top grandeur of Gyöngyös was lacking, though. Perhaps the congregations had not been able to afford anything more exciting; perhaps it had been too soon after World War I, when Hungary lost much of its provincial territory (including half its Jewish population), for outward architectural celebration. Then, too, there had been the upsurge of anti-Semitism in Hungary in the early 1920s, in the wake of Béla Kun's short-lived Soviet-style Bolshevik government. The right-wing overthrow of Kun's government touched off the anti-Jewish and anti-leftist pogroms in many towns that Israel Cohen described. It also laid the groundwork for official anti-Semitic attitudes that grew over the coming years. In 1920, for example, the government imposed so-called *numerus clausus* restrictions limiting the percentage of Jewish students allowed to enter universities to the percentage of Jews in the population as a whole. "Lipót Baumhorn in one of his more restrained moments," I had noted about Nyíregyháza.

The Páva Street synagogue was damp and extremely cold, bone chilling. It still belonged to the Jewish community—next door there was a community day care center for elderly people—but it hadn't been used for services for years. All the decoration and fittings were intact but run-down, stained by seeping water and flaking from the damp. Here, instead of the costly marble, mosaic, stained glass, and precious wood Baumhorn had used in Szeged, I found plaster walls and pillars painted with swirling, varicolored lines to look like marble. The use of stained glass was minimal, and other decoration also simply was painted on in a largely geometric scheme that covered every surface in tones of blue, white, cream, and russet. Gilding highlighted the Ark, and the ceiling and upper portions of the walls were sprinkled with a galaxy of six-pointed stars.

IN BUDAPEST, I HEADED TO THE LIBRARY at the Rabbinical Seminary, where I hoped I would be able to find the one article I knew of about Baumhorn, a brief study published in a Hungarian Jewish magazine in 1980. The seminary, established before World War I in a sober, three-story brick building near the Danube, was a symbol of Budapest's primarily Neolog Jewish community, conspicuously different in style and educational emphasis from traditional Orthodox *yeshivas.* Rabbinical training here involved secular scholarship as well as religious studies. After the Holocaust, it remained the only rabbinical seminary in Eastern Europe. I first visited there years earlier, when Rabbi Sándor Scheiber, a Jewish scholar of international renown, was its director. I vaguely remember Friday night services in a small prayer room and a Sabbath meal with a bunch of rabbinical students. Scheiber died in 1985, and I hadn't been back to the seminary since.

The library is two flights up in a building that now also serves as a Jewish high school. The street door is monitored by a guard in a little booth who buzzes you in. Books line the hallways—books of all types, many in disintegrating leather bindings. They are stuffed helter-skelter into shelves, and whether or not they are all listed and catalogued, I never found out. The research rooms are small and stuffy and overheated and also lined floor to ceiling with books. I was told the seminary library contains 150,000 volumes. The librarian, an older man with whom I spoke Italian and who enjoyed joking that his last name, Remete, came from the Italian *eremita*, meaning "hermit"—a good name for a librarian—had never heard of Lipót Baumhorn, but he was easily able to find the article I was looking for and made a photocopy of it for me.

It was a ten-page article, including pictures, co-written by György Somogyi, the architect who had been Baumhorn's son-in-law as well as his partner in Baumhorn's later years, and a certain János Gerle. From it I was able to add more names to my list of towns in which Baumhorn had designed synagogues.

Baumhorn was known to have designed about two dozen synagogues. In *Synagogues of Europe,* Carol Herselle Krinsky listed the following: (1) Esztergom, 1888–1889; (2) Zrenjanin (in Vojvodina), 1895; (3) Szeged, 1899–1903; (4) Budapest Dózsa György utca; (5) Budapest Páva utca, 1923; (6) Rijeka (in Croatia); and—in partnership with Somogyi—(7) Gyöngyös, 1929; (8) Budapest Csáky utca, 1927; and (9) Budapest Bethlen Square, 1931.[7] The last two, I found out, are prayer halls inside other buildings. I read elsewhere that the synagogues in both Rijeka and Zrenjanin had been destroyed during World War II. Krinsky also noted that Baumhorn had entered the design competition for the synagogue in Žilina, Slovakia (he did not win), and I knew that he had also competed for the never-constructed Great Synagogue planned for Budapest's Lipótváros district, a wealthy downtown neighborhood along the Danube. Many other architects submitted designs for this project; all of them were for opulent temples of gargantuan proportions. Baumhorn's entry had come in third.

From my own experience and Hungarian sources, I added to Krinsky's list (10) Lučenec, 1926; (11) Cegléd, 1905; (12) Szolnok, 1898–1899; (13) Nyíregyháza, 1923; (14) Novi Sad, 1906–1909; (15) Eger, 1913; (16) Makó, 1914; (17) Nitra (in Slovakia), 1914; and (18) the reconstruction and dome of Kecskemét. The Eger synagogue was destroyed in 1945; the Makó synagogue was pulled down in the 1960s.

According to the Hungarian article and the few other sources I dug up in the library, Baumhorn also designed the synagogues in (19) Braşov and (20) Timişoara, in Romania. In addition, various other towns were listed, including Kaposvár and Liptovský Mikuláš (in Slovakia), where, apparently, Baumhorn carried out restoration or reconstruction work.[8]

I learned, too, that Baumhorn was born in Kisbér, a small town west of Budapest. He studied for a time in Vienna and then became a disciple of Ödön Lechner, the most influential of Hungary's late-nineteenth-century architects, whose experiments with flowing lines, bright color, and decoration incorporated as part of a building's structure had tremendous impact on Hungarian architecture as a whole. I also discovered a possible reason, aside from Lechner's influence, that Baumhorn's synagogue style changed so radically in just a few years following his first synagogue at Esztergom. In the 1890s, I read, he made architectural study trips to Italy. He undoubtedly visited Italy's great Renaissance and baroque churches, but, knowing his interest, I had visions of him also taking notes in front of what then had been the new Great Temple in Florence, a Moorish-style synagogue built between 1874 and 1882 with a richly decorated interior, a massive arch over the facade, and a tall central dome flanked by two domed towers—all motifs that appeared frequently in Baumhorn's later work.

Somogyi and Gerle's article ended with the information that Baumhorn was buried in Budapest's Kozma utca cemetery, in a tomb

LIPTOVSKÝ MIKULÁŠ: Ruined interior, from afar *(above)* and close up *(below)*, of the synagogue, showing decoration designed by Lipót Baumhorn.

designed by Somogyi himself, and on which was written a poetic epitaph by the great Rabbi of Szeged, Immánuel Lőw:

Ihlett müvészünk: Ájtatkeltő zsinagógák
Égkereső vonalát ihlete, szíve szülé!
Békés hajlékán lebegett áhítatos érzés:
Égkereső vigaszát férj és apa lelke szülé.

These four incomprehensible lines haunted me. Epitaphs are meant to sum up a person's life, and these lines, I felt, might tell me something about Baumhorn the man, aside from what I could deduce about him from the buildings he designed and the few scraps of biographical information I found during a couple of days of searching through the library collection. I had to get it translated.

I took the epitaph to a friend, a Hungarian journalist. She puzzled over what she described as extremely flowery, poetic language. She tried to piece together a translation word by word: *skyline; sky-seeking; artist; husband; father; comfort.* But she gave up. "I can understand it, yes, but I can't translate it," she said. "It is very, very poetic."

I carried a copy of the epitaph with me and pulled it out to show every bilingual friend or colleague I met in Budapest—two, three, four, five, six people. No one could quite figure it out; some took one look and refused even to try.

Gáby, a young English-speaking student doing his own research at the library—the son, I found out, of Rabbi József Schweitzer, the director of the seminary—tried to help, but when he looked at the little stanza he too threw up his hands. "I can't translate that stuff," he said. "But," he added, "there is a book I know, which you may find useful."

He disappeared into another room and returned with a thick volume, packed with pictures, on turn-of-the-century Hungarian architecture, co-written by the very János Gerle who had co-written the magazine article on Baumhorn.[9] There were entries on scores of architects, arranged in alphabetical order, plus an insightful introduction in English as well as Hungarian.

"Lipót Baumhorn . . . led Lechner's achievements in structure and form back in the direction of historicism," I read. This indicated that rather than being full-fledged examples of the innovative Hungarian style of his era, Baumhorn's eclectic designs were instead rooted in earlier tradition. "It is quite easy to trace how, from the first few years of the century, he shook off the influence of the Lechner atelier and how historicism became predominant in his works. . . . On his synagogues, Lechner's influence is apparent for another decade."

I flipped through the book, hoping to find further critiques or biographical information or pictures of Baumhorn buildings I had not seen, or possibly a complete list of his work.

What I found was his photograph.

I felt like Stanley meeting Livingstone in the heart of the African jungle.

There he was, in a formal, posed portrait against a background shaded from gray to black. He was a stocky, almost chubby, contented-looking fellow with his head cocked slightly back, giving him a rather imperious air. He must have been in his forties when the picture was taken. His short, slightly graying hair was swept back from an egg-shaped forehead; his eyes were sleepily (or knowingly) half-lidded; his nose was short and turned up a bit, and his lower lip was slightly underhung. He wore a full, dark mustache, pointed at the ends (I could imagine him twirling the points), and a dark, pointed Vandyke beard. I could tell from the picture that his cravat and starched white collar were tight; a tiny roll of flesh bulged under his ear. He reminded me of someone I couldn't quite place: an architect friend of mine in Wales, perhaps, or maybe an English painter I had once been half in love with many years ago.

I WENT TO DINNER A FEW NIGHTS LATER at the home of Miklós Haraszti—a Jewish writer, political theorist, and now member of Parliament—whom I have known since the days, a decade and more ago, when he was a leading activist in Hungary's anti-Communist dissident intellectual movement. Miklós was a favorite target for anti-Semites; even a non-Jewish relative of his by marriage had reported receiving hate mail. Also at dinner was the architect László Rajk, another former dissident and current member of Parliament, the son of Hungary's postwar Communist interior minister (also named László Rajk), who had been executed for anti-Moscow "Titoism" in October 1949.

I pulled out my by now well-worn copy of Baumhorn's epitaph, and they too attempted a translation. They pieced together the following, which neither found a satisfying rendition:

LIPÓT BAUMHORN (photo provided by János Gerle, from the collection of the late György Somogyi).

Our inspired artist: gave birth to the heaven-searching skyline of
   rapturous synagogues.
The husband and father searching for heaven's comfort gave birth
   to the feeling of inspiration.

"Let me explain it," said Miklós. "What he's saying is that 'our
artist' carried out the creation. It is his inspiration and heart that gave
birth to the skyline of synagogues that produce rapture. And it's his
husbandly and fatherly soul that gave birth to sky-searching consola-
tion (or comfort), while his raptures (or reverential feeling) embraced
his peaceful home."

"What it is, is two interpretations of him," chimed in László.
"There is the person and the architect. Both interpretations refer to
heaven and sky—there is a play on the words 'sky' and 'heaven';
when he writes 'skyline,' he doesn't just mean 'silhouette.'"

"So," Miklós concluded, "it is an epitaph that praises the heart
and inspiration to create architecture, plus the fatherly and husbandly
feeling to create a home, which both help him to create synagogues."

László then added a final touch by telling me that he himself had
used the sports facilities in the Baumhorn synagogue on Dózsa
György Boulevard when he was a teenager. "It was an absolutely
run-down sports hall in the 1960s, when I used to go there. It was a
cold sports hall, very shabby."

A FEW DAYS LATER, THROUGH LÁSZLÓ, I met János Gerle himself, the architectural historian who at that point could probably have been considered Hungary's—indeed, the world's—expert on Lipót Baumhorn. It
was he who had co-written the magazine article on Baumhorn as
well as the book on turn-of-the-century Hungarian architecture. He
was a thin, wiry man with a sharp profile broken by dark-rimmed
glasses and an enormous black mustache. We met amid packing
cases in the apartment he was just vacating, five floors up in a building near the Hall of Parliament, with a spectacular view of the
Danube.

"Baumhorn didn't have any descendants," he told me. "And I
don't know anyone living in the family, though there may be some
distant relatives living in Miskolc. Also, a few months ago there was a

Baumhorn from France trying to find out if he was related in any way. György Somogyi, his son-in-law and partner, died in the early eighties, when he himself was eighty or so." Somogyi had been married to Baumhorn's daughter Margit, an industrial designer. As an old man, decades after Baumhorn's death, Gerle told me, Somogyi had criticized his father-in-law for having refused to evolve his style and for having recycled the same stylistic elements and plans in his later work that he used in earlier designs. These, Gerle explained, included an almost trademark use of four pillars, arches, and tambour below a double cupola. According to Somogyi, he told me, the Gyöngyös synagogue was the first design that departed from that basic structural concept. In the Gyöngyös synagogue, the cupola is laid upon four flat, reinforced concrete beams.

I asked Gerle where Baumhorn and his work fit into both the history of Hungarian architecture and the history of Jewish life in Hungary. He had described Baumhorn's style as dominated by historicism, bucking the trend of his contemporaries; Somogyi had criticized his lack of innovation. Was Baumhorn indeed an important figure or just a synagogue-building hack?

"He was a conservative person for his time," Gerle replied. "Baumhorn had three or five synagogues, though, which have really a great architectural value. There is a series—Novi Sad, which is somehow following Lechner in his bit more dry style—it's really modernistic architecture. In this series is also the synagogue on Dózsa György Boulevard in Budapest, which has been horribly transformed. The entire decoration reveals the structure of the building. Cegléd also belongs to this series, and it too is horribly transformed."

And Szeged, Baumhorn's opulent masterpiece?

"Of course Szeged is very nice, with all its details, so very rich," Gerle replied. "It belongs to the historical heritage of Europe. It was old-fashioned for its time. You know, there are many tendencies within the Jewish community—this is illustrated when I think of how the synagogues in Szeged and Subotica were built at the same time. One of them, Szeged, was conservative. The other, Subotica, incorporated new ideas."

I thought back about how, yes, the Subotica Jewish community had constructed its joyful, folk-art–inspired art nouveau synagogue as part of the entire art nouveau complex of buildings in the town center, after the Jews in Szeged had rejected an almost identical design for their own new synagogue.

As others had, Gerle also noted the correlation between Jewish emancipation and optimism and the explosion of cultural (including architectural) innovation at the turn of the century.

"In Hungary, the Jewish community was always strong, with many freedoms compared to other countries," he said. "After the 1860s, they were granted civil rights, so of course they became really a leading part of development. Nowhere else in Europe was there a tendency like there was here. Jews wanted to be Hungarian; assimilation was very strong. There were many wealthy [Jews] who became supporters of the new arts and of the new architecture. They had strong communities, and all civil rights, and money, and could build—they wanted to support the Hungarian style."

Many—most—of the leading Hungarian architects of Baumhorn's day were Jewish, and Gerle's book on the Hungarian architecture of the time includes numerous examples of synagogues and Jewish family tombs designed by the same people who designed banks, apartment buildings, hotels, theaters, and town halls.

"The book includes about two hundred architects," he said. "At least two thirds of them were of Jewish origin, the overwhelming majority—much more than the Jewish proportion of the population."

But he rejected my suggestion that this might mean that the distinctive Hungarian art nouveau was actually created by Jews. Though most of his followers were Jewish, he pointed out, Ödön Lechner— the great pioneer of this style—was not.

"There was, in fact, controversy that the followers of Lechner destroyed his 'Hungarian' style and that these followers—Jews—created something not really Hungarian but Jewish," he said. "It's true [that they destroyed Lechner's style], but not in this way. What Lechner's followers did was to make a more commercial architecture; it became routine."

IN ORDER TO FIND ONE SPECIFIC TOMB among the hundreds of thousands spread out among the vast acres of Kozma utca Cemetery, you go first to the little office in the ceremonial hall and ask the attendant for help. "Lipót Baumhorn," I told the man, a youngish fellow in rough clothes with a long, thin straggly beard and a dirty yarmulke pinned on his greasy, light brown hair. He turned to a wall cabinet of wooden drawers packed solid with file cards arranged in alphabetical order; there were three hundred thousand or more tombs, he told me.

"Baumhorn, Baumhorn . . ." He fingered through the B's. "This one?"

I glanced at the card. "No—this is a Lipót Baumhorn, but it's the wrong death date. This is 1931; I'm looking for a Lipót Baumhorn who died in 1932."

"This?" He pulled out another card and handed it to me. "It also has his wife on it."

"Yes, this is the one." The card was handwritten in old-fashioned script. The brown ink was faded.

The attendant took back the card, which apparently contained notations as to where the grave was to be found, and motioned for me to follow him. I followed him for what seemed like a half hour. We walked clockwise around the perimeter, past the outer circle of family mausoleums against the cemetery wall, past the Holocaust memorial with its poignant lists of names, past tombs of martyrs, tombs of rabbis, tombs of the mourned, tombs of the forgotten. It was gray and cold, and it seemed as if the gray stone of the tombstones had absorbed the weather. From time to time planes rumbled low, directly overhead, on their approaches to the airport a few miles away. The attendant walked far ahead, consulting the card occasionally, checking its notation with on-site markers that to me were invisible, finally stopping to wait for me to catch up.

"I made a mistake," he shrugged, and smiled a little sheepishly. "This is the wrong side of the cemetery."

Back we went, past graves of soldiers, graves of salesmen, graves of doctors, graves of loving wives and mothers and little children. Another attendant, wearing a big fur hat, joined us. My breath came as puffs of gray steam.

Finally, somewhere in the middle, my guide consulted the card in his hand, turned off the main path to the left, and stopped. He stepped into an expanse of graves, looked around, stepped back, consulted his friend, moved forward again, and then returned to the path.

"He should be here," he told me. "This is the plot. His grave should be here, but I can't find him." He shrugged. The plot was relatively well tended. Most of the tombs were horizontal slabs marked at one end by simple, rather low, stone uprights whose names and epitaphs were clear and easy to read. There was very little of the ivy and weeds and uncontrolled brush that choked much of the cemetery and shrouded many of the other tombs.

"You are sure?"

"Yes, that is what is written." He shrugged again.

Just across the path on the other side, the name Baumhorn leaped out . . . but it was the wrong first name, the wrong person completely.

What did I want to do?

"I have to find him," I said. Here? Amid all these thousands of tombs? I turned slowly around, 360 degrees. "Yes."

"Wait," the attendant said. "Maybe it's that over there."

He pointed to the middle of the plot, to what at first glance seemed simply a tall shrub, a mass of dark green leaves some eight or ten feet high. It was, in fact, the only tomb in the plot that was totally enveloped by ivy, so completely covered that it was impossible to make out any of the stone beneath.

The attendant threaded through the surrounding tombs and pulled away some of the glossy leaves. Parts of three carved letters emerged: . . . HOR . . .

"This is it!"

The man beamed at his discovery—the old card filing system had been right after all.

I felt paralyzed. "I have to stay here awhile," I told him. I spoke quite calmly, but my voice felt as if it came from a distance, and I could feel my heart beating fast.

The two attendants headed back through the graves, leaving me with Lipót Baumhorn.

Ivy, thick ivy, encrusted the tombstone like a darkly shimmering outer shroud, a living cocoon as tightly concealing as linen strips wrapped around a mummy. Not even the full size or shape could be determined. In the cold, I began clawing at the stems and creepers hugging the stone. Brown and brittle, the smaller shoots put up resistance, but finally tore away.

I felt like a liberator, and I guess I was, restoring to the light of this cold, gray day the chiseled memory of this man. It was a highly

personal liberation. For more than three years I had followed a trail of monumental buildings whose style, number, and significance had made Lipót Baumhorn successful in life and more than just a footnote in the history of his profession. His synagogues were his survivors; he was honored on gilded marble plaques in their entryways. He wore pointed mustaches and a tight white collar. The person was here, shrouded in ivy.

I tore at the clinging vines. Little by little the face of the tomb was exposed. It was far taller than I am, with a gothic-style point at the top. In the upper section was a carved relief: the vast dome of the synagogue at Szeged floating on a heavy mass of clouds. In the lower part was a list of twenty-three synagogues, described there as those that Baumhorn had planned: the most comprehensive list I had seen:

> Budapest Aréna [Dózsa György] Boulevard, Bethlen Square, Csáky and Páva Streets; Szeged [set off on a line of its own as befits the designer's masterpiece]; Gyöngyös, Braşov, Esztergom, Kaposvár, Cegléd, Kecskemét, Szolnok, Eger, Liptovský Mikuláš, Timişoara, Rijeka, Murska Sobota [now in Slovenia], Nyíregyháza, Lučenec, Zrenjanin, Novi Sad, Nitra, Újpest [a Budapest suburb].

"I'm sure the tomb was paid for by the communities where he designed synagogues," János Gerle told me, "so the list was their names. It's therefore partly a list of his works and partly a list of those who paid money for the tomb." A couple of places, like Makó, were missing—maybe they had not contributed.

On the back of the tomb, added years later, was a simple inscription of the name and dates of Baumhorn's wife, a much younger woman, who survived the Holocaust: Blanka Schiller, 1874–1958; nothing more.

Rabbi Lőw's epitaph occupied the middle part of the tomb face.

János Gerle had helped me put together yet another translation. ("It's not easy," he said. "Immánuel Lőw was a very great person, but this poem is not nice.") I found that the strange lines had more meaning when viewed within the context of the tomb, designed by Baumhorn's son-in-law, with Szeged's great dome hovering in the clouds and the simple name and dates of the architect's widow on the rear.

(Facing page)
BUDAPEST: The tomb of Lipót Baumhorn, partially cleared of ivy.

BUDAPEST: The tomb of Lipót Baumhorn, cleared of ivy.

Our inspired artist: His inspiration and heart gave birth
To the lines of synagogues that look toward heaven and awaken
    piety.
Above his peaceful home hovered devotion;
The soul of a father and husband gave birth to heaven-seeking
    consolation.

The inch-thick stems of ivy at the top of the tomb were too
strong for me to break or even to cut back with a penknife I found in
my bag. I left them and their trailing tendrils and glossy green leaves
in place, like a crown or a hat with pluming feathers or a head with
unruly hair, waving in the cold wind.

MONTHS AFTER I LEFT BUDAPEST, János Gerle sent me the following
list, which he had compiled from his files. Some of the dates are
not certain, he wrote, and not all data have been checked, but
the list represents the most complete catalogue available of Baumhorn's work. Where possible, I have noted the present use of each
synagogue.

Lipót Baumhorn's Career and Architectural Work

1883–1884	In the office of Ödön Lechner
1888	**Synagogue,** Esztergom (offices)
1890	Grünfeld residence, Komárom
	Royal Court, Győr
1893	Glass factory, Salgótarján
1895	**Synagogue,** Rijeka, Croatia (destroyed)
1896	Paper industry pavilion, Budapest Millennial Exhibition
1898	**Synagogue,** Szolnok (art gallery)

(continued)

1899	*Synagogue* competition, Szeged, first prize (built 1903; now a synagogue/concert hall)
	Lipótváros *Synagogue* competition, Budapest, third prize
	Gyárváros *Synagogue,* Timişoara, Romania (synagogue)
1901	*Synagogue,* Braşov, Romania (synagogue)
1902–1904	Construction, Szeged synagogue and Jewish community building
1903	Szeged-Csongradi Bank, Szeged
	Bank competition, Hódmezővásárhely
	Water regulation company headquarters, Timişoara
	Girls' school, Timişoara
	Residence, Timişoara
1904	Residence, Szeged
1905	Wagner residence, Szeged
	Two residences, Timişoara
	Synagogue, Cegléd (sports hall)
1906	Enlargement of *Synagogue,* Kaposvár (stands empty)
	Remodeling and restoration of *Synagogue,* Liptovský Mikuláš, Slovakia (under restoration)
	Synagogue, Makó (destroyed)
	Synagogue, Jewish school, residences, Novi Sad, Yugoslavia (concert hall)
1907	Tomb of Újhely family, Kozma Street Jewish cemetery, Budapest
	His own residence and office, Budapest[10]
1908	Aréna [Dózsa György] Boulevard *Synagogue,* Budapest (sports hall)
	Two residences, Novi Sad
1910	Elementary school, Budapest
	Building competition, Budapest, second prize

Bank, Baja

Music school competition, Szeged, third prize

Residence, Szeged

1911   ***Synagogue,*** Eger (destroyed)

1912   Lloyd Palace, Timişoara

1912–1913   Restoration of ***Synagogue*** after earthquake, Kecskemét (conference center, offices, and art gallery)

1913   ***Synagogue,*** Trenčin, Slovakia. (This is open to debate: The large, domed, Baumhorn-style synagogue standing in Trenčin today, and now used as an exhibition hall, bears a plaque stating that it was built in 1909–1912 by the architectural firm of Fuchs and Nigrais and does not mention Baumhorn.)

1925   ***Synagogue,*** Lučenec, Slovakia (ruin)

1926–1927   ***Synagogue,*** Hegedüs Gyula [Csányi] Street, Budapest (the first collaboration with Somogyi; still a prayer hall)

1928   ***Synagogue*** competition (with Somogyi), Žilina, Slovakia, second or third prize

Ferenc Klén residence, Budapest

1929   ***Synagogue*** competition, Váli Street, Budapest, second prize (with Somogyi)

1931   ***Synagogue,*** Gyöngyös (with Somogyi) (department store)

1932   ***Synagogue,*** Bethlen Square, Budapest (with Somogyi) (prayer hall)

Albert Márkus residence, Budapest

1932   Dénes residence, Budapest

In Addition

Synagogue transformation, Nagykanizsa
Synagogue, Nyíregyháza (synagogue)
Synagogue transformation, Zrenjanin, Yugoslavia (destroyed)
Synagogue, Nitra, Slovakia

(continued)

Synagogue transformation, Murska Sobota, Slovenia
Synagogue enlargement, Budapest-Újpest
Synagogue, Páva Street, Budapest (with Somogyi) (empty)
Bank, Novi Sad
Casino competition, Lipótváros, Budapest, first prize
State Girls' High School, Szeged
Ceremonial hall, Szeged
Seven residences, Szeged
Béga Canal Society building, Novi Sad
Residence, Győr
Enlargement of Jewish Hospital, Budapest (before 1926)
Hospital, Szövetség Street, Budapest (before 1914)
Residence, corner of Honvéd and Kálmán Streets, Budapest (before 1914)
Residence, Sziv Street, Budapest
Tomb of Wagner family, Szeged Catholic Cemetery

∽ 4 ∽

What's to Be Done?

Cracow

∽∽∽

I've drunk gallons of coffee with people who have ideas about
what to do with Kazimierz.
—Stanisław I. Zohar
American Jewish Joint Distribution Committee
representative in Poland

 AZIMIERZ, THE ANCIENT JEWISH QUARTER of Poland's historic
capital, Cracow (Kraków), is a Jewish ghost town.

It is unique in East-Central Europe: a once-teeming,
big-city "Jewish town" whose Jewish population vanished virtually overnight during the Holocaust, but whose
entire Jewish infrastructure—houses, markets, streets, shops, synagogues, schools, cemeteries—was left intact, to crumble and molder
slowly through the decades of Communist neglect: to become, in the
words of Henryk Halkowski, one of the handful of Jews still left living
in the city, a powerful and very eloquent "symbol of Jewish absence."

"Right here in Cracow, especially in Kazimierz, that absence
seems more painful than anywhere else," Halkowski has written.

There are no Jews in Warsaw, either, but then Warsaw has no Jewish houses and streets. Jewish Warsaw does not exist. In Cracow,
the very buildings exist, the doorways, the streets, the synagogues,
the schools—destroyed, derelict, gutted, with the jagged wounds
showing where houses have been pulled down—but it is the same

Jewish Cracow, the same city. Jewish tourists drive through Cracow on the way to Auschwitz, and what they see in Kazimierz provides them with a sort of prologue to their visit to the death camp. In Cracow they see the ruins of Jewish life in Poland, and then they arrive at the place where Jews were murdered, gassed, and burned. In Cracow, they see the old Jewish district: the destroyed, ruined buildings; there, where the inspired faces of sages and prophets could once be seen, they see a gray, decrepit existence. They look, and say, 'Churban Bayit ha'Shlishi' (The Destruction of the Third Temple).

Those Jews are gone. One can only try to preserve, maintain, and fix the memory of them—not only of their struggle and death (as in Warsaw and Auschwitz), but of their life, of the values that guided their yearnings, of the international life and their unique culture. Cracow was one of the places where that life was most rich, most beautiful, most varied: and the most evidence of it has survived here.[1]

For years, particularly since the ouster of Poland's Communist regime, the means and manner by which Kazimierz and its memories should be, as Halkowski put it, preserved, maintained, and fixed, have bedeviled scholars, city planners, Jews, Jewish organizations, monument preservationists, businessmen, tourists—and many others.

Kazimierz as it stands today includes seven synagogues, the oldest of which dates back to the fifteenth century; nineteen shtibls, or small prayer rooms; numerous other ritual and community buildings; two cemeteries; and various market squares, all set in a matrix of centuries-old housing. The physical condition of these buildings is so bad that more than eighty percent, it has been calculated, are in serious need of repairs or renovation, and at least eight percent should simply be demolished.

What to do—what can be done, what should be done—with this crumbling unique ghost town so full of ancient specters has become a debate, a round and round discussion, that encompasses much more than architecture and urban development; it embraces the whole sphere of memory and Jewish memory and the relations between Jews and Catholic Poles. In this most historic of Polish cities, it embraces life and legend and raises more questions than answers. Interests and personalities clash, too, and so, sometimes, do egos.

CRACOW: A dilapidated building in the Kazimierz district.

"What should be done?" easily turns into "Why should it be done?" and "How should it be done?"—and indeed, "Who should do it?" The questions spin out to regard not just Kazimierz, not just the dying Cracow Jewish community, but all of Poland and beyond—surviving Jews, individual surviving Jewish buildings, and Jewish monuments scattered throughout Poland and the countries beyond its borders.

"What are you trying to do?" asked Jonathan Webber during a Sabbath walk around Kazimierz. A Jewish scholar at Oxford University, Webber also teaches and carries out Jewish studies research in Cracow and elsewhere in southern Poland. He was one of the researchers whose study of how Jews were remembered in Polish Galicia had been so important in the formulation of my own interest in such questions. We stood at Plac Nowy, the Jewish Square, the former Jewish market, in whose center still stands a low, round, many-windowed building once used as a kosher slaughterhouse for poultry.

White clouds scudded across a blue June sky; a few gnarled stall keepers at a few metal stands sold fruit and vegetables and curiously antiquated sets of women's underwear. "What are you going to do? A 'roots' service? A place where American tourists can go Friday night? Shall we simply point out: This is the last Jewish building, that is the last Jewish building? What should we do with it? Should we destroy it? Should we let it fall down? Bury it? There are many answers; I don't know."

THE SINGULAR, TROUBLING QUESTION of Kazimierz derives in part from Cracow's own unique situation. Of all major historic Polish cities, Cracow was the only one to emerge largely unscathed from World War II. Gdańsk and Warsaw, for example, were leveled; what stands today as their picture-perfect "Old Towns" was painstakingly reconstructed after the war, brick by brick, from photographs and paintings. Warsaw's once crowded Jewish quarter, the congested, vital, chaotic, poverty-stricken home to most of the city's 330,000 Jews, is today a neighborhood of drab, decaying glass-and-steel apartment buildings.

Cracow's historic Old City, a beautifully harmonious complex of narrow streets and ancient buildings centered on the vast Rynek Główny, or main market square, and anchored by hilltop Wawel Castle, dates back to medieval times. And despite decades of deliberate neglect under the Communists, it is, locals are quick to point out, original. I vividly recall how the thin young man with long straggly hair, my guide in the summer of 1980 on my first trip to Cracow, stretched out his hand at one point during a walk through town and affectionately patted the soot-blackened, crumbling wall of a building. "It might be falling down," he smiled, displaying bad teeth and local pride, "but at least it's real."

Cracow, Poland's royal capital for more than five hundred years, suffered under the Communist regime for its "reality" and all that it represented. In a sense, the Communist leadership took out its animosity against all that communism opposed by deliberately debasing the city, which had long symbolized Poland's national, intellectual, and religious identity. Here stand Wawel Castle and the royal cathedral within its turreted walls, which are considered by many Poles to be the very heart of the nation. Polish kings and national heroes are buried here—a religious, cultural, and political pantheon—ranging from the country's patron saint, the eleventh-century bishop St. Stanisław, to the beloved Romantic poets Adam Mickiewicz and Juliusz Słowacki to the eighteenth-century military hero Tadeusz Kościuszko and the revered pre–World War II leader Marshal Józef Piłsudski, who died in 1935. Under the Communists, Cracow's historic buildings were left to rot and crumble. It was more important, it

CRACOW: General view of the Rynek Główny (main market square).

was deemed, to reconstruct what had been lost in its entirety than to repair and maintain what had managed to escape destruction.

Worse, though, the Stalinist-era Communist state in the early 1950s built as part of its massive industrialization programs the immense Lenin steelworks and a complete new steel mill town, Nowa Huta, right on the edge of ancient Cracow itself. Several villages dating to medieval times were bulldozed to clear the way. Nowa Huta—whose very name means "new steel mill" and whose construction by work brigades was immortalized in Andrzej Wajda's famous film *Man of Marble*—was established as a model socialist workers' settlement, and its placement next to Cracow was determined by a deliberate decision of Communist ideology. The huge steel mill and surrounding "workers' paradise" were to be a direct contrast and counterweight—a challenge, as it were—to the ancient city's stronghold of Catholic, intellectual, aristocratic, and historic cultural traditions. Infamously, in fervently Catholic Poland, the new paradise was to be "a city without God." It was built without a church; one of Pope John Paul II's most clamorous successes when he was Archbishop Karol Wojtyła of Cracow was to fight for and finally achieve the construction of the Church of Our Lady of Poland, consecrated in 1977 as the first newly built church in Nowa Huta.

Just as infamously, the steel mill, said to account for about half of Poland's current iron and steel production, belched out constant clouds of deadly pollutants, which helped turn Cracow, otherwise set in fertile farmland, into an environmental disaster area for both people and the historic buildings they hold dear. One of the first news articles I ever wrote about Poland, in the summer of 1980, detailed what I described as "a combination of ignorance, neglect, and shortsighted city planning" that threatened a city which in its first millennium of existence had survived floods, fires, earthquakes, and invasions.

"The problem is that so many buildings need emergency first aid just to keep them standing that there is not enough money to complete the overall block-by-block restoration, and the pollution is the worst problem," I quoted a member of a nationwide committee founded in 1978 to raise money for Cracow's restoration as saying. He told me that local industrial plants had by then been fitted with basic antipollution filters. "But they were installed very late. And they are not enough; they limit the toxic dust but not the gases."

CRACOW WAS FOUNDED AS EARLY AS the seventh century. Legend has it that it was established by a powerful prince named Krak or Krakus who built a castle on Wawel hill overlooking the Vistula River. Unfortunately, according to the legend, a fierce and hungry (some say fire-breathing) dragon lived in a cave within the hill under the castle. It devastated the surroundings, preying on livestock and even young maidens to appease its voracious appetite. Krak, the wily prince, thought up a ruse to destroy it. (Or, according to one version, it was a local cobbler who came up with the idea; another version says it was Krak's two sons.) He ordered a sheepskin (or cow or ram skin) filled with sulfur (or a mixture of sulfur and tar, or sulfur, tar, and wax), which was set alight and thrown into the cave. The dragon immediately snapped it up in one gulp. One version of the legend says the burning sulfur made the beast so thirsty that he drank and drank from the Vistula until he blew up in a fantastic display of sparks. (One version specifies that he burst into a thousand pieces; another says that the fiery meal alone was enough to cause him to explode.) The town was saved, and the dragon became its symbol. The version of the legend that says the cobbler thought up the trick to kill the dragon duly notes that the cobbler then married Prince Krak's beautiful daughter. (Another version states that the daughter, Wanda, married nobody but took the throne after her father died. She committed suicide by drowning herself in the Vistula after a German prince whose offer of marriage she had rejected threatened to invade Cracow. The legend says she is buried under a mound built by her grieving subjects that still exists outside the city.)

Legends aside, by the year 1000 or so a cathedral as well as a castle stood on Wawel hill, and in 1038 the city became Poland's royal capital. In 1079, Bolesław the Bold (the first king to be crowned in Wawel Castle) murdered one of the first bishops, Stanisław (later canonized as St. Stanisław, the Polish patron saint whose tomb is in the castle). Cracow continued as the royal seat until the Polish capital was moved north to Warsaw in the early seventeenth century, a move that added considerable fuel to a rivalry between the two cities that persists to this day.

Cracow lives and breathes historic memory. Even if you close your eyes, you will hear homage to the past: Every hour on the hour, day and night, a trumpeter climbs to the top of St. Mary's church tower in the market square and blows the beginning bars of a medieval hymn, the *Hejnal*. He blows it four times, to the north, south, east, and west. Each time, the melody is cut off in the middle of a note. This commemorates the moment in 1241 when the Tartars, swarming in from the east, invaded Cracow and a Tartar soldier shot an arrow into the throat of a Polish trumpeter at just that point as he was sounding the hymn. The music broke off as the trumpeter fell dead.

In a sense, the Tartars gave us the Cracow we see today. They destroyed the city in 1241, burning it to the ground, and ravaged it in further attacks later in the century. In 1257, Duke Bolesław the Shy drew up a comprehensive reconstruction plan for a new, fortified city whose checkerboard grid layout, centered on the 200-meter by 200-meter main square, has survived intact through nearly eight turbulent centuries.

JEWS PROBABLY LIVED IN CRACOW by the latter part of the thirteenth century, and by 1304 there was already an established "Jewish street" near the main market square, along what is now the street of St. Anna. For the next two centuries, a Jewish community—consisting mainly of craftsmen, merchants, money lenders, and other financial operators—grew up in the heart of the medieval city, where, however, they were subject to increasing hostility on the part of their Christian neighbors. The preaching of St. John of Capistrano in 1454, for example, touched off violent anti-Jewish riots, which left many dead and caused much damage to property. A few decades later severe restrictions were imposed on Jewish business activities.

Given this climate, by the fifteenth century many Jews had already begun moving south from the center just beyond the city walls to the "twin city" suburb of Kazimierz, which had been founded as a separate town by King Casimir (Kazimierz) the Great in 1335. Casimir was held in high respect and affection by the Jews because he acted in many ways as their protector, issuing several edicts that granted them privileges. He also, according to legend, had a Jewish lover named Esther, described as the beautiful daughter of a tailor. Casimir is supposed to have built castles (or a castle) for her and to have allowed her to bring up the children they had together as Jews. And Esther herself is said to have founded three synagogues. Legend has it that the house in Kazimierz where Esther lived was connected to the royal castle by a secret underground passageway. To this day one of the streets in Kazimierz bears her name.

In 1495, anti-Jewish hostility in Cracow proper—this time triggered by accusations that Jews had started a fire that devastated parts of the city—led King Jan Olbracht to expel all Jews from Cracow. Most of them moved only the few hundred yards to Kazimierz, and here they developed into one of the most influential and respected Jewish communities in Central Europe. Thriving in their enforced residential isolation but still permitted to trade and carry out business in Cracow's main market, the Jews of Kazimierz became great merchants, using family and religious ties to forge links all over Central Europe. Many immigrants from Bohemia and Moravia, driven out of their homes by the authorities there, settled in Kazimierz. In the sixteenth to mid-seventeenth century, Cracow's golden age, the Jewish merchants of Kazimierz practically monopolized trade between Cracow and Prague, then Central Europe's most glorious Jewish center, which was enjoying a golden age of its own.

Kazimierz was home to great sages and fostered the development of important Jewish scholarship. The first Hebrew printing press in Poland was set up here in 1534. Beautiful synagogues were built, as well as study houses and ritual baths. The dead were buried in what is now the Old Cemetery, founded in 1551 in the heart of the town, under tombstones richly carved with elegant epitaphs and ritual imagery. The greatest sage was Moses ben Israel Isserles, known as Remuh, Poland's most famous Talmudic scholar, who lived from about 1520 to 1572. His tomb still stands in the Old Cemetery, and pilgrims still come to pay homage at his grave. They pile its ledges with memorial pebbles and tuck petitions and prayers on folded slips of paper into crevices in the stone. It was Remuh who amended, adapted, and wrote commentaries on the Shulchan Aruch, so that this landmark codification of Jewish law drawn up by the Sephardic scholar Joseph Caro could be used as a guide for Ashkenazic Jewish practice as well as for the somewhat different Sephardic observance.

It was also Remuh who, commenting on the relatively good situation for Jews in Poland compared to the rest of Europe, asserted that it was preferable to live on dry bread and in peace in Poland than to enjoy better material conditions amid the greater danger and insecurity outside Poland's borders. And it was Remuh, too, according to one story, who noted that the Hebrew word for Poland, *Polin,* could be made up of two other, separate Hebrew words, *poh* and *lin,* meaning "here he shall stay." (Other versions say these words, formed by leaves falling from the sky, or heard in the twittering of birds in the air, indicated to Jews fleeing eastward from medieval German persecutions that this was where they should settle.)

Jews stayed in Kazimierz until the Holocaust swept them out of existence; more than sixty-four thousand Jews lived in Cracow at the outset of World War II. By that time, Kazimierz, which had long since been incorporated into Cracow proper, was home mainly to the mass of the city's poorer Jews, many of them Hasidic. More acculturated middle- and upper-class Jews had tended to move out, closer to the main market square, as residency restrictions confining Jews to Kazimierz alone were gradually lifted in the nineteenth century.

In Kazimierz, the Jews lived in crowded, tenement-style apartment houses built around dank courtyards with wooden or iron balconies on each floor. There were, a Jewish travel writer wrote in the 1930s, "numerous Hasidic study-halls and prayer-rooms lost in a maze of courts and alleys, where Jewish mysticism still beats its wings."[2] At about the same time, a non-Jewish American travel writer made Kazimierz and similar Jewish quarters sound much less romantic:

> Interesting as I found the ghettos, as much fun as it was to go poking around in twisting medieval streets and alleys, peering into courts, walking slowly when I came to open doorways, sometimes I fear staring when I met some very rich or some very poor Jews, I found that half an hour was as long as I could stay. Now my sense of smell is subnormal. For the average tourist, ten minutes would be enough. Acute smellers had better get glimpses from the street-car and be content. For the ghettos I saw in Warsaw, in Wilno, Lublin, Krakow are not only ugly and dreary, they're smelly—an ancient medieval odor plus a sour odor. The streets are dirty (even in Warsaw), they're crowded, too, and with people who are not always clean. Not that the houses are small or poorly built; but they're discolored, squalid, neglected—unattractive to the maximum degree. . . . I know that the Jews in Poland are nearly all wretchedly poor, facing a terrible struggle just to exist. I know that nearly all of them live in very crowded rooms, without baths; that they must carry up many flights of stairs every drop of water for cook-

ing, laundry, bathing. But many Poles live under the same conditions, yet give no such impression of permanent dirt as do the Jews. If one of these Jews sat down by me in the street-car I would move or stand up; what with the dirt, the smell, the fear that something would crawl over on to me, I couldn't ride next them, but cringed and drew away as I never do from negroes. There's something sinister about them.[3]

This writer may sound superfastidious and even anti-Semitic, but Cracow-born Jewish intellectual Rafael Scharf has also written that Cracow's acculturated, progressive, middle-class Jews viewed the majority of Kazimierz residents with ambivalence, if not disdain:

That human landscape . . . did not, at that time, appear to us to be attractive. On the contrary—I am ashamed to admit—many of us looked on these people with a sense of embarrassment. Those

CRACOW: The remains of Yiddish writing on a flaking wall in the Kazimierz section.

beards, side-locks, crooked noses, misty eyes, what do our non-Jewish fellow citizens make of this? It is now clear that those faces, lined with care and wisdom, glowing with some inner light, as if they stepped down from portraits by Rembrandt, were beautiful. We realize that now, when they are no more.[4]

Old photographs of Kazimierz from the late nineteenth and early twentieth centuries show residential buildings with shop after shop on the ground floor: shops with signs in Polish and Yiddish, shops one after the other selling everything—groceries, leatherware, hats, beer, fish, clothing, umbrellas, salami, tallises, wine, bagels, shoes. What was not sold in the shops was bought and sold in the crowded marketplaces: the fish market in front of seventeenth-century Izaak's Synagogue; the vast flea market on the long square called Szeroka Street, the heart of Jewish Kazimierz, with the massive, fifteenth-century Old Synagogue at one end and the Old Cemetery and sixteenth-century Remuh Synagogue—built in 1553 by the father of the scholar for whom it is named—at the other; the food market in what is today Plac Nowy. The photos show clean-shaven Jews in modern European dress walking the same streets alongside pious Jews in their beards, caftans, big fur hats, and sidelocks. The buildings in the old pictures look much as they do today: scuffed and shabby, needing repair. It all looks much the same, in fact, except that today there are few shops, few people, and no Jews. Indeed, only about two hundred people identifying themselves as Jews, their average age seventy-five, live in all of Cracow today. The eighteen thousand people who now live in Kazimierz are a fraction of the prewar Jewish population there, though they too, like the Jews before the war, are among the city's poorest residents.

"YOU SHOULD HAVE SEEN THIS NEIGHBORHOOD before the war," Rafał—Ralph—Immerglueck told me, relishing the memory. A Holocaust survivor from Cracow who emigrated to the United States after the war, Immerglueck now spends part of the year in his old hometown. "There was movement, everything was moving. It was all Jewish businesses. You could buy everything—and cheap! Not just salami, but *goose* salami. You can't believe how good it was. And pastries?

Fantastic! The people here were all very, very poor. . . . But on Shabbos everything was closed. No one was afraid of anyone, and there were lots of religious schools."

I met Immerglueck, a frail-looking man with black-rimmed glasses and a nervous smile, during a visit to Cracow in early June 1993. I had come to Cracow not only because I wanted to revisit Kazimierz and walk once again through the strange cityscape of that Jewish ghost town, but because I also wanted to investigate the status of the debate on the district's future.

I had last spent time in the city about a year earlier. During visits that summer, I spoke at length with a whole roster of people, ranging from city officials to members of private foundations to individual Jews who were interested in "doing something." But the questions, "What should be done?" "How should it be done?" "Why should it be done?" "Who should do it?" had lingered in the air, largely unanswered. I had come away, too, with the uncomfortable impression that Kazimierz (and perhaps Jewish memory, or the exploitation of Jewish memory as a whole in Cracow) was regarded as something of a prize and that competing interests were priming themselves to stake their individual claims.

"The situation is changing in Kazimierz," I was told by Joachim Russek, deputy director of the Center for Research of Jewish History and Culture in Poland at Cracow's Jagiellonian University, Central Europe's second oldest university, founded in 1364. The center, established in 1986 and supported in part by the Washington-based Project Judaica Foundation, Inc., sponsors research work and publications, runs an intensive summer course of lectures and on-site study of Jewish history in southern Poland, and works out of a well-equipped facility in one of the Jagiellonian's buildings. One of the projects it had sponsored was the ethnographic study of attitudes toward Jews in present-day Galicia. Although it was a major player in efforts to encourage Jewish studies and to reinsert a Jewish presence in Cracow, none of its staff was Jewish.

One of the Jagiellonian's projects was the construction of a large Jewish cultural and study center in a former study house in the heart of Kazimierz near the old Jewish market. When Russek and I talked, construction had begun on this center but had not progressed very far. He said he expected it to be ready by the autumn of 1993, however, and told me that it would eventually include a whole range of exhibition, study, information, and hospitality facilities.

"The number of visitors to Kazimierz is growing," said Russek, a youngish, articulate man with reddish hair and beard. "What's there now can't provide what needs to be provided. Our new center is so far the only investment to deal with people going to Kazimierz who are not just casual tourists.

"I think we in Cracow should take care of [Kazimierz]," he continued. "The Jewish community is nearly gone. Our center for Jewish culture is a step toward providing in-depth information to those who need it."

During another of my talks, Zbigniew Zuziak, an energetic architect and city planner associated with the new International Cultural Center situated on Cracow's main market square, outlined a study he was putting together for the center on—precisely—what should be done with Kazimierz.

"The essence of the topic is a cross-cultural study," he said. "The main difficulty in revitalization is not just the physical aspect, but how to revitalize the social space without its population. The architectural sense is there, but the Jews are gone. I'm now at the stage where I know what should be done. We have a vision but are lacking the proper political climate to carry it out. The authorities have to express their will on Kazimierz."

That summer Zuziak was coordinating a conference sponsored by the International Cultural Center on managing tourism in historic cities, and he tied much of the theoretical aspect of this topic with the Kazimierz situation. Kazimierz, being a historic area that was virtually undeveloped, represented virgin territory.

"The idea is how to combine tourism with historic preservation," Zuziak said. "There is always the risk that a place will end up like Disneyland. How should we put the plans in operation? I think there should be a form of community development trust, along the lines of the concept of a historic district. Kazimierz could be a useful pilot study."

Jacek Purchla, the director of the International Cultural Center, pointed out to me some of the basic, underlying problems concerning Kazimierz that were holding back its development.

"Until World War II, Kazimierz was overpopulated by a very

poor population," he explained. "The whole population was murdered by the Nazis. After the war, this district again was inhabited by very poor people. The problem of ownership of the property there has not been solved, so since 1939 those houses have been in a permanent state of devastation. We know that ninety percent of the prewar owners went up the chimneys of Auschwitz. Now, the question of ownership in Kazimierz should be solved. It means negotiating internationally. . . .

"I'm deeply convinced that Kazimierz has a future," he said. "Maybe as a sort of Latin Quarter. But it will be a long-term process; it needs investment, and Poland is considered high risk for investors. . . . I'd love to see Kazimierz booming, with Jews coming to study their roots."

A Jewish source in Cracow, a man who had been born in Cracow, survived the Holocaust, moved away from Poland, and then returned a few years earlier to live in Cracow again—added more depth to the issue from his own, Jewish, perspective.

"Nothing can be accomplished in Kazimierz until the question of ownership is settled," he stated bluntly. "There's the problem of ownership and then, too, the question of resettling the people who live there now. They are very poor people—super lower class—living there. What can be done with them?"

I knew that the question of who owned what now in Poland (indeed in all post-Communist countries) was a touchy and highly emotional one—and not just where former Jewish-owned property was concerned. What today has cynically become known as ethnic cleansing had taken place at various times and to various degrees against various people over the past half century. First the Nazis leveled towns and cities and killed three million Polish Jews and three million non-Jewish Poles. After the war, refugees and other homeless people took over their vacant dwellings and business premises. The Communists confiscated or nationalized Jewish religious and community property and abandoned Jewish private holdings, as well as farmland, factories, pharmacies, mines, industrial complexes, business enterprises, commercial property, residences, landed estates, and other private property that had belonged to Jews and non-Jewish Poles alike. To complicate matters further and add to the reciprocal pain, millions of ethnic Germans living in that part of western Poland

199

which was Germany before the war but was awarded to Poland afterward were expelled and forced to move to Germany, often leaving homes they had lived in for centuries. Their property, too, was taken over by Polish settlers and the Communist state. An estimate made in 1991 put the total value of property that could eventually be returned to private owners as between $9.9 billion and $17.4 billion.[5]

The problem of what property should be returned to its prewar owners, whether it should be returned, how this return should be regulated, and what should be done with the people who had lived in or used the property for fifty years was a serious source of concern and even fear. Jewish Holocaust survivors simply going back to visit their hometowns have, for example, reported hostility on the part of current residents, who feared they had come back to take over their former property.

The attitude of the government, the Jewish man I questioned said, was to give back the synagogues to the Jewish community, including those that had been confiscated and converted over the years for secular use.

"But what to do with them? As a Jewish community, you can't turn a synagogue into a swimming pool; you can't rent it out as a department store. Maybe someone should ask for a rabbinical opinion: When is a synagogue not a synagogue? so they can be rented out. But what happens when a synagogue is restored? How is it going to be maintained? One idea is to use one of the synagogues in Kazimierz as an ethnographic museum of Jewish traditions. Do you know, I once overheard a kid in the Jewish museum that is here, in the Old Synagogue, asking, 'What does a Jew look like?'"

Meanwhile, it had become clear that some things were already being developed in and around Kazimierz. Increasingly during visits to Cracow over the years I noted evidence of both scholarly and intellectual interest in local Jewish history, as well as a tendency to "market" Jewish history and memory as part of the city's attractions. There was an ever-growing number of books on Jewish topics, both in Polish and English, prominently displayed in Cracow's many bookstores. Cassettes of Jewish music were on sale; and, as elsewhere in Poland, tunes from *Fiddler on the Roof* were by now standard for restaurant violinists. An art gallery specializing in works by Jewish artists and on Jewish themes opened in the Old City in 1989. Also in 1989, the National Museum in Cracow put together a magnificent exhibition on the Jews of Poland, which also traveled to Warsaw. On a separate level, the numerous Cracow stalls and shops selling examples of Polish folk art and woodcarving increasingly included figures of Jews among the standard images of Jesus, Mary, and Polish peasants. A number of these figures, with their long beards, big noses, and sad eyes, were for me rather too close to stereotypical caricature to be comfortable. But what was significant was that they, *Jews,* were seen as a marketable facet of Poland that tourists might want to buy to take home.

My visit to Cracow in June 1992 coincided with another major example of this rediscovery of Jews and Jewish tradition as part of local tradition. For a week and a half that month Cracow was host to its third Jewish Culture Festival, an international extravaganza of klezmer music, films, exhibitions, performances, seminars, and talks on a wide range of Jewish themes, all hailed by some as a Jewish Woodstock. The festival, begun in 1988 and staged every two years, has grown in scope, audience, and enthusiasm each time and is now a standard feature in the summer cultural scene. Striking posters for the 1992 festival, depicting a braided loaf of challah with a Star of David baked into the crust, were plastered on walls all over the city, and billboards advertised it along main roads. Most events were centered in Kazimierz, with concerts and performances taking place in several of the former synagogues and in the open air on Szeroka Street, the long, rectangular square that had been the heart of Jewish life before the war. Here, on Szeroka Street, surrounded by the dilapidated houses in which Jews had once lived, hundreds of fans, mostly young and overwhelmingly non-Jewish, danced and clapped along at a riotous grand finale concert by top klezmer bands from the United States, Israel, the Netherlands, and Ukraine that went on past midnight. Addressing the crowd from a stage that was decorated with blown-up reproductions of Marc Chagall paintings of shtetl life, violinist Alicia Svigals, of the Klezmatics group from the United States, bridged past and present. "We dedicate tonight's concert to those who lived in these houses and could not complete their full lives," she said. "May their memory be blessed."[6]

I TIMED MY JUNE 1993 TRIP so that I would be able to meet up in Cracow with my brother, Sam, the director of the Jewish Heritage Council of the World Monuments Fund. The Council—and thus Sam—were active players in the what to do with Kazimierz dilemma: The Council had announced the year before that, at the invitation of the Cracow Jewish community, it would be taking on as its biggest preservation project to date the restoration of the Tempel Synagogue in Kazimierz, the only intact nineteenth-century synagogue in Poland. Sam was leading a group of American Jews on a week-long study tour of Poland, visiting a score of Jewish sites to examine some of the best and worst examples of how these places are cared for today and to explore the wide range of issues surrounding the preservation and conservation of Jewish cultural relics and memory. The trip culminated in Cracow, where the group—whose fee for the tour included a donation toward the Tempel Synagogue restoration project—could get a detailed look at the synagogue and learn what needed to be done. In Cracow Sam was also talking with the local Jewish community and city monuments preservation officials concerning the start of work on the building.

Sam, an architectural historian, had been instrumental in getting me interested in Jewish historical relics and their fate. It was while traveling with him in Hungary and Poland in 1989 and 1990 that I became both fascinated and overwhelmed by the wealth of tangible evidence—the symbolic mezuzahs of cemetery and synagogue, ghetto and shtetl—that remained to bear witness to a thousand years of Jewish history in the region. What I discovered on those trips, and in my ensuing thousands of miles of travel documenting these places, evolved into a deep concern for the fate of these stone survivors. Sam and I have spent hours during family visits and over transatlantic phone lines discussing aspects of this frustrating and tragic problem. *What can be done? What should be done . . . ?*

Cracow and Kazimierz loom with particular importance in this discussion because, just as Cracow was the only major Polish city unscathed by World War II, Kazimierz is the largest and most complete historic Jewish quarter to survive. The only comparable place is not Prague, with its famous complex of Jewish buildings, but Venice. In Prague, the Old Jewish Cemetery and a number of extremely valuable and historic synagogues survive, but the medieval ghetto surrounding them was demolished and totally rebuilt with new buildings and streets around the turn of the century. The ghetto in Venice, however, is a complex of a half dozen synagogues, plus Jewish dwellings and marketplaces dating back to the sixteenth century, forming an intact, well-maintained whole that looks much as it did four hundred years ago.[7]

"The Venice ghetto balances tourists and the local Jewish community," Sam said. "The problem in Kazimierz is that there is too much for the Jews here. There are too many synagogues, too many historic buildings."

Of the seven synagogues in Kazimierz, two—the Tempel and the sixteenth-century Remuh Synagogue—are still consecrated for worship. Of the rest, the seventeenth-century Kupa Synagogue, a dilapidated building long used as a workshop, was recently given back to the Jewish community, but it is in terrible physical condition. Restoration would be expensive, and the Jewish community has found that it

CRACOW: Beautiful Hebrew calligraphy in the partially restored Izaak's Synagogue.

CRACOW: Soaring lines of Izaak's Synagogue.

now must pay property taxes on it. The sixteenth-century High, or Tall, Synagogue is a workshop; Popper's, or Bocian's, Synagogue, built in 1620, is a culture center, but all the rich interior decoration has been destroyed. Izaak's Synagogue, built in 1638 and the biggest synagogue in Kazimierz, is in a sort of limbo. The city started to restore it but ran out of money; the cavernous building with its lofty, barrel-vaulted ceiling and graceful women's gallery with stone arcade and balustrade—described in the 1930s by Marvin Lowenthal as looking as if "poured in molten rock at one splash"[8]—now simply sits empty. No one knows if or when restoration work will continue, or to what use the synagogue will be put once it is restored. None of these synagogues is marked by a plaque saying what it used to be.

The splendid, gothic Old Synagogue, built in the fifteenth century and devastated during and after World War II, was fully restored in the 1950s and turned into a Jewish museum, but here too there are problems. The museum, like many Jewish museums, displays a fascinating collection of Judaica—silver and ceramic ritual objects, paintings, embroidered tapestries, and textiles—but they are displayed primarily as art objects, as artifacts, as exotica, with little descriptive information and little attempt to teach or explain what these objects were used for, by whom, how, and why.

"It could be an exhibition of exotic Indian artifacts or material from the South Sea islands," Sam commented when we visited the museum. "There's a need to 'humanize' Jews, to teach that Jews were people. To show what Jews did, who they were. To look at this, you'd think that Jews just sat around menorahs all day. Until there is understanding about what is or was a Jew, stereotypes will be perpetuated."

I recalled how the Jewish man I spoke with in 1992 had overheard a child at the museum asking what a Jew looks like.

CRACOW: The historic Old Synagogue in the Kazimierz district, built as early as the fifteenth century and now used as a Jewish museum.

Said Jonathan Webber, "The problem is not how Poles present Jews, but how we Jews represent ourselves in a country where we lived for eight hundred years, how we Jews lay our memory to rest."

"I WAS BAR MITZVAH IN THE OLD SYNAGOGUE," Stanisław Zohar told me. The Polish representative of the American Jewish Joint Distribution Committee, Zohar was born in Cracow, escaped from a Nazi concentration camp during the war, and went to Israel, where he lived until he returned to Cracow in 1990 for the JOINT, a key Jewish aid organization that provides social services and help to needy Jews worldwide. We talked over late afternoon cognac in his apartment-cum-office a few steps from the main market square. "My grandfather was *gabbai* [a senior lay official of the congregation] there. He had a seat on the eastern wall.[9] When I visited the Old Synagogue when I first came back in 1990, I saw this. I felt OK. But when I saw the seat there . . . I felt a *kvetch* in my heart when I saw the seat."

Zohar, a small, wiry man with large, heavy-lidded eyes and deep facial wrinkles, said that when he moved back to Cracow he tried to find an apartment on Szeroka Street in Kazimierz. "I was begging the municipality to rent or sell me a flat on Szeroka. I wanted symbolically to live in Kazimierz, to be the only Jew living in Kazimierz, but they had nothing," he said.

Reiterating what I heard from others the year before, Zohar said not much could be done on a grand scale in Kazimierz until the ownership question and the question of what to do with current tenants were cleared up. The year before, he said, Cracow's mayor had sent a letter to international Jewish organizations inviting former Cracow Jews or their heirs to come back and claim their property. "There was lots of noise, but that was the beginning and end of it," he said.

Like everyone connected with Kazimierz, Zohar has spent much time theorizing on the district and listening to the theories of others. "I've drunk gallons of coffee with people who have ideas about what to do with Kazimierz," he told me. "I think from the Jewish view the only place that has a meaning and that can be saved for us is Szeroka Street. There's the Remuh Synagogue and Cemetery, and the Old Synagogue—the exhibitions in the Jewish museum there have to be changed, but I'm told that there's no money. In addition, there's already a very nice little café on Szeroka. There's room on Szeroka Street for a good Jewish bookstore, and there's a need for a good book on Kazimierz, on Cracow Jewry, in English, Polish, and Hebrew. There needs to be a good kosher restaurant, too . . . and a hotel catering to Jews. It's a problem for Orthodox Jews who come and visit, you know. The nearest hotel catering to Jews is the Forum, across the river. But it's a problem. It's far, and it's an unsafe walk, among other things. I'd like to see a Jewish hotel with a kosher kitchen—a forty-room hotel would have seventy to eighty percent occupancy all year round. Groups come. That's the way you can make Kazimierz alive."

THE "GOOD LITTLE CAFÉ" THAT ZOHAR MENTIONED is the Ariel Café, a thriving oasis amid the derelict buildings, with umbrella-shaded tables set up right on Szeroka Street, a few steps from the Old Synagogue. Its sign is in Hebrew-style letters and also in Yiddish. Founded a few years earlier in a privately owned building as an art gallery specializing in Judaica, it was transformed into a coffeehouse in the autumn of 1992. I found it a dimly lighted, intimate place serving drinks and snacks, ideal for idling away long hours in thought or conversation. It still included a small art and Judaica gallery, as well as a selection of Jewish-interest books for sale, ranging from photography books on Jewish cemeteries to esoteric biographies of Polish rabbis.

"Some people think it's sick to have a café here, but I disagree," the Ariel's manager, Wojtek Ornat, a youngish man, a non-Jew whose wife is descended from a Jewish family that converted to Catholicism, told me. Along with Sonia Lucas, a young Englishwoman living in Cracow doing research for her doctoral degree in Jewish studies at Oxford University, we sat talking, drinking tea, and making our way through a platter of fresh strawberries at one of the wickerwork tables outside.

"Forty years have passed now," Ornat said. "Until recently, you couldn't think of doing something like this. Kazimierz spatially is identical to how it was before the war. Now Jews are coming back to visit here; they recognize places where they were as children. Now I can open a café."

Ornat said he felt himself a pioneer in both the revitalization of Kazimierz and the general revitalization of interest in Jewish culture and Jewish memory. So isolated a venture was the café that Jewish visitors occasionally mistook it for a synagogue or other religious facility, he said. Another of his projects was managing a new klezmer band, called Kroke, the Yiddish name for Cracow. The group was enjoying considerable local success playing traditional Jewish music—their concerts at Ariel were generally sold out—but it was klezmer music in a vacuum; in practically Jewless Cracow, all the musicians were young Polish Catholics.

Unlike most of the people I spoke with, Ornat did not feel that the question of property ownership was the most serious one confronting those who want to develop Kazimierz. "It's a problem but not a big problem," he said. "Twenty to thirty percent of the ownership has already been cleared up. The main problem is money, money, money. Szeroka would be completely different now if there was money to spend. . . . Eventually, this will become a very snobby, elegant neighborhood, with very expensive property prices. Now people are already looking at the area; with the way the Polish economy is going, within five years professional people will have the money to buy properties. It will be gentrified—already there's a well-known composer who's bought a place here. And artists will come, too. . . .

"Another problem right now," he said, "is that there are still a lot of drunks and alcoholics living in this area. But once normal people begin moving in, this will change too. My café is a first step: Suddenly it's a normal street. A serious problem," he went on, "is that the people who have money don't understand that this was a Jewish area. I'm afraid that they'll put up fancy shop signs, that they'll kitsch up the neighborhood. To make it like Prague is today [highly commercialized and directed toward tourists] is not the solution. . . . I'd like to see it here more like Montmartre, but everything with a Jewish feel. It will never be able to go back to the way it was before the war, but there are interested people who will come. For my wife and me, we find it very warm and nice here, running the café. I sit out here, talk to people about Jewish things—and *that's* what's important today! Of course, I'm running a business, but it's not some place like a disco or a bar—it's a place of good feeling."

Sonia Lucas, an attractive woman in her mid-twenties, dressed all in black and with long, dark hair, had brought some photographs to look at as we drank our tea and polished off the plate of strawberries. Her doctoral project, supervised by Jonathan Webber, was an ethnographic study of the Cracow Jewish community, with an emphasis on exploring Jewish memory, particularly the memories Cracow Jews retained about the Holocaust and prewar times.

"How can you understand the loss of six million people and not know what was there, what was lost, recognize the chasm that exists between then and now?" she said.

The pictures she brought related to her project. They were shots she had taken during the recently completed filming in and around Cracow of Steven Spielberg's film *Schindler's List,* the story of how a German industrialist saved a thousand Jews from the Płaszow concentration camp near Cracow. The filming had created a brief storm of controversy during the winter when Spielberg attempted to film inside Auschwitz. Some members of his crew also had reported anti-Semitic incidents involving local Poles.

"Spielberg reconstructed memory for six months here for the movie," Sonia said. "The Jewish community here had daily contact with the set."

Sonia had taken her pictures surreptitiously, before being thrown off the set and warned not to publish them. The images were extremely eerie. They showed Szeroka Street—where we were sitting—catapulted back fifty years to represent the wartime Cracow ghetto. For the movie this part of Kazimierz had been populated again—by dark-haired movie extras pretending to be Jews, wearing yellow stars. Shop signs once again advertised goods in Yiddish, sold in shops whose proprietors had Jewish names. But this reconstructed memory, however accurate the signs and costumes, Sonia pointed out, was false. The wartime ghetto had not been set up in Kazimierz, and particularly not on Kazimierz's most recognizable square, but deliberately some distance away across the river to the south in the Podgórze neighborhood. This cinematic relocation back to Szeroka Street made some Jews in Cracow considerably uneasy. "Kazimierz was a place of life, not death," one man told me. "The Jews were *expelled* from here; it wasn't the ghetto."

I considered the various ways in which wartime memory was reconstructed and the uses to which these reconstructions were put.

A day or two earlier, I had met in passing Bernard Offen, a Holocaust survivor from Cracow who now lives in San Francisco, where he was associated with a Holocaust oral history project. A strikingly handsome man, he was wearing a gray silk shirt, and his silver hair was pulled back in a ponytail. He had had some success creating a multimedia presentation on the Holocaust, *The Work,* in which he examined the murder of six million Jews from the personal viewpoint of what happened to himself and his family. Offen was in Cracow this summer, where he was based at the Jagiellonian University and was carrying out another Holocaust-related project drawn from his personal experience. From material I received on this project, it seemed clear that its aim was to make the horror of the Holocaust more clearly understandable by explaining it in terms of individual human tragedy, putting the wholesale murder of six million Jews—a fact so vast that it becomes abstract—into a more personal perspective, and trying to draw lessons from it for the future.

"Join a Survivor," an advertising leaflet read, "Revisit the former Concentration Camps and the 'Killing Fields' of Poland. Seminars on Self-Healing and Creating Peace. Join a Walk," it went on:

> Join with me, Bernard Offen, in guided walks, in my family's footsteps, from the former Cracow Ghetto in Poland to Auschwitz and other concentration camps we were in. Before the walks we will review the Jewish historical context in Poland; following the walks, we will process our feelings and insights, creating a larger context for our experience. We explore how to use our experience to create a world in which we don't recreate this suffering.

"Join a Film Project," it concluded:

> This film will tell the story of a single individual's disappearance during the Holocaust. One of the six million was my father. My father and I were enslaved and forced to build shoes for the German army during WWII. The name of the film is "Jacob, the Shoemaker."

I did not discuss the project with Offen, and I certainly recognized the value of what he appeared to be trying to do. Nonetheless, it made me feel uneasy. Maybe it was just how his advertising pamphlets were worded, but I felt vague undertones reflecting a commercialization of personal tragedy, which didn't sit quite right with me. This wasn't by any means the blatant sale of one's own tragic experiences to make a television miniseries, but I was slightly repelled, nonetheless.

"Working on memory here is a very difficult task," Sonia said, discussing her own research. "You could interview people, but there is a problem with interviews. People will simply tell you what they want. Now it is very popular for Jews to come back and visit the sites here, to make a pilgrimage. People like this are reconstructing Jewish memory in a very different way. . . . Some of the visitors who come back are very disoriented. Many visitors are wealthy; they can stay in the Grand Hotel. Then they come back here, where they spent their poor and often very difficult childhood. . . . Many of the visitors come and want to see hatred [toward Jews] and nothing else. Israeli visitors, especially young people, want to see hatred; they look for it and expect it."

THE TEMPEL SYNAGOGUE, ALSO CALLED the Postępowa, or Progressive (Reform), Synagogue, was originally built in 1860–1862, by the Association of Progressive Jews in Cracow and was enlarged and remodeled several times. It is the only "modern" synagogue in Kazimierz, the only one in which the congregation worshiped following the Reform ritual. And, along with the Remuh, it is one of only two in Cracow still consecrated as a synagogue. Here, amid what would have been splendidly colorful, Moorish-style fresco, bas-relief, and stained-glass decoration, the men sat in their up-to-date European suits and top hats—not by any means the long black caftans and sidelocks of the Hasidim and other traditional, pious Jews—listening to sermons preached in Polish. Women in the Tempel were still separated from the men in an upper gallery, but the synagogue choir was composed of men and women—something that shocked the Orthodox community. Shocking, too, was the use of an organ, which didn't go so far as to provide music on Sabbath and Holy Days, but was played at weddings and other nonreligious events.

An inscription on the main facade of the synagogue further set it off from Orthodox houses of worship. It quoted the book of Kings: "In the eighth month, he completed the temple with all its splendor." This deliberate linking of the synagogue to the biblical Temple in Jerusalem almost defiantly proclaimed the synagogue as Reform. Reform Jews call their synagogues temples, regarding them in a sense as replacements for the Temple of Solomon destroyed in Jerusalem. For Orthodox Jews, Solomon's Temple is, was, and will be the *only* Temple: They live in the hope of rebuilding it and would never dream of referring to any present-day, temporary house of worship by that name.

The Tempel's most outstanding rabbi was Ozjasz Thon, who served there from 1897 until his death in 1936. A handsome man with a high, bald forehead, wire-rimmed glasses, and a neat, trimmed beard, Thon was a gifted orator, writer, and scholar. He was a dedicated Zionist who even as a student was a close associate of Theodore Herzl and had helped Herzl organize the First Zionist Congress in Basel in 1897. Recognized as a national Jewish leader, he served as a member of the Polish Parliament from 1919 until 1931.

In a diary memoir about a 1919 mission to Poland to observe Jewish conditions in the unsettled, violent aftermath of World War I— a time when Polish nationalism and anti-Semitism were on the rise and young Jewish people in Cracow organized armed defense units to protect the community—Jewish writer and Zionist activist Israel Cohen described attending one of Thon's electoral campaign rallies in Kazimierz:

> Went to a public meeting in Kahal (community) building, addressed by Dr. Thon in connection with his candidature for Polish Constituante (Parliament). On the way met Jews with guns (militia), even orthodox men wearing flat hats and caftan also with guns. Building packed. Jewish officer, Dr. I. Schwarzbart, forced way for us. Dr. Thon dealt with war, Palestine, Jewish national autonomy in Poland. Interrupted by Socialists. A P.P.S. (Polish Socialist Party) Jew caused booing when he called himself a Polish nationalist.[10]

Thon, though one of the most respected Polish Jewish leaders of his day, was ultimately considered a tragic figure by some people because his sense of ethics and belief in the power of reason made him unable to fight back on the same tough level as the nationalists and anti-Semites he opposed:

> He wanted to be a statesman, to negotiate, to discuss, to win influence, but he was forced into a policy of radical opposition which had sometime to explode out of the framework of defense and defensiveness. Sometimes it happens that your opponent does not

appear to attack you, but ignores you, overlooks you completely, doing so gracefully under a hypocritical mask. He must then be unmasked and his true countenance revealed. Mere defense will not do in that case, for defense must sometimes also be attack. That was Thon's tragedy: he began with peace and never ceased to wage war; he wanted to build and had also to destroy. That tragic predicament brought him sorrow and suffering which only few understood or were aware of.[11]

"BEFORE THE WAR, THIS SYNAGOGUE was very beautiful," said Rafał Immerglueck, looking up at the sooty facade with its decorative pillars, pilasters, arched portals, and windows. "It was packed with people—

CRACOW: Detail of the facade of the Tempel Synagogue.

213

one thousand! The better, richer Jews came here. I came here because I had to. It was far to come from where I lived, but my Hebrew teacher said that I had to come to this synagogue, so I did. . . . There are no Jewish people here anymore, just Jews from outside. There are no young Jews—those who were left married Catholics. No one wants to come back here," he said. "But the synagogue is different. It will be good to restore it; it will be for the future. It has memory; there must be something left over. The Jewish community in Cracow will die out in five, ten, twenty years. But at least you'll be able to come here and see how the Tempel looked!"

Today, when Cracow's Jewish community consists of only two hundred or so mainly elderly Jews—Sonia Lucas defined it as "nonregenerating"—the originally separate Orthodox and Reform congregations have joined together, and the Tempel Synagogue has been fitted with a bimah in the middle of the sanctuary, as in Orthodox practice, rather than in the front, near the Ark, as in Reform, so that Orthodox services can be conducted. There is no rabbi in Cracow. Services, I was told, were usually held in the small Remuh Synagogue, with one of the congregants leading the prayers. There were usually enough men present to form a minyan, at least on Friday nights, and it was not rare for tourists to make up a sizable portion of the congregation. The Tempel Synagogue was rarely used, except on special occasions and when there were large groups of visitors.

Jonathan Webber led Sabbath services in the Tempel the Saturday morning that I was in Cracow. About half the members of the congregation were participants of my brother's study tour; the other half were locals, mainly elderly men. There were one or two Israeli tourists and a few Pentecostal Polish girls who, I was told, were interested in Judaism and thinking of converting. They wore Stars of David around their necks and whispered to each other. There was also a middle-aged man—also not Jewish, I was told—who solemnly strode in and out of the sanctuary several times, a yarmulke perched on his head and a battered briefcase clutched in his hand. No one quite knew who he was or why he was there, though he appeared to be a Sabbath regular. The evening before, we attended services in the Remuh Synagogue. There, as for hundreds of years, we women sat in a small side gallery, screened from the men praying in the little sanctuary by windows that were curtained with a sort of net fabric. In the

Tempel, on Saturday, we sat in the wooden pews to one side of the bimah; the men sat in the pews to the other side.

Enveloped in a blanketlike tallis, bearded and wearing horn-rimmed glasses, Webber, a man about my own age, led an Orthodox service. It was, somehow, a thrilling experience. I myself am not a religious Jew, and I do not go frequently to services. But I was moved that morning in a powerful way, much more so than by services I had attended in much more historic shuls—in the Old-New Synagogue in Prague, for example, or even in the Remuh Synagogue the night before. Perhaps it was because, by some trick of light or situation (or ancestry), Webber in his tallis, with his beard, with his stance, bore an uncanny resemblance to a figure in a famous nineteenth-century painting of Polish Jews in the Cracow National Museum: He could have been a ghost. Perhaps it simply was that because of the improvised conversion from Reform temple to Orthodox synagogue, or because the smallness of our congregation in this cavernous old sanctuary made it impractical for women to sit high above in the gallery, we were there on ground level, "next to the action." There was no participation in the service, of course; not the slightest possibility of feeling part of the intimate, clubby atmosphere among the various men around the bimah as Webber read the Torah. But for once I could see the men's faces as they prayed, and somehow, even just by this, feel involvement in the poignant sense of continuity that reached back so far into the Jewish past.

There was a Kiddush after the service, and we said the blessing over what during the past year had become a fashionable drink in Poland: kosher Polish vodka. Indeed, there was a craze in Poland for kosher food and, particularly, drink. In a land of few Jews, few of whom followed Jewish dietary laws, as many as twenty different brands of kosher vodka were now on sale, with names like Polnisskosher, Dawid, Rebeka, Judyta, Cymes, and Travka. They were considered purer and healthier, of better quality, than regular vodka—less likely to produce hangovers. The word "kosher" had become imbued with an almost superstitious significance. In what had to be one of the most curious and to a certain extent troubling marketing strategies I had ever seen, beer and even, incredibly, *water* advertised as kosher were also now in the shops: Polish yuppie drinks and incongruous souvenirs for Jewish visitors to take home.

We drank our delicious, smooth vodka from thimble-sized plastic cups, ate fresh-baked challah, and wandered around the melancholy Tempel. It resembled many of the old Jews who themselves had lived through the war and through communism: structurally more or less sound, but shabby and rather sad. The walls, stained by rising damp, were painted or faded the color of dried blood. A dull, dark shadow coated all the extremely elaborate Moorish-style decoration, too. The Ark was a vast construction with a big central dome encircled by a crown topping the case for the Torahs. All was gray, gray, gray. "It's marble," hissed an Israeli woman who had sat in front of me at services, apparently oblivious to history, to costs, to current conditions. "It's marble! Can't they clean it? Can't they scrub it? Why do they let it get in this state?"

TWO DAYS LATER, SAM MET AT THE TEMPEL with representatives of the local Jewish community, city authorities, and local monuments preservation experts. Everyone seemed relaxed and nervous at the same time. And no wonder. It was, Sam told me, the first time that representatives of all these parties involved in the restoration met together, although plans for the project had been announced more than a year before. The points raised at the meeting, and the meticulous discussion of costs, responsibilities, preservation priorities, and procedures, vividly demonstrated the delicacy of balancing the various interests, sensitivities, and needs of the various parties. Much more was involved than simply scrubbing sooty marble.

Sam recalled to the group that it had been in April 1992, at a gala concert held in the synagogue by the Cracow Symphony Orchestra, that the World Monuments Fund announced it would help with the restoration and oversee it from start to finish. That concert was dedicated to the memory of Cracow's sixty thousand Jewish Holocaust victims and also honored today's remnant community of survivors. The program included Arnold Schönberg's "Survivor from Warsaw" and Leonard Bernstein's "Chichester Psalms"; the Cracow Festival Choir sang the *"Shema Yisroel"*—("Hear, O Israel," the key profession of Jewish faith in one God). The concert was conducted by Gilbert Levine, an American Jew who spent four years as the director of the Cracow Symphony Orchestra, during which time he became deeply and energetically committed to promoting dialogue between Jews and Polish Catholics. To this end, Levine organized several landmark concerts in the synagogue, at which Jewish and Catholic dignitaries sat side by side, united by music.[12]

"The World Monuments Fund was invited by the Jewish community to help with the restoration," Sam said. "We believe that this is a very important building architecturally, and that it is important for Cracow, important for all Jews worldwide, that this building be saved. The building is owned by the Jewish community. Every decision on its future rests ultimately on the community.

"In the end," he stressed, "every decision [on the restoration project] rests with the World Monuments Fund, but I expect to arrive at these decisions through consultations. I won't make decisions that are counter to the desires of the community, but we must decide together what steps to take."

Away from the meeting, Sam described to me how important he felt it was—and how difficult—to make sure that the Jewish community felt involved in Kazimierz restoration and redevelopment projects, particularly those of the synagogues and other sites with religious connotations.

"In the community there are only a few people with the energy to set a course to the future," he said. "All the older members of the community are Holocaust survivors. They have horrible stories. Then came fifty years of communism when being Jewish, if not a crime, was at least difficult. Their whole existence is living in a world that doesn't want them. People tell them what to do, but expect something from them."

I had already heard murmurings of suspicion and misgiving voiced by and about various people and organizations: The Jagiellonian Research Center was faulted by some for the non-Jewish makeup of its staff, for example, and some feared that the Joint Distribution Committee was planning to cut back on its aid contributions. Various private foundations were faulted for promising to carry out restoration projects but instead simply putting up plaques in their own honor. The city was criticized for giving back to the community property that was so dilapidated that it became a financial hardship.

"Now," Sam went on, "every group coming through Cracow

talks, makes promises, boasts to them, teases them—but they haven't seen too much in return. . . . They see a lot of groups coming in, and they resent it. . . . They're skeptical, realists rather than cynical. It puts strains on cooperation because they are not familiar with how things work in this new context. . . . But I feel that no one who is not of the Cracow Jewish community has a right to speak for the Cracow community."

HENRYK HALKOWSKI DESCRIBED HIMSELF to me as "inside and outside" the Jewish community. A stocky, bald, outwardly jolly man in his early forties, with thick glasses and a gray-flecked beard, Halkowski looks a little like pictures of the great Rabbi Thon and is one of the few younger Jews in the Cracow congregation. Extremely knowledgable about Cracow and its Jewish history, he pointed out lingering details, such as the one or two last Yiddish inscriptions on Kazimierz's walls and the ruined doors of an abandoned prayer house tucked into a courtyard on a street near the Rynek Główny, Cracow's main market square. Articulate despite a pronounced stammer, Halkowski is something of a modern-day *luftmensch*—literally a person who lives "on air," doing this and that, with little visible means of support: a classic figure in prewar Jewish Eastern Europe. He works a few hours a day as the salaried secretary of the Jewish Club, the local branch of the Social and Cultural Association of Polish Jewry, or TSKZ, a nonreligious Jewish cultural organization founded under—and, until the political changes at the end of the 1980s, controlled by—the Communist state. He makes extra income by writing and translating. "I don't need too much money," he told me. "I'm not married; I don't have a car . . . the only thing I spend money on is books."

The Jewish Club is situated in a big, plainly furnished room near the Rynek Główny. It contains some simple tables and chairs, a kettle to make tea. On the walls hang a poster for Israel and stiff charcoal portraits of former TSKZ officials. Hanging apart, above Halkowski's desk, is a similar portrait of Mordechai Gebirtig, a Cracow carpenter killed by the Nazis in 1942, who was one of the greatest of

(Facing page)
CRACOW: Viewed through a crack in a locked gate, the entrance of an abandoned prayer house in a courtyard near the main market square.

218

CRACOW: Charcoal portrait of Yiddish bard Mordechai Gebirtig, who died in the Holocaust, hanging on the wall of the Jewish Club.

all Yiddish poets and songwriters. His chilling song "*Dos Shtetl Brent*"—
"Our Town's On Fire"—became an anthem of the wartime ghettos.
Another of his lyrics mourns Cracow as he is forced to leave it:

Farewell, Cracow, farewell!
A horse cart is waiting for me out in the street.
I'm driven out of here like a dog,
Driven out without pity toward an unknown destination.

Farewell, Cracow!
It's time to take our leave.
Will I ever see you again
This place so dear to my heart.
I've wept my heart out on my Mother's grave
    and shed my last tear on my Father's tombstone.
Where my grandfather lies, I don't know; his grave is probably
    covered over with sand . . .

Farewell, Cracow!
This hallowed ground!
The place where the tombs of my mother and father will lie
    forever;
My resting place will not be with them. . . .[13]

Halkowski said a few people generally turned up at the club
each afternoon to sit and read or socialize. I was surprised that even
a few people came: The room was stale and cheerless, a relic, somehow, of Communist days. Maybe in the winter, or on a rainy day, it
would provide a heated haven, but there were far more cheerful
places in Cracow these days to sit and read or talk.

"There are problems with one old man," Halkowski said, "His
idée fixe is to make a union between the club, which is secular, and
the religious community." There were also occasional problems with
anonymous anti-Semitic phone calls, he told me, and strange letters.

"We got a really crazy one two years ago," Halkowski said. "A
man wrote asking me to help free him from the mental institute and
to give him half a million dollars because he wanted to marry a Jewish woman. He wrote that he was put into the mental hospital
because he destroyed Hebrew inscriptions at Auschwitz–Birkenau.

He accused Jews of sending mental waves to inflict pain on him after he said that the Jews ruled Poland and that Jews should get out of positions of power and go back to keeping shop. This wasn't an anti-Semitic statement, he wrote, because it would be better both for Jews and for Poles. Anyway, he wound up saying, don't condemn some poor Jewish woman to die without children or to marry someone worse than he was."

Halkowski was born in Cracow after the war. "My grandfather was religious, and when I was young he used to take me to synagogue. He ate kosher; he would buy live chickens and take them to the shochet, which at that time was in the building of the Kupa Synagogue. My parents, though, were not observant and had no contact with the Jewish community. After my grandfather died in 1962, I lost all sense of Jewish identity. I began to feel Jewish again, though, in 1967–1968 [the time of the Six Day War and subsequent anti-Semitic campaign in Poland that forced most of the country's remaining Jews to emigrate]. I began to feel Jewish—not in the religious sense but in the national sense. So I went to Israel in 1980–1981, but it was a disappointment. When I came back here, though, I really started to get involved with Jewish culture, etc."

Halkowski, like other Polish Jews of his age and younger whom I have met over the years, said he had the impression that foreign Jews, particularly those from North America, often seem uncomfortable meeting younger Jews in Poland. They can't, he said, understand why—or how—these younger Jews stay. "American Jews have a stereotype about Polish Jews who stayed here," he said. "It's as if we are seen as 'traitors' to the nation."

What interested me was that in Cracow there seemed to be so few younger Jews. In cities like Warsaw, Wrocław, and Łódź, particularly since the ouster of the Communists in 1989, a number of totally assimilated people in their twenties and thirties had discovered or rediscovered their Jewish roots and had formed active Jewish study groups, similar to *havurahs*, but no such group was active in Cracow. (A small group began to coalesce some months after my visit.) The New York–based Ronald S. Lauder Foundation coordinates many of these activities and runs a highly successful summer camp program aimed at providing Jewish experience and education to these people. Ambassador Milton A. Wolf, the president of the Jewish Joint Distribution

Committee, recently referred to them as "hidden children," children, he said, "who were [not] hidden during the Holocaust, but children whose Jewish identities were hidden from them. They are now men and women . . . who only recently learned of their Jewish roots. Though most are married to Catholics, they are determined to learn what it means to be Jewish." Wolf spoke of seven hundred of these people.[14]

To a certain extent Halkowski was part of the first wave of this Jewish rediscovery, which took form at the end of the 1970s and early 1980s, centered on the semiclandestine, Warsaw-based "Flying Jewish University," a Jewish study group of several dozen people who essentially educated themselves from scratch in Jewish practice and culture. I was living in Warsaw at the time and vividly recall my first encounter with members of this group. It was at Kol Nidre services, the eve of Yom Kippur, in 1980, just three weeks after the Solidarity union, represented by Lech Wałęsa, and the Communist government signed the historic agreement in Gdańsk that allowed the formation of Solidarity as the East Bloc's first legal free trade union. There were only a few people my age in the congregation. Three of them talked to me eagerly after services and took me home to continue the conversation. "You're a real Jew," one of them told me. "You can tell us how to do things."

Halkowski had a definite theory as to why such a Jewish revival had not caught on in Cracow. "For one thing," he said, "I have a theory that a lot of Jews left Cracow in 1968. Then, vis-à-vis Warsaw: Warsaw was a mecca of Jewish Communists, and after the crisis of communism, there was this discovery of Jewish identity. Cracow, on the other hand, was the capital of Jewish Catholics—Jews who converted. It was probably easier for Jewish Catholics to live here, with Cracow's traditonal situation of liberal Catholicism, rather than in Warsaw, where the Church is more rigid," he said.

"The young Jews who remain in Cracow are Christians," he said. "I know cases where both parents are of Jewish descent but feel a strong Christian identity, and so do the children. Maybe they feel something of their Jewish origin, but it's history. As for the Jewish community now: Their children are gone or Christian or not active."

This theory was paraphrased by another Jewish source: Jewish Communists, he said, had an easier time converting back to Judaism than did Jewish Catholics.

Like everyone else I talked to, Halkowski had an idea of what to do with Kazimierz: Restore all the synagogues and use them as a network of exhibition halls to house an expanded Jewish museum—as in Prague—and perhaps to designate this a national museum of Judaism or Jewish life.

"I think that the right place for a museum of Polish Jews is Kazimierz, not Warsaw. Warsaw is all connected with the Holocaust, the Warsaw Ghetto Uprising," he said. "The Ghetto Uprising has been so mythologized; I think the Holocaust has been Christianized by Jews—the Holocaust is equated with the Crucifixion, and Israel is the Resurrection. In this framework, the Ghetto Uprising is the first battle toward resurrection. I think every Jewish museum in Warsaw must be seen from this perspective, but I think that it is the wrong perspective. In Kazimierz, there are those points of Jewish heritage that can convey something of Jewish heritage to Poles and to tourists," he said. "Kazimierz can be a place where meaning can be materialized. There's no other place in Central Europe where there are so many Jewish sites in such scale and size and number."

THE CRACOW MUNICIPALITY IS, IN THEORY, the biggest player in the issue of Kazimierz's redevelopment, and indeed, in 1991 the mayor's office established a special city agency for the development of Kazimierz. But despite a lot of detailed plans, paperwork, and analysis, the twin demons, lack of money and lack of ownership clarification, prevented the implementation of any large-scale, coordinated projects.

"It is a circle," Janusz Smolski told me. Smolski is a monuments-preservation expert who served for eight years as chief conservator for the city of Cracow and the surrounding region before taking on the onerous job of chief architect for the renovation of Wawel Castle. "Kazimierz is neglected. It needs money and investment. But people don't want to invest if no one knows who is the owner of the buildings."

In 1985–1986, Smolski was part of a team of city architects who drew up a master plan for the rehabilitation of Cracow's Old City and Kazimierz. His expertise is being used in the restoration project for the Tempel Synagogue, and I met him during my brother Sam's meeting at the Tempel with the parties involved in that restoration.

Later, I sat with him in a café at Wawel Castle, discussing the master plan and the concrete problems inherent in its implementation. A handsome man with piercing eyes, Smolski described the plan as a huge and, in theory, very strict zoning and historic-preservation ordinance. It doesn't go into how development should be undertaken, but it shows what the buildings must look like when development takes place. "It's a basic plan for all buildings in the district—that is, all new buildings and restorations must obtain a design approval based on the master plan. . . . We were a group of four or five architects, and we made our plan according to contemporary ideas of conservation knowledge, based on profound historical research by the huge staff of the State Monuments Preservation Office. Our project was called a "Master Plan for the Rehabilitation, Renovation and Revitalization" of the districts . . . and it was accepted by city and regional authorities."

Kazimierz was a major part of the project, he said, particularly given the extreme state of dilapidation and neglect of the historic buildings. "We emphasized protecting the Jewish area of the city," he said. "The whole area of the Jewish city was protected and described in the plan as a monument of Jewish heritage. You couldn't do anything in the area without special permission; you could not change the plan. The most important element was to preserve all the synagogues and all the houses connected with the Jewish religion. For example, the plan said improper uses of the synagogues must be rectified. We wrote that any improper businesses or activities set up in a synagogue had to be removed. The synagogues are objects of Jewish heritage and must be given back to the Jewish community; and, of course, they cannot be changed architecturally. They must be left as monuments of historical importance. This is now the law," he said, "signed by town authorities."

"But what happens?" he said, with a gesture of resignation. "The Kupa Synagogue, for example, has nice nineteenth-century frescoes. It was given back to the Jewish community. But the community has no money, so the money for restoration has to come from the town, the state. . . . The Izaak Synagogue is a big problem. It's a very big synagogue. The plan was for the State Monuments Restoration Office to make it into a conservation workshop, but the town administration refused permission for this. So they asked the Jewish community to take it back, but they didn't have the money. Then Rabbi Joskowicz in Warsaw said he wanted to open a yeshiva there, but this didn't work out. The State Restoration Office made the plans for a total restoration rehabilitation. The idea was to restore the artistic elements and then use the building as a synagogue again. But all work is stopped. There's no more money for reconstruction. The situation was the same for the Tempel Synagogue."

Smolski again stressed the basic problem of clarifying property ownership before any major projects could be undertaken, and he noted that this question of reprivatization, as it is called, has affected other areas of Cracow too. "The situation is almost resolved in the Old City," he said. "Kazimierz is the worst case, as the Jews disappeared as owners. This district was very neglected even before the war. Things are going very slowly," he went on. "But I am an optimist. We have in our imagination how Kazimierz will look. Step by step the ownership is being clarified, and many houses are being restored.

"The most important problem now," he said, "is how to keep this Jewish city as a whole urbanistic complex, how to retain this local identity of Jewish culture here. We are afraid that someone will come in with a lot of money, put up houses, invest, and that the Jewish city could disappear as a unique quarter. . . . I am not concerned that renovation is going slowly. Rapid intervention could mean too much modernization. For forty-five years it was all totally neglected. Now the renovations have to be done very carefully."

Already, he said, the strict zoning was sometimes ignored in the construction of new buildings. "We presented a special description in our plan, that the area must be under care, that every element must be controlled by conservators and architects so that nothing destroys the atmosphere, the climate, the forms of architecture," he said. "But, for example, there are new houses being built next to the Izaak Synagogue. We said that they had to be constructed conforming to the old style of building. The plans we were shown for approval look a lot different from the way the houses are being built. . . ."

I WAS ABLE TO EXAMINE THE DETAILED DRAWINGS and blueprints of Smolski's master plan in the offices of the International Culture Center on the main market square. I was interested in following up the Culture Center's plans vis-à-vis development of Kazimierz and developing it as a tourist center, as Zbigniew Zuziak had outlined to me the year before. I found that ambitious plans, at least on the theoretical level, had been drawn up. The ideas Zuziak outlined to me had jelled into a full-fledged, internationally funded pilot project on regenerating historical districts, coordinated by the center's Institute for Urban Studies.

Representatives of city authorities from Cracow, Edinburgh, and Berlin were cooperating in research work and in drawing up a regeneration plan; a series of seminars was being held throughout 1993. Only two months before, at one of the seminars in April, Zuziak presented a formal outline, or methodological framework, entitled "Towards an Action Plan for the Revitalization of Kazimierz District in Cracow." Among the numerous research papers presented along with the outline were analyses of the existing structures in Kazimierz; a series of suggestions for specific, building-by-building restoration possibilities; and historic surveys of the area.

One of the papers presented a detailed analysis of the pros and cons, strengths and weaknesses, opportunities and threats that will influence any potential revitalization plans. These, I found, set forth in a black and white, schematic way much of what I had heard in my various talks and interviews about what should be done. They were presented coldly and without emotion, however, and points of strictly commercial significance on a touristic and urban-planning level were also indicated. "Threats" to the development of Kazimierz, for example, included not only the problem of clarifying property ownership and controlling gentrification and wildfire real estate speculation but also the fact that there were few international air and rail links with Cracow, and that the city had to compete for tourists with other Central European cities like Prague and Budapest.

"Weaknesses" included what was termed the "fundamental question": "Can the social space of the Jewish District be revitalized considering that the Jewish community in the area is too small to create its social identity?" Also noted were "lack of publicly accepted vision and public consensus regarding the policies of revitalization" and "lack of effective institutional, organizational, and financial framework of revitalization." This heading included what to me seemed a good summary of the problems that had been outlined to me by so many people:

Potential actors of the process are not mobilized (lack of financial or other incentives that could mobilize them).

Community-based planning is practically nonexistent; there is no participatory framework, and [the] community is not involved in the discussion of the future of the area.

There is a lot of skepticism or even lack of confidence regarding the effectiveness of any public action.

[The] local community is highly fragmented; multiple groups are claiming to represent local Jewish residents, and there is a lack of consensus regarding the future use of former synagogues and other buildings significant for cultural heritage.

[The] idea of public/private partnership is too novel.

[The] disposable income of the local residents/business is too low to be regarded as a base of/for local investments. The economic structure of the local population is typical of centers with social problems: [a] high percentage of [the] elderly, welfare-dependent, and [people with a] low education [level].

[There is a] perceived strained relationship between Christians and Jews.

Tourist infrastructure is practically nonexistent.

Most of the workshops and craft-based industries as well as small shops (corner shops) and cooking traditions characteristic of the area were lost.[15]

"Under the new [post-Communist] economic conditions, the city has to prepare a new strategy for the revitalization of Kazimierz," Krzysztof Broński of the Culture Center's Institute for Urban Studies told me. "Until now only a few separate buildings were done. There was no all-embracing concept of revitalization. . . . We want to see Kazimierz, now, in the context of the whole city of Cracow and as part of the whole strategy of the development of Cracow, [so] it is essential to establish the function and role Kazimierz is to play—cultural, touristic, festival, residential."

He said proposals being drawn up suggest turning former workshops, stores, and other nonresidential buildings in the zone into exhibition halls and other centers for cultural and touristic use. "There are plans to move the offices of some municipal authorities to the district, and there is also a plan to establish a Hungarian consulate there, plus hotels, hostels, pensions. The whole strategy is to use existing buildings, not to build new ones." All design and renovation work, he said, would conform to the master plan drawn up by Smolski and his team of architects.

Something did seem to be happening on this theoretical level, but the trouble in implementation boiled down to the same problems: clarifying ownership, attracting investors, and determining what to do with the population now living in Kazimierz.

I WALKED AROUND KAZIMIERZ and tried to imagine how it used to be, how it might become. I let my imagination run wild with schemes and models I hoped no one would ever consider, not even if they would bring in a fortune in hard currency and make every one of Cracow's remaining Jews a millionaire: Spielberg had reconstructed Szeroka Street, making it believable as the wartime Jewish ghetto, populating it with false-front Jewish shops and non-Jews posing as Jews. Might anyone propose to make this permanent? To reconstruct Kazimierz as an open-air museum—what they call a *skansen*—of prewar Jewish life, with guides dressed in caftans and sidelocks, with shops turning out traditional Jewish crafts, with restaurants exclusively serving herring and gefilte fish along with the kosher vodka? After all, Central Europe was dotted with skansens showing vanished village life—and theme parks from Colonial Williamsburg and Sturbridge Village to Dollywood did good business in the United States. . . . I shuddered.

What should be done? What can be done? How should it be done? Who should do it? Why?

Standing on the site of the Old Jewish Market, Jonathan Webber summarized some of the needs any redevelopment of Kazimierz should or might or must attempt to fulfill: memorializing the vanished Jewish population; maintaining a physical Jewish presence; offering possibilities to encourage dialogue on Jewish and Jewish-Polish issues; teaching today's local population about the Jews who once lived there and everywhere else in Poland.

"It has to serve the existing Jewish community, the world Jewish community, Jewish tourists," Webber said. "We have to remember, to affirm the Jewish identity here, and to think of the future."

"You have to do what you can do, and do what can be done," said my brother Sam. "There are many constituencies and many needs to be served."

ON VISIT AFTER VISIT TO CRACOW, I've walked around Kazimierz, along the streets still named for Jewish heroes—Esther, Isaac, Jacob, Joseph—looking into courtyards and taking pictures. In one dark hallway, and one alone in the entire district, a peeling Yiddish sign still advertises a café. On one street wall, and one alone in the entire district, three faded Hebrew letters remain, the final traces of an

CRACOW: Crumbling tombstones in the overgrown New Jewish Cemetery.

unknown word. Strings of laundry hang limp from rickety balconies.
A few old drunks sit belching and passing a bottle in a park.

In the New Cemetery, a 47-acre walled expanse laid out originally at the beginning of the nineteenth century, the dead sleep in a
forest: Rampant shrubs and trees create a green cocoon, cool and
soothing; summer breezes ruffle the leaves. The Nazis destroyed the
graveyard, but it was restored in the 1950s. Burials take place here
today, but the vast enclosure is largely untended. Here, nestled in
green, lie rabbis and politicians, artists and intellectuals, businessmen
and builders, Orthodox and Hasidic leaders and followers of the Jewish enlightenment. Rabbi Thon, passionate Zionist, Jewish statesman,
and rabbi of the Tempel Synagogue is here. His tomb also bears an
inscription commemorating his wife, Maria, and his son-in-law and
grandson, who were killed by the Nazis.

In the Old Cemetery, next to the Remuh Synagogue, I aim my
camera at almost too neat rows of gravestones. The cemetery was
founded in 1551 and remained in operation until 1800. By the 1930s,
it was already in bad repair. In a guidebook to Jewish Cracow published in 1935—perfect facisimile editions of which are on sale in
Cracow bookshops today—distinguished Jewish historian Majer
Bałaban described the Remuh Cemetery as

> a depressing view; most tombstones are in ruin, sunken into the
> ground, or lie toppled at the foot of those still standing. Some mon-
> uments to rabbis and sponsors of synagogues have been renovated
> many times over . . . without respect for their artistic value. On
> some tombs, new gravestones have been erected with old epitaphs,
> known from literature. The majority of monuments, however, have
> been lost irrevocably. In the cemetery which, for 250 years, was the
> only one in such a densely populated community, there remain
> very few monuments, and only a few dozen of them with legible
> epitaphs.[16]

Less than a decade later, the Nazis finished the devastation, smashing
or uprooting almost all remaining tombstones and turning the area
into a dump. Bałaban himself died in 1942 in the Warsaw Ghetto.
Only a few tombs in Kazimierz's Old Cemetery still stood at the war's
end, among them the tomb of Moses Isserles, Remuh.

But during postwar restoration work, archeologists excavating
under the surface made a tremendous discovery: more than seven

CRACOW: Neat rows of restored tombstones in the Old Jewish Cemetery in the Kazimierz section, with dilapidated buildings in the background.

hundred tombstones and fragments of tombstones buried under the earth, probably hidden there deliberately in the seventeenth or early eighteenth century to protect them from feared depredations during a Swedish invasion. The intact tombs were set up again in neatly spaced rows, forming a collection of Jewish art rather than a real graveyard. Reconstructed memory again; the fragments of stone that could not be pieced together were affixed like a giant memorial mosaic on the cemetery's inner wall.

The epitaph on Remuh's tomb reads:

Light of the West, the greatest of the generation's wise men,
   Rabbi Moses
Shepherd of the flock of Israel
On the 33rd day of the counting of the omer among Israel
Pride was exiled from Israel
Moses herded the flock of Israel
He did righteous deeds and taught law to Israel
He spread Torah among Israel
He established scholars for thousands among Israel
From Moses to Moses there has not been such a Moses in Israel
And this is the law of the sin-offering and of the whole-offering
Which Moses set before the people of
Israel the year [5]332 [1572]
May His Soul Be Bound Up in the Bond of Life.[17]

I aim my camera and am approached by an elderly man through the graves. "No!" he says, almost shouting. "You can't photograph here! You need a permit! You can't take pictures here without a permit." I try to ignore him; I know he is not telling the truth, but he stays there, trying to stop me. I know all he wants is money. He and several cronies are *shnorrers*—beggars—contemporary examples of what used to be a traditional component of many Jewish communities. Cracow's schnorrers are a handful of old men, and at least one woman, Holocaust survivors like most other Jews in Cracow today. They sit around the synagogue courtyard outside the gate leading into the cemetery, passing the time and waiting to prey on tourists. They latch onto visitors, generally offering to guide them around the cemetery, and then demand a handout. They may put up an argument if they think the handout is too small or, like the man who accosted me demanding a nonexistent

CRACOW: Mosaic of broken tombstones in the Old Jewish Cemetery.

permit for photography, they may try other methods of getting money.

These beggars are a permanent fixture, tolerated by, yet embarrassing to, other members of the community. Czesław Jakubowicz, the slow-moving, sweet-faced president of the community—a Holocaust survivor himself—shrugs: What can be done with them? "The community is so small that they need these people in order to function," Henryk Halkowski told me later. "One of them digs graves; one of them knows how to wash and prepare bodies for burial; one can drive on errands for the community. The schnorrers are not necessarily poor, but they feel unstable. They are survivors of the Holocaust. They never feel as if they have enough."

I WALK THROUGH KAZIMIERZ, have a cup of tea at the Ariel Café, repopulate the town with ghosts, the Jews Marvin Lowenthal described in the 1930s:

Red Jews, black Jews (Chagall with his "Green Jew" is no doubt an unimaginative copyist); Jews in every and no degree of health and prosperity. . . . Unlike the Gentiles about them, their diversity and interest lie not in their costume, but their character, in the planes and shadows of their faces, in their speaking eyes, in their cunning, sorrow, wisdom, patience, fire, and impenitent despair. Their gesticulations are the Book of Job, and their immobility the rock which brought Moses to his sinful grave.[18]

I resurrected these ghosts, then laid them again to rest. But the ghost town remained, and the questions: What should be done? Jewish tradition discourages excessive personal mourning, lest the mourner appear to be more compassionate toward the dead than God himself. Commemoration and memory are something different: The mourner's Kaddish, the prayer said in honor of the dead, does not mention death at all, but praises God, and prays for peace, life, and the establishment of God's kingdom. Jewish graveyards are crowded with elaborately carved monuments listing the virtues of the departed. And according to tradition, family members or followers of a deceased rabbi pray there, meditate there, leave pleas and petitions for intervention. The Jewish calendar is studded with feasts and fasts commemorating great tragedies, and Jewish literature is rich with lamentations and elegies commemorating the pogroms and other tremendous calamities that for thousands of years have marked Jewish history with unrelenting regularity.

What should be done with a Jewish ghost town, skeletal, like a grinning skull in the middle of one of Poland's great cities?

Roberta Brandes Gratz, a writer on preservation issues, urban affairs, and the changing face of cities, was one of the American Jews on my brother Sam's study tour that wound up in Cracow. She had never been to Poland before, but for years has been involved with the restoration project for a synagogue in New York, on Eldridge Street, on the Lower East Side, once the quintessential immigrant Jewish neighborhood, now a district with few if any Jews.

"The issue," she told me, "is not what is to be done. There is a place here, Kazimierz. It exists. It functions—much more so than one would have thought. It is a living, breathing community. It may not be a Jewish community, but neither is the Lower East Side. I saw very vivid signs of life here, though. Not a life of poverty; maybe of lower income. But when I walked around Kazimierz, I saw mothers and children, people washing windows, several people at a café, a lot of real businesses—a machine shop, tiny stores. . . . There are scattered empty buildings, scattered deteriorated buildings . . . but scattered renovation, too.

"These are not the signs of a dead or moribund area," she said. "Just the opposite. To me, it's not a question of what to do with the district, but what to do with a couple of sites. And that's very tricky. The art of doing something with sites in a living community is an art. Very few people, and no plan, have mastered it. The people drinking gallons of coffee discussing ideas for Kazimierz are maybe pontificating with grand plans, none of which is relevant."

It really wasn't that important, she said, that Jewish buildings be restored for Jewish or religious use. They could be used, for example, as a library or bookstore, or even for noncultural functions "if only because it would mean that the buildings would be open."

Gratz was fascinated by the manifestations of Polish interest in Jewish culture, in what she called the absorption issue—the books, the kosher vodka, the carved souvenir folk figures, the restaurant orchestras striking up tunes from *Fiddler on the Roof*. She also drew parallels between Jewish "memory" issues in Poland and in the United States. "We face some of the same preservation dilemmas at home," she said. "How to treat history as well as preserving buildings. Preservation is a very recent issue with Jewish communities in America."

The best element in Poland, in Kazimierz, she added, "is that there is not enough money to do all the wrong things."

Life, in effect, goes on. I thought about ordering myself a kosher Polish vodka and giving the traditional toast, "*L'Chaim!*"

❦ 5 ❦

Snowbound in Auschwitz

❦❦

The Nazi murderers . . . twisted and changed the respected and
time-honored name of Oshpitsin into the terrifying name
Auschwitz.
—*The Memory Book of Oświęcim*[1]

N THE LAST WEEK OF MARCH 1993, I was snowbound in Auschwitz for nearly four days.

I had not intended to spend time at Auschwitz. I was on a purely journalistic assignment and expected to stay there a few hours or possibly overnight. I planned to do an interview or two concerning the continuing controversy over Carmelite nuns and their convent at the former Nazi death camp, and then drive on to the Czech Republic. I did not intend to revisit the state-run memorial and museum at the Auschwitz camp, nor to return once more to the vast, dead field of nearby Birkenau, where Jews were brought by the trainload from all over Europe and led off to be killed in the Nazi gas chambers.

Plans change.

Snow was already falling lightly when I set out from Warsaw in the late morning for what should have been a three-hour drive. I felt a compulsion, somehow, to get on the road despite the weather. My friends urged me to reconsider, but it wasn't really cold, and the falling flakes were melting as soon as they hit the ground. Most of the trip would be on a four-lane highway, and I didn't think there would be much trouble. After all, it was spring.

I was already nearly three quarters of the way to Auschwitz when conditions suddenly deteriorated. Here, just south of Częstochowa, the road began climbing through an upland region of low, gently rolling hills. A few feet of elevation was all it took; the snow became dense, and the road surface was suddenly clogged and slushy. A fierce wind slapped the wet snow thickly across the windshield. The four lanes of the highway narrowed to two because of the accumulation, and every so often I passed a small group of people at the side of the road, trying to tug a vehicle out of a ditch.

I decided that if I found a hotel I would stop for the night and give Auschwitz a miss altogether. But there were no hotels. I crept along, clutching the wheel, through empty forest and farmland, and then finally into the grimy built-up area of factory and mining towns around the great industrial center of Katowice. At this point, I knew, I was only twelve or fifteen miles from Auschwitz, so I made the indicated turn-off onto a two-lane secondary road and followed the signs to Oświęcim, the Polish name for the town whose German name has become synonymous with the Holocaust.

When I awoke the next morning it was still snowing hard. The freak spring storm had dumped at least nine inches on the immediate area, and even more on towns not far away. Everywhere it lay—a heavy, cold, wet, white blanket. In Auschwitz, the scene of so much tragedy, the symbol of so much loss, it was tempting to think of the snow as a shroud.

I considered my situation.

When I began work on this book, as I noted in the introductory chapter, I decided I didn't want to write about the Holocaust per se. I didn't want to write about ghettos, deportations, concentration camps, gas chambers. I therefore did not want to write specifically about Auschwitz. Chance brought me here, though, during a freak spring snowstorm; chance forced me to stay. If I were superstitious, and sometimes I think I am, I would call it something other than chance. For from what better place, I realized, to survey the sweep of Jewish life in East-Central Europe than from the place synonymous with its death? From what better place to contemplate the Jewish present than from the place that serves as a reference point dividing present from past?

I decided not to worry about snow-blocked roads or missed appointments in the Czech Republic. I was snowbound in Auschwitz, forced to remain until the sun came out. I decided I would use the time to explore the surroundings—not so much the camp, perhaps, as the shadow of the camp. Or, rather, the matrix of town and people and history in which the camp was embedded; the tapestry surrounding the big jagged hole that here, on the spot, fifty years later, has not at all been mended.

Day One

I arrived in Oświęcim in the late afternoon and drove directly to the museum at the former Auschwitz I main camp, located across a river and a mile or two away from the town itself. The museum was already closed for the day, but a taxi driver in the snow-clogged parking lot directed me to a new Center for Information, Meetings, Dialogue, Education, and Prayer a few hundred yards away. There, he said, I would be able to find a room for the night. The center, run by the Catholic Church, had opened nine months earlier as part of a complex of buildings that also includes the new convent for the Carmelite nuns whose presence in a building abutting the Auschwitz camp—an old theater used by the Nazis as a warehouse for Zyklon-B poison gas crystals—had been a source of bitterness between Jews and Polish Catholics for nearly a decade. Indeed, the fact that the nuns had still not moved into the new convent six years after Jewish and Catholic representatives had signed an agreement to that effect was the reason I had come here on this trip.[2] The Polish media had been playing up reports that the World Jewish Congress was threatening to boycott upcoming ceremonies marking the fiftieth anniversary of the Warsaw Ghetto Uprising if the nuns had not moved, and I wanted to see the situation for myself.

The center, located on a street named after St. Maximilian Kolbe, a Polish Catholic priest killed in Auschwitz, was a three-story brick building with white stucco outer walls, dormer windows in the peaked, red-tile roof, and a tall, modernistic pillared entryway. It looked brand new and squeaky clean, but the snow softened the sharp lines. Behind it, across a lumpy field littered with construction material, squatted the much larger convent building itself, still raw, bare brick and obviously incomplete. The center looked closed—after all, it was late Sunday afternoon—but the front door was unlocked, so I entered. Hanging in the vestibule was a framed, poster-sized print of a Star of David strikingly depicted in red and sooty black, as if made of blood and ashes.

I was welcomed enthusiastically by a woman at the reception desk on the far side of the high-ceilinged lobby. She was about my own age, dark-haired like myself, and soberly dressed in a sweater, below-the-knees skirt, and slippers.

"Do you keep kosher?" she asked, as she took my passport and registered me as a guest in the center's pension—ten dollars for bed and breakfast or twenty-five dollars for bed and all three meals. "If you keep kosher, I'll want to make sure that the kitchen knows."

She was American, and after assuring her that I would eat whatever they provided, I asked how it was that she was working here. She looked to me a bit like a lay sister or a member of a religious order. Was she a nun? "No," she replied. "I'm not married, but I'm not a nun." She was, she told me, a Polish-American who had left the United States five years earlier to come to Poland, to return to her roots, and to teach English in a small village near Warsaw. "When I heard that this center was being set up," she told me, "I wrote to Cardinal Macharski in Cracow and told him I wanted to work here. He said yes. So here I am, and I can say that here I have finally found my vocation, that this is where I belong."

I went out to haul in my bags from the car.

I knew about the center already. One of its stated goals was to promote interfaith dialogue, and I had been there briefly the summer before, during its first week of operation, with a delegation of American Jews and American and Polish Catholics: two archbishops, a bishop, various monsignors, and a dozen rabbis and other Jews traveling around Poland on a bus whose air conditioning had broken down, during four of the hottest days of a blazing hot summer. An American couple, Polish-born Jews who had survived the Holocaust and were making their first trip back since the war, were also part of the group. They were nervous to be in Poland; they admitted their trepidations and comforted each other with loving looks and little warm pats of the hand throughout the journey.

The trip had been arranged under the auspices of a new center for Jewish-Christian dialogue based at Sacred Heart University in Fairfield, Connecticut; the organizers characterized it as the highest-level joint delegation of American Jews and Catholics ever to visit Poland. The group included well-known representatives of both faiths who had dedicated distinguished careers to improving interreligious relations; even those just along for the ride were at least dedicating these four days. We had formed an ecumenical road show that rolled from meetings to memorial services, from hallowed sites of Holocaust tragedy to strongholds of contemporary religious faith. Deeply moving learning experiences were interspersed with almost bizarre moments of banality. I found it fascinating.

In Warsaw we held a memorial service at the starkly simple sidewalk monument at Umschlagplatz, the point from which scores of thousands of Jews had been deported to Treblinka from the Warsaw Ghetto. The text had been written and edited for the occasion by one of the rabbis on the trip; folded photocopied sheets were passed out. It had been a long time since I had heard prayers expressed in American synagogue English, and I found the form and language of the responsive readings uncomfortably reminiscent of the bland suburban synagogue I'd gone to as a child. I had trouble connecting the flowery yet sanitized solemnity of the pious English phrases with that hot, sunny, traffic-clogged morning in downtown Warsaw and with the memory of the brutal and horrible things that had taken place at that very spot fifty years before.

From Umschlagplatz we moved on for lunch at Poland's one and only kosher restaurant, which had opened a year before, the first kosher restaurant in Poland for thirty years, on a square that before the war had been the heart of the teeming Jewish district but now was simply an ordinary run-down neighborhood of Warsaw's ubiquitous concrete high rises. The menu included gefilte fish, kreplach soup, and pale green new pickles, but Mrs. Menkin, the Auschwitz survivor making her first trip back to Poland, was not able to eat. She put down her fork and made little gestures with her hands. The fish was too hard; it was not sweet enough. There was no horseradish, not even grated horseradish and beetroot, as the waitress, obviously non-Jewish like the other restaurant personnel, had promised. The new pickles were bitter, too. Her complaints were the stuff of Yiddishe mamma humor. "My daughter-in-law's gefilte fish is better than this," she sniffed. But I realized that it was an act, the wary, whistle-in-the-dark sniff of the survivor. She was nervous, even fearful, to be back, to be in Poland—

but here she was, despite everything. She didn't know quite what to do with her eyes, her voice, her thoughts. She looked around at the rest of us to back her up in her complaint, to give her strength. Her husband, meanwhile, a survivor from Vilna, recounted to us strange, almost hallucinogenic sensations he said he had been experiencing ever since he got to Warsaw. "I look around and I don't see empty streets and modern apartment buildings," he said, a note of wonder in his voice. "No. I see streets that are full of Jews, windows with Jewish people looking down, shops, schools, synagogues, markets. Yes, this is what I see."

In Cracow, we met with the non-Jewish scholars doing research on Polish-Jewish history at the Jagiellonian University's Jewish Research Center. In the elevator of our hotel, a Hasid in sidelocks and beard stepped in along with several of the American rabbis in their summer sports jackets and business suits. No one made eye contact or said a word.

In Częstochowa, we attended mass celebrated by the priests from our group in the holiest shrine of Polish Catholicism: the oppressively ornate, black, gold, and silver chapel at Jasna Góra Monastery, which houses the famous Black Madonna icon. Here we were surrounded by hundreds of sobbing, ecstatic Polish pilgrims, many of whom walked dozens of yards on their knees down the sides of the chapel to pass close to the holy picture. For many of the Jews in the delegation it was their first real contact with the fervent Polish faith they had so often read about. Some seemed a little shocked by the full immersion. "After having heard about the Polish Catholic soul, this for me crystallized in a very real way the Polish Catholic national and religious experience," one of the Jewish lay representatives, the child of Holocaust survivors, told me afterward. "It crystallized the experience of one thousand years of Polish history in one moment," he said. "It enhances my understanding of some of those areas that are troubled in the Polish-Jewish encounter."

For the Catholics in our group it was the best way they could have had to show the Jews, in a sense, what they all were up against in their mutual commitment to break down ancient barriers: Polish Catholicism, highly conservative and to a large extent closed within itself, was quite different from the Catholicism encountered in America's pluralistic society. "You can't understand Poland without understanding Częstochowa," Polish Archbishop Henryk Muszyński, president of the Polish episcopate's Commission on Dialogue with the Jews and one of the leaders of the delegation, told me later. "It was very important to come here; it was [also] very important for Poles to see a Polish bishop bringing Jews to Częstochowa." He could have said "bringing Jews *back* to Częstochowa." Did anyone remember, I wondered, that about thirty percent of Częstochowa's population before the war had been Jewish? In this holiest city of Polish Catholicism, the Nazis chose Christmas Day, 1939, to destroy the monumental, domed Great Synagogue; they set up a Jewish ghetto here in 1941, from which tens of thousands were deported to Treblinka and other camps. Today the Jewish cemetery is virtually inaccessible, enclosed by the grounds of the Częstochowa steelworks.

We spent much of a full day at Auschwitz. One of the rabbis got up in the front of the bus when we were still a few miles away and, taking the microphone, felt compelled to describe in detail how his heart was pounding and his stomach was tied into knots and he couldn't control his emotions as we neared this place. His words gushed out; I was sure that they would end up as part of a sermon when he got back home. "Stop it!" I wanted to shout at him. "Shut up! Save it for your congregation!" But I recalled, too, how the author of a guidebook to Poland had been similarly overcome. "It was with a coward's beating heart," he wrote, "that, early one morning, the sky stained yellow with dawn, I caught a train from Cracow to Oświęcim."[3] My parents, when they visited, would not even consider taking a train to Auschwitz, even one of the modern semicommuter trains that make regular trips back and forth to Cracow; the memory of all those hundreds and hundreds of thousands of doomed Jews packed into cattle cars for the last rail journey of their lives was still too strong.

The rabbi relinquished the microphone and sat down as our overheated bus rumbled closer to our destination. No one spoke. There was dead silence except for the droning of the motor and soft sobs coming from somewhere. I looked out the window at the typical drab, industrial Polish townscape slipping by, no different from a hundred other small cities throughout the country—the junky cars on the street, the groups of people in cheap summer clothes milling about on the hot sidewalks; obscene graffiti on the walls.

OŚWIĘCIM: A group of Israeli students about to enter through the *Arbeit Macht Frei* gate.

At Auschwitz, the Jews and the Catholics of our group held two joint memorial services. The first was at the Auschwitz I camp, the original concentration camp set up in abandoned Polish military barracks in 1940 mainly for Polish and other political prisoners. It is at this camp that the infamous slogan *"Arbeit Macht Frei"*—"Work Makes You Free"—arches over the iron gate. In 1947 the camp was turned into a museum; placards still say, with heavy, unintentional irony, that children under thirteen are not permitted. It is this museum that, under the Communists, minimized the Jewish presence at Auschwitz, scarcely mentioning the fact that ninety percent of its victims were Jews, exterminated here simply because they were Jewish. Indeed, the decree by the Polish state establishing the museum in 1947 stated simply that "on the site of the former Nazi concentration camp a Monument of the Martyrdom of the Polish Nation and of Other Nations is to be erected for all times to come." Until the fall of Communist rule brought the possibility of changes, exhibit captions and informational material referred to Jews simply as one of a number of peoples deported to Auschwitz from more than two dozen countries. An exhibition hall that opened in 1978 devoted to the suffering of the Jews under the Nazis was given the same prominence as similar halls detailing the suffering of, for example, the East Germans and the Austrians. The official guidebook to the camp referred to "six million Polish citizens" killed in the war, not mentioning that half of these were Jews, representing nearly all of the Polish Jewish population.

Here, near Block 11, the so-called Block of Death where thousands of Poles had been tortured and executed, our group recited Psalm 130 in Latin, English, and Hebrew—*De Profundis*: "Out of the deep I have called unto thee, O Lord: Lord, hear my voice." Heaps of withering memorial flowers, brought by visitors, were lying against the brick of the execution wall, as if they too had been victims of the firing squads' bullets. Not far away, on the other side of the barbed-wire–topped perimeter wall of the camp, we were able to see the anonymous brick building that since 1984 housed the controversial Carmelite nuns living their cloistered lives praying for these victims. I wouldn't have known what it was if it hadn't been pointed out to me. I tried to glimpse the twenty-foot cross next to the convent, which also had drawn protest, but found that I would be able to see it only if I jumped into the air to catch a look over the wall.

The second ceremony took place at Birkenau, the Auschwitz II camp, two miles away. It had been to Birkenau that, starting in 1942, the infamous Nazi rail transports brought Jews from all over Europe, most of them to be led immediately from the rail siding to the gas chambers. At the time, word seeped out only slowly as to the extent and horror of what was going on. In April 1943, the Jewish Telegraphic Agency carried a chillingly laconic item datelined "Somewhere in Europe":

> Three large labor camps for Polish Jews have been established by the Nazis at Lublin, Auschwitz and Birkenau, a report reaching here today disclosed. Jewish men and women from all parts of Poland

are being driven to these camps, and assigned to difficult physical labor. . . . The greatest rate of mortality is in the Birkenau camp.[4]

Birkenau, the death camp, is part of the Auschwitz museum but is its own exhibit. The enormous area, 425 acres, has been left as it was: a rusting rail line surrounded by row upon row of tall, skeletal chimneys rising on the sites of demolished wooden barracks. At the far end are the ruins of the crematoriums and a huge, ugly monument—described in a Polish guidebook printed as late as 1989 simply as an "International Monument commemorating the victims of Fascism."[5] Just across the street from Birkenau, the building that served as the SS commandant's headquarters has been turned into a church. Atop the roof, above the door, a huge cross stands like a beacon.

I often recall what the Italian writer and Auschwitz survivor Primo Levi wrote after revisiting Auschwitz decades after the war:

> I didn't feel anything much when I visited the central Camp. The Polish government has transformed it into a kind of national monument. The huts have been cleaned and painted, trees have been planted and flowerbeds laid out. There is a museum in which pitiful relics are displayed: tons of human hair, hundreds of thousands of eyeglasses, combs, shaving brushes, dolls, baby shoes, but it remains just a museum—something static rearranged, contrived. . . .
> I did, however, experience a feeling of violent anguish when I entered Birkenau Camp, which I had never seen as a prisoner. Here, nothing has been changed. There was mud, and there is still mud, or suffocating summer dust. The blocks of huts (those that weren't burned when the Front reached and passed this area) have remained as they were, low, dirty, with draughty wooden sides and beaten earth floors. There are no bunks but bare planks, all the way to the ceiling. Here nothing has been prettied up.[6]

We stood in a group in front of one of the destroyed ovens and read a memorial service prepared by two members of the delegation especially for interfaith groups commemorating the Holocaust. It included passages from the Old Testament but also quoted Pope John Paul II and a Protestant pastor. While stressing that the Holocaust was primarily directed against Jews, it noted that "millions of Poles and Gypsies, Russians, and other Europeans also lost their lives as victims of Nazism's diabolically efficient technology of death."

During the service Mr. Menkin, the Holocaust survivor from Vilna who had seen visions of Jews in Warsaw, stepped forward. He could not control his tears. Think of Holocaust victims as individuals, not as an anonymous mass of millions, he urged. "I want you to look instead at the dress of a little girl, the shoes of a baby. . . . This is a life. This was a life. This little baby had a father and a mother and a brother and an uncle. She went with her mother to the crematorium. One person. One little child. Think of one case. Because there were millions. And this impression should remain with you."

Nine months later, as I looked through a mist-streaked window of the Auschwitz interfaith center and later trudged out through the storm, I thought about these victims in terms of snow. The thick, wet, white layer that covered the city and the camp smoothed and softened and obliterated details, creating an anonymous winter landscape. Yet this featureless expanse of snow was composed of individual flakes. I watched them fall and fall on the ground, on my sleeve. Each snowflake, I knew, was unique; none was identical to another. Each was a six-pointed crystal—like the six-pointed Star of David—but no two were exactly the same. Each of the millions put to death by the Nazis was a separate individual, too; each individual was a member of a separate family, a separate community. Behind each stretched a separate history, generation before generation—even here, even in Auschwitz, I realized, for there had been Jews in Oświęcim long before the Nazis brought them to the gas chambers in cattle cars.

I TOOK MY BAGS UP TO MY ROOM, a large, airy, obviously brand-new chamber arranged like a dormitory. Five single beds, each covered with a bright woolen blanket, were arranged neatly in two rows, and a new, peasant-style wooden table and chairs stood on a separate raised platform under the window. A small, discreet crucifix hung over the door. I washed up in the big bathroom, drank a beer, and then went down for an early supper. I was the only person in a refectory-style dining hall big enough to seat two or three tour groups. The meal, served by a giggling blond teenage girl, was delicious: hearty homemade soup, a sautéed cutlet, tangy salad, and creamy mashed potatoes—among the best food I had ever had in Poland. I relaxed and had another beer.

Later, in an upstairs office, I spoke for awhile with the Reverend Marek Głownia, the director of the center, whom I had met briefly the summer before. An owlish-looking, youthful priest with big eye-glasses, he was casually dressed in a patterned pullover sweater. Our conversation focused inevitably on Jewish-Polish relations and the unique, troubling role of Auschwitz as a symbol of both dialogue and discord; it was a theme that, with variations, became a constant during my entire snowbound stay.

"We, Poles and Jews, we speak different languages where Auschwitz is concerned," Głownia said, succinctly summarizing the issue. "The very word has two different meanings."

For Jews, Auschwitz means the ultimate symbol of the Holocaust, the Shoah; the ovens, the six million. At the same time, for Poles it represents the ultimate symbol of Polish suffering under the Nazis: three million non-Jewish Polish dead, whole cities destroyed, a culture suppressed, a people subjugated and conquered. The camp, in a sense, exists in two parallel universes. Poles under communism—as witnessed by the way the Auschwitz museum was set up—were taught little if anything of the Jewish universe; Jews worldwide learned little about the Polish one. Both claimed Auschwitz as their own.

The summer before I had been taken rather aback by how little even the American rabbis—thoughtful individuals involved in seeking to better Jewish-Polish relations—seemed to know about this basic dichotomy.

"I, for one, came on this trip as someone with much to learn," Rabbi Jack Bemporad, one of the organizers of the delegation, admitted at a news conference in Warsaw at the conclusion of the trip. "I've learned how heroic Poles were during the war, the degree to which Poles were victims. It's a mistaken stereotype that only Jews were victims and that all the rest were perpetrators—it is simply not true."

Głownia brought up his own parallel ignorance.

"Until I came to work here at Auschwitz three years ago," he told me, "I had never met a Jew. I'm sure there are many, many people my age who don't know anything about Jews or understand anything about Jews. . . . A group of young Poles came to our center this month, for example. I talked to them, I told them that Auschwitz was an important symbol for Jews, and I'm sure it was the first time that they had heard this."

THE POSITION OF THE CHURCH VIS-À-VIS JEWS and anti-Semitism in Poland today is ambiguous. The official policy of the Polish Church, as set forth in a pastoral letter issued in early 1991, firmly condemns anti-Semitism and pledges to work toward bettering Polish-Jewish dialogue. The letter, signed by all 244 Polish bishops and read from pulpits all over Poland, expressed "sincere regret over all cases of anti-Semitism that were committed at any time or by anyone on Polish soil" and said that "all cases of anti-Semitism are against the spirit of the Gospel . . . and are contrary to the Christian vision of human dignity." It stressed that Jews could not be held responsible for the death of Jesus Christ and added that the bishops were "especially disheartened by those among the Catholics who in some way were the cause of the death of Jews. They will forever gnaw at our conscience. . . . We must ask forgiveness of our Jewish brothers and sisters."

This attitude is of a very recent date, however, and despite the efforts of some committed clergymen has not yet been instilled into the thinking of most parish priests, nuns, and other grass-roots members of the Church: The trickle-down effect has not yet trickled down.

It must be—and often is—recalled that the intense Polish anti-Semitism before World War II was fostered by the Church, among others, and that priests on all levels of the hierarchy preached anti-Semitism from their pulpits. In February 1936, the primate of Poland, August Cardinal Hlond, issued a pastoral letter much different from the one issued in 1991: It essentially sanctified anti-Semitism—nonviolent anti-Semitism, to be sure—as official Polish Church policy:

A Jewish problem exists, and will continue to exist as long as the Jews remain Jews. . . . It is a fact that the Jews fight against the Catholic Church, they are free-thinkers, and constitute the vanguard of atheism, of the bolshevik movement and of revolutionary activity. It is a fact that Jewish influence upon morals is fatal, and their publishers spread pornographic literature. It is true that the Jews are committing frauds, practicing usury, and dealing in white slavery. It is true that in schools, the influence of the Jewish youth upon the

Catholic youth is generally evil, from a religious and ethical point of view. But—let us be just. Not all Jews are like that. . . .

I warn against the fundamental, unconditional anti-Jewish principle imported from abroad [i.e., Nazi Germany]. It is contrary to Catholic ethics. It is permissible to love one's own nation more; it is not permissible to hate anyone. Not even Jews. One does well to prefer his own kind in commercial dealings and to avoid Jewish stores and Jewish stalls in the markets, but it is not permissible to demolish Jewish businesses, destroy their merchandise, break windows, torpedo their houses. One ought to fence oneself off against the harmful moral influences of Jewry, to separate oneself against its anti-Christian culture, and especially to boycott the Jewish press and the demoralizing Jewish publications. But it is not permissible to assault Jews, to hit, maim or blacken them. . . . When divine mercy enlightens a Jew, and he accepts sincerely his and our Messiah, let us greet him with joy in the Christian midst.[7]

"Between the two wars, many priests were involved actively in anti-Semitic propaganda in Poland," the Reverend Stanisław Musiał, a member of the Polish episcopate's Commission on Dialogue with the Jews, told the interreligious dialogue group apologetically the summer before. "We are now ashamed of it. Now, in 1992, no priest is active as writer or journalist in this sad field," he asserted. This may have been so, but recent evidence has shown that priests and Catholic activists are still involved in other forms of anti-Semitic activity.

Warsaw-based Konstanty Gebert, one of the most eloquent of contemporary Poland's Jewish intellectuals, discussed with me on numerous occasions the gap between official Church policy and grassroots belief and practice. He wrote, for example, of the anti-Semitic bias of a small, right-wing Catholic political party, the Christian-National Union, and how some priests played "an important role in the dissemination of anti-Semitic rumors" during the Polish presidential campaign of 1990.[8] He quoted a Catholic lay activist, Jan Turnau, as writing in the Polish newspaper *Gazeta Wyborcza*, that "Not only the laity, but also clergymen used anti-Semitic tricks. . . . During the presidential electoral campaign they produced them straight off the pulpit, which—contrary to the position adopted by the episcopate—was abused for political purposes in at times a truly devilish manner."[9]

One Polish Church figure lauded by Gebert and other Jews is Archbishop Muszyński, a chief architect of current Polish Church policy on the Jews and a prime mover behind the 1991 pastoral letter. His ground-breaking efforts over two decades to bridge the often bitter gap between Jews and Polish Catholics have not, however, gone without criticism from conservative elements in the Polish Church.

In a series of conversations during our interreligious road show the summer before, Muszyński told me there were a number of levels of perceptions about Jews and Judaism in Poland, all of which were complicated by stereotypes, inherited memories, and ideas distorted by four decades of Communist rule. "Many people think, 'We have no more Jews in Poland, so there is no Jewish problem here,'" he said. "We have to explain to them why there is Jewish interest in Poland. That's a major problem here. We have to explain to Poles why they should be interested in Jewish things."

He described the differing perceptions of the Holocaust and suffering under the Nazis as almost a "competition of suffering." Poles, he said, feel that the Jewish emphasis on the uniqueness of Jewish suffering in the Holocaust minimizes Polish suffering. As a result, he said, if the Poles say, "we suffered too," Jews feel that this in turn is a belittling of their own suffering. "So you have to explain to them, and it's not easy to explain; because it's not necessarily who suffered the most," he said. "The difference, as I try to explain to everybody, is that *all* Jews *had* to die, but Poles could survive."

In the half century since the war, he said, "We lived in perfect isolation, without any contact. And so we have a fixed history, Polish history and Jewish history, and everyone takes into account only their own perspectives. So what we [in Poland] need the most is contact with living Jewish people—and from my point of view, living Jewish people who believe in God."

He added that in Poland there is often a sharp difference between how the intelligentsia view the situation and how it is seen on a popular, mass level. "It's not just a problem of mutual prejudices, but also generalizations, terrible generalizations. The ideas that Jews have about Poles and that Poles have about Jews," he said. "It's because we don't have contacts."

Muszyński stressed that in order to get Poles to know more about Jews and thus break down stereotypes, it is important to reach the broadest mass level of the population, through both preaching and teaching. He therefore underscored the need for improved training programs for Poland's priests and teachers—programs that were being developed with input from Jewish organizations such as the Anti-Defamation League and the American Jewish Committee. "We have to revive our own history, and we have to teach history in the correct way, because until now we were taught the history of totalitarian movements. We have a terrible heritage of Communist mentality in all fields," he said, adding that this has abetted the persistence of anti-Semitism through what he termed the "scapegoat theory, which makes enemies of imperialists, capitalists, and Zionists. . . . We have very nice documents now," he said, "but we have to implement them in daily life."

NINE MONTHS LATER, REV. GŁOWNIA ECHOED much of what Muszyński had told me, and he related the general situation, the gap in understanding, to the specific case of the Auschwitz convent. The Church hierarchy was determined that the nuns, as agreed six years before, should move to the new convent, parts of which were now finished enough for habitation. But the nuns still did not understand why they had to move. Głownia described them as simple women whose dedication to their cloistered, monastic vocation and lack of contact with the world made it hard for them to understand why their presence at the convent overlooking the concentration camp created so many problems. They did not understand how or why a Roman Catholic religious presence such as theirs at an otherwise "Godless" place could offend Jewish sensibilities; they lived in a different universe. "They made the decision to spend their lives next to the camp in prayer," he said. "It is very, very hard for them to understand why there is this problem. For them, life devoted to God and prayer for the good of everyone is not a problem."

He said, too, that whereas the main concern at the moment was the transfer of the nuns to the new convent, he was also concerned about how local people would react when the twenty-foot cross set up next to the old convent by the wall of the death camp was removed and transferred to the new building.

The nuns, he said, "can get into a car and go to the new place, and that's the end of the problem. But you can't just put a cross like that into a car and leave. In Poland, the cross is a great symbol. It's both a religious and a patriotic symbol, and that's the problem." Changing the position of a cross of that size and significance—it was used during the ceremonies conducted by Pope John Paul II when he visited Auschwitz–Birkenau in 1979—would be a major event in the spiritual and civic life of the entire town, he said. "We have already planned a place for the cross at the new convent, but we must prepare the transfer with local Catholics. We must explain— and explain well—why the best place for this cross is next to the new convent. I feel that the best way to handle the transfer of the cross would be to make a great religious festival out of it, with a solemn procession from one place to the other, involving senior Church dignitaries."

I SAID GOODNIGHT TO GŁOWNIA and went upstairs to my room. The heater wasn't working too well, so I piled blankets from all the other beds onto mine. I wanted to read, but there was no reading lamp, just an overhead ceiling light, and my reading matter was limited: serious research books I was reading for work or a trashy paperback trilogy of Dracula novels a friend had given me earlier on the trip. It had been a long day, and I was tired; my mind was already too full of serious matters. I chose the Dracula.

Day Two

The snow was coming down hard when I woke up and looked out the window. The roads were invisible, and my car was a smooth white lump in the parking lot. I had made an appointment with Głownia to take a look at the new convent building, and we walked

OŚWIĘCIM: The unfinished kitchen of the new convent.

there across the open field between the two buildings, following the footsteps of workmen who had tramped a path through the snow earlier in the morning.

Głownia took me from top to bottom in the new convent, a large, red-brick building constructed behind a high wall and around a central courtyard. One two-story wing included living quarters for the fourteen nuns from the old convent, common rooms, and other facilities, which had been readied for use but were empty of furnishings. For each nun there was a small, rectangular bedroom with a large window, wooden floors, and a sink. The bedrooms were arranged along two corridors, with a common bath for each hallway. Głownia told me that the central heating system was fully functioning, as were the stoves in the otherwise largely unfurnished kitchen. Rooms to be used as an infirmary, a laundry, and pantries were also ready but empty. The chapel, the vestibule, and another wing of bedrooms were incomplete, and there was the air of a building site about the place. The new convent was only a few hundred yards away from the old one; from an upper-floor window in the new building, I could easily look across and see the old one, at the edge of the camp.

BACK AT THE CENTER, I FOUND AN EXHIBIT of old photographs of Oświęcim displayed in an upstairs lobby. The pictures dated from the late 1800s through World War II. Many were old postcards, typical small-town postcard views of the market square, the castle, churches, a man waving from the river bank with a panorama of the town behind. Summertime in the Polish provinces.

On one postcard, a turn-of-the-century beauty, draped in a toga-like robe, posed as if she were the body of a butterfly, while four scenic views of the town spread out around her, forming her wings. On another card, multiple townscapes were arranged like the tail of a peacock. *Pozdrowienie z Oświęcima!* they read in Polish. *Gruss aus Oświęcim!* the same cards read in German. "Greetings from Oświęcim!" Most of the postcards, even those dating back to before the turn of the century, bore printed greetings and captions in both languages. This reflected the fact that for much of its eight-hundred-year history, Oświęcim was a border town that passed back and forth between Polish- and German-speaking territory; its population, too, was ethnically mixed.

Situated thirty-two miles west of Cracow, near the point where the Soła River flows into the Vistula, Oświęcim was founded in the twelfth century as a fortress and in the Middle Ages became the capital of a duchy. The castle, originally built in the thirteenth century, still rises on an escarpment overlooking the Soła. Oświęcim was subject to Silesian and then Bohemian domination before it became part of Poland in 1457. When Poland was partitioned among Russia, Prussia, and Austria at the end of the eighteenth century, the town came under Austrian rule. It was right on the western edge of Austrian-held Galicia, just at the border with Upper Silesia, which was German.

Oświęcim became part of Poland again when the independent Polish state was resurrected after World War I, but it was still located not far from the German frontier, and some of its citizens were *Volksdeutsche,* or ethnic Germans. When the new Polish state was founded, part of Upper Silesia—just west of Oświęcim—also was incorporated into Poland as the result of a controversial referendum. Upper Silesia's population was a dense mixture of Germans and Poles, and the industry-rich territory had been hotly contested. In the 1930s, some 750,000 ethnic Germans lived within Poland's borders, forming a minority that, particularly in Upper Silesia, remained "sour and disaffected . . . dangerously unreconciled to the very existence of the Polish state."[10] German allegations of Polish mistreatment of *Volksdeutsche* living in Poland and incidents—or manufactured incidents—between Poles and Germans on both sides of the border in the summer of 1939 were among the pretexts used by the Nazis to launch their invasion of Poland on September 1, 1939, which touched off World War II.

Jan Karski—a young Polish artillery officer who eventually became a legendary hero of the Polish resistance and who in 1942 brought chilling word of the plight of Polish Jews to the outside world—was sent to Oświęcim with his regiment when Poland secretly mobilized in August 1939, a week before the German invasion. Decribing the aftermath of the Nazi blitzkrieg and the retreat of Polish forces from Oświęcim, Karski wrote bitterly about the *Volksdeutsche* in the town:

> Our reserve battery received orders to leave Oswiecim in formation and to take our guns, supplies and ammunition in the direction of Cracow. As we marched through the streets of Oswiecim toward the railroad, to our complete astonishment and dismay, the inhabitants began firing upon us from the windows. They were Polish citizens of German descent, the Nazi Fifth Column, who were, in this fashion, announcing their new allegiance. Most of our men instantly wanted to attack and set fire to every suspect house but were restrained by the superior officers. When we reached the railroad, we were compelled to wait while the track was being repaired. We sat down under the blazing sun and gazed back at the burning buildings, the hysterical population, and the treacherous windows of Oswiecim until the train was ready. We boarded it in weary, disgusted silence and began crawling eastward—toward Cracow.[11]

Oświęcim was deep within Polish territory annexed by the German Reich, and the Nazis called the town only by its German name, Auschwitz. They brought in Germans from elsewhere in the Reich to settle there, in many cases taking over the houses of Jews and Poles. The marketplace—*Rynek* in Polish, *Ringplatz* in German—became, as attested to by a postcard dating from the Nazi occupation, *Adolf Hitler platz*.

PREWAR OŚWIĘCIM-AUSCHWITZ had another name, too: a Yiddish name, *Oshpitsin,* which appears on no map or old postcard, and has space in few memories anymore. Jewish history in Oświęcim, however, is almost as old as that of the town itself. Jews settled here in the fifteenth century or even earlier, and a permanent community of Jews was established by the 1560s. They were drawn by the important fairs that attracted merchants and traders from all over, though local rulings at that time barred Jews from living in the immediate vicinity of the marketplace and also forbade new Jewish settlers from taking up residency. Nonetheless, by 1588 the community had grown large enough to build a synagogue and establish a cemetery. Two hundred years later, when the town came under Austrian rule, nearly 150 Jews lived in Oświęcim. By the eve of World War I, the number had risen to more than three thousand. More than five thousand Jews lived in Oświęcim just before World War II, making up fifty to sixty percent of the population.

Oświęcim was, in effect, a shtetl, a small town with a large Jewish population, little different from many other such towns scattered throughout Poland. The Jews here were, as in most Polish towns, mainly workers and peddlers, small merchants and artisans, but there was a middle class, too, of white-collar professionals, and there were also a few prosperous businessmen and factory owners. Numerous Jewish clubs and associations, business organizations and political parties, schools and trade unions existed alongside similar non-Jewish organizations. There were prayer houses and two synagogues; one of them was shown in a picture in the exhibit of old photographs. A number of Jews served in the city government, and there is a persistent belief among local people today that Oświęcim's most prominent mayor between the wars, Roman Mayzel, was at least of Jewish ancestry.

Oświęcim was also the site of a major railway junction, one of the main reasons the Nazis decided to situate their concentration camp there. In the winter of 1919, the English Zionist activist Israel Cohen found himself stranded for a few hours at Oświęcim as he made his circuitous way from Cracow to Vienna. It was in the volatile period immediately following World War I, when bloody local skirmishes raged around the new borders of the newly independent Polish state. Jews, too, found themselves the targets of widespread violence, and Cohen was on one of several missions he made to Poland and elsewhere to investigate the situation:

> February 1—Caught train at 7 A.M. for Oswiecim: compelled to go there instead of travelling to Vienna direct, owing to Czech-Polish war. At Oswiecim had to wait few hours for train to Kandrzin (in German territory), so went into town, looked up secretary of Jewish community. He told me of attempts at pogroms, warded off on the first occasion by Cracow Jewish Militia, on the second pogromists were injured. Was conducted to Jewish cemetery, saw damage to many tombstones done by gang of roughs. General violation of graves. In Oswiecim station official wanted to subject me to "body search" in a cubicle, but I protested that as I was on an official mission I should be exempt, so he gave me stamped disk, allowing me to go on platform. Left Oswiecim at 4, reached Kandrzin at 9 P.M., left 10:30 for Annaberg. . . . Arrived Annaberg 1 A.M., changed again for Oderberg, arriving 2 A.M. Changed at Oderberg [today Bohumin, Czech Republic], left 3 A.M., in Arctic frost, arrived in Lundenberg [today's Breclav, Czech Republic] 10 A.M. Long wait in warm station restaurant until 3 P.M., then left for Vienna, arriving 7:30 P.M.—36 hours from Cracow to Vienna, about twice as long as previous [direct] journey from Vienna to Cracow.[12]

The Jews of Oświęcim shared the fate of three million other Polish Jews. According to *The Black Book of Polish Jewry*, a contemporary account of Nazi atrocities against the Jews that was published in 1943, before the full reality of the Nazis' "Final Solution" became known, the Nazis ordered all Jews to leave Oświęcim on the eve of Passover 1940. The Jewish council in the nearby town of Sosnowiec "invited all Jews of Oświęcim to celebrate the Passover with them," and sent wagons and a thousand volunteers to

> help carry out the deportation as efficiently as possible. The moving was done during the Passover week in several wagon-caravans, the

Nazi authorities having forbidden the use of the railways. Some of the wagons were used to move the sick, the aged, and the small children; others were loaded with light furnishings. The heaviest furniture had to be left behind. The able-bodied had to make the journey on foot. The cobbled road from Oświęcim to Sosnowiec was for several days crowded with wandering Jews followed by a procession of small, primitive wagons.

It transpired later that the expulsion was bound up with the Nazi plan to establish a concentration camp at Oświęcim, where thousands of Poles and Jews, mostly of the educated classes, were tortured, many of them to death.[13]

I had some coffee and went to look over the center's little library. There were a few English-language books on Holocaust-related subjects. I leafed through one book and stopped as I came across an eyewitness account of that expulsion, as recounted right after the war by a Jew who was fourteen years old at the time. As he told it, the expulsion took place in two waves—and he, too, like Jan Karski, recalled with astonishment the violence of local ethnic Germans.

They ordered that the *shtetl* of Auschwitz must become *judenrein,* so gradually, everyone was forced to leave. The selection of the first 1,000 deportees took two weeks. Whole families were led away with all their things. Whoever had large sums of money tried to buy their reprieve. The people were taken near the city of Lublin and confined in the small villages of the area. This transport took away my grandparents—my father's parents. It was the first really terrible ordeal the people suffered. Every family mourned, each home was filled with weeping. The rabbinate called a day of fasting, loud prayers rose from every *Shtibl* [small prayer house], *Tilim* [psalms] was heard from every window. Everyone felt this was the beginning of the destruction of Jewish life. We all kept repeating the phrase: "Who knows if we'll ever meet again?"

To assemble in the *shiel* [shul, synagogue] was outlawed—the Germans saw to this right away. Then, they set the *shiel* on fire and tried to burn it down. At the start of 1940, we suddenly heard this explosion rip through the *shiel,* but we were able to put out the fire. The community leaders carried out the *klei koydes* [holy objects], as well as the *sifre toyres* [Torahs] from the *shiel* and distributed them to different Jewish families for safekeeping. All gatherings of Jews were forbidden, and we couldn't *daven* [pray] publicly in the *kloizn*

[Hasidic prayer rooms], but had to gather privately in each other's homes to make up the *minyen* [quorum of ten men]. We kept watch at the door in case a German stole by. The neighbors close by used our house for the *minyen*. The *sifre toyre* was hidden in a small cupboard in the wall. When the order was given for the 1,000 Jews to leave town, everyone fasted. Women and children, too. . . . The family was in a total state of shock. I could never have imagined a sorrow like that which descended on us after they took my father's family away.

In the week of *Paysekh* [Passover] 1941, the *Judenrat* [Jewish council set up under the Nazis to carry out their orders] made an announcement for all the Jews to be ready to leave the town within three days, taking along whatever they could carry. The people were divided up in three groups headed for different destinations: Bendien [Będzin], Sosnovits [Sosnowiec], and Chrzanów. The *Judenrat* arranged for the local Jews in these towns to accommodate us. The Germans hitched together a few dozen carts. and horses for the old and sick people, because it was over two kilometers to the train. People couldn't stop crying on the march out of the *shtetl* because they were being forced from a home their ancestors had settled and lived in for centuries. The way was littered with abandoned belongings the people couldn't carry anymore. Many fainted and collapsed in the streets. The Jewish doctors tried reviving those who'd had attacks. The *sfurim* [prayer books] and *gemures* [Talmuds] were all buried earlier, for the most part. Many *sfurim* were buried in the *shiel* courtyard to prevent their being desecrated by enemy hands. The *sifre toyre* and *mezuzes* [mezuzahs] the people took themselves.

The expulsion from Auschwitz was carried out by the German border patrols. They were correct toward us and some even tried to help. In contrast, the *Volksdeutsche*—most of them former local Polish subjects who lived alongside the Jews—trailed after us with anti-Semitic slogans and curses, rejoicing over their "revenge." They were only looking for people to drop their belongings so they could swoop them up and steal them. Mostly, we were stunned by the correct behavior of the German field gendarmes toward us— that was why so few tried escaping. It was only inside the train that the transport was taken over by the German SS, dressed in black, skull and bones.

Of all the Jews who had been in the *shtetl* before this deportation, only the *Judenrat* was left behind now with another fifty people to clear out the deserted Jewish homes. What they did with the Jewish belongings they gathered together, I don't know.[14]

"The Jews from Oświęcim were removed to the nearby towns of Sosnowiec, Będzin, Chrzanów. They shared the fate of these communities, gradually liquidated, brought back to Auschwitz in 1942 and 1943," I was told by Polish Holocaust scholar Franciszek Piper. "They came back to Auschwitz, their hometown, but they came back to the gas chambers."

Piper, director of the research department at the Auschwitz museum, had had a brief burst of fame a few years earlier when he published research that convincingly revised the number of Auschwitz victims down from the long-quoted figure of 4 million to about 1.1 to 1.5 million, at least one million of whom were Jews and seventy thousand of whom were Poles. His bluntly titled, sixty-eight-page pamphlet on the subject, *Auschwitz: How Many Perished, Jews, Poles, Gypsies . . . ,* was published in Yad Vashem Studies in Jerusalem in 1991, and I found it on sale in various translations at the Auschwitz museum. It is a grim work containing list after detailed list of extremely large, extremely precise numbers, in which Piper occasionally managed nonetheless to break out of the dry recitation of horrors to inject some of his personal feelings.

His findings, he wrote, confirmed that Auschwitz was "the largest center for the extermination of Jews: about one million innocent men, women and children were deliberately put to death by the Nazis, for political purposes, merely because they were Jews."

But, he added,

For Poles, who for six years of German occupation were being murdered in thousands of prisons and other execution sites, Auschwitz is also a symbol of the sufferings of the Polish people. Its very name spread terror among the Polish population—the place where tens of thousands of Polish patriots, members of the resistance movement and the intelligentsia, including prominent representatives of cultural, scientific and social life, met their deaths.

Nor should we forget that Auschwitz is of special significance for the Gypsies. Nearly 20,000 of this small people lost their lives in the camp due to starvation, illnesses and being killed in the gas chambers.

But Auschwitz was a tragedy not only for entire nations; equally it remains a tragedy for all individuals whose loved ones perished there. For humankind as a whole, Auschwitz looms large as an ominous warning against indifference to all forms of violence and racial, religious and national hatred.

Piper is a self-effacing, soft-spoken man with thick glasses; he looked that day a little like an aging rockabilly singer with his pompadour hairstyle and loud plaid jacket. We spoke in his comfortable office, a bright room with a big desk, book-lined shelves, and a bulging file cabinet, situated in one of the brick barracks blocks of the Auschwitz I camp. Bundled up, I walked there in snow that came up to my boot tops and soaked through the leather to my skin. Walking through the camp gates, I tried to cast my mind back fifty years, to what I had read about camp conditions, about prisoners forced to stand barefoot in the snow in their thin, striped uniforms.

Piper told me there were still important traces left of Oświęcim's Jewish history. "The Nazis destroyed the main synagogue, but there is still a small synagogue standing; it's an office now or something, across from the castle. There's also a Jewish cemetery," he said. "I live near it, and pass it every day on the bus when I come in here to work." (Passing by the Oświęcim Jewish cemetery every day on the way to work at the Auschwitz death camp—I admired the lack of irony with which he described this normal bit of daily routine.)

"Once I gave a lecture in Germany," he went on. "Someone asked me, 'Were really so many Jews killed in the war?' So I answered: 'We know exactly how many Jews fell into the hands of the Nazis and how many survived. Before World War II, there were 3.3 to 3.5 million Jews in Poland. In many towns, like Oświęcim, Jews made up half or sometimes more of the population. Now in Poland, one finds only cemeteries.' I mentioned the cemetery in Oświęcim, where I live now. It's a big one. And no one has been buried there after the war. There was a Jewish community here, which is remembered by the old people. And there are cemeteries like this all over Poland."

We spoke a little about the changes that were being made at the Auschwitz museum in order to rectify the distortions and disinformation inherent in the Communist-era exhibits. I knew that for three years an international committee had been working on how to modify the museum, particularly how to make it better reflect the reality of the site's Jewish character. Many things had been done already; much still had to be agreed on and implemented. Things were going slowly, he said; money was short, and each change had to be carefully debated. It was a painful, emotional, and very sensitive process. Piper said the Auschwitz museum was working on a new exhibit, too, as part of its effort. "It will show something of the daily life of Jews, show who they were. Show that they were normal people—not just these shapes in striped uniforms."

Piper told me that if I was interested in the Jewish history of Oświęcim, I should go to the town's archives, which were located almost next door in another brick block of the former concentration camp. So when I left his office I trudged there, to Block I, through the snow.

Every time I visit Auschwitz, I feel the same sensation as soon as I step through the gates. It's a constriction in my chest, a tightness; a sense of anger, too, wells up; I feel as if I want to lash out. It's enough just to be on the grounds of the camp. I felt the constriction this time even when I didn't actually visit the museum or look at the painful displays of relics, but simply walked from one building to the next.

I was thus already a little tense when I rang at the door to the archives and was admitted into a small library. The corridor leading to it was decorated with facsimiles of ancient town charters and documents. I introduced myself to a young librarian, one of several people there, a pleasant-looking man with a small mustache, who spoke English. I told him that Piper had said there was material on Oświecim's Jewish history in the archives and asked if I could see books and documents.

The man disappeared into a back room and returned. "Do you have a letter of authorization from Warsaw?" he asked.

I was surprised and perplexed. Why no, I told him. Why should I need a letter all the way from Warsaw to look at local reference material?

He was adamant. "Then it's impossible," he said. "Without a letter of authorization from the state archives, you cannot see documents here, because you are not a Polish citizen."

What? I tried to control my temper, but I found my hands beginning to tremble and the tightness in my chest becoming unbearable.

"Do many people come here to do research?" I asked.

"No, very few. But you must write to this address in Warsaw to get permission."

"What is it here, secret information? Only for Poles?" I was really having trouble breathing, and my heart was beating very fast. A sudden pressure pounded in my head. I took out my notebook to take down exactly what he was saying, but I was shaking so much it was hard to write.

"Yes," he replied, blandly. "It is secret Polish information. I don't know what information we can get for a person who is not a Polish citizen."

I left, feeling sick. "If this had happened in a library in the town," I told someone later, "I would have been angry, I know. But this was different. It wasn't just stupid bureaucracy. It was something else. It was incredible to me that this smug, officious bastard was acting like that right in a block inside the concentration camp—and apparently wasn't fazed in the least."

THAT AFTERNOON, I WENT INTO OŚWIĘCIM PROPER to take a look at what was left of the one-time Jewish presence. Before the war Oświęcim had apparently been a pleasant town. Jan Karski, the Polish artillery officer who became a resistance hero, has recounted how pleased he was to learn he would be posted there:

> I brightened up. It might even turn out to be fun. I remembered that Oswiecim was situated in the middle of an expanse of fine, open country. I was an enthusiastic horseback rider and I relished the notion of galloping about in uniform on a superb army horse. . . .

Once he arrived he recalled, he enjoyed himself

> in the pleasant Officers' Club at Oswiecim. Army routine and drill were more than usually severe and caused considerable grumbling but did not exhaust us sufficiently to mar our leisurely evenings and even left enough free time . . . to indulge our desire for excursions on horseback into the beautiful surrounding country, under the brilliant and cloudless sky of the Polish summer.[15]

Today Oświęcim is a major industrial center. Of its prewar population of ten thousand, more than half—the Jews—were killed by the Nazis, and there were victims, too, among the Poles. The local ethnic Germans and the Germans brought in to live there under the Nazi occupation fled or were expelled back to Germany, like hundreds of thousands—millions—of other ethnic Germans, after the war.[16] It is estimated that at least seventy to eighty percent of the nearly fifty thousand people who live in Oświęcim today are newcomers, people who arrived in recent decades from elsewhere in Poland seeking work at the huge chemical and other factories that have grown up outside the town. The old downtown center looks much as it did decades ago, with its market square, castle, and churches, but the city of Oświęcim itself now sprawls out in a drab welter of new high-rise housing developments.

I toured Oświęcim with a man in his seventies, a Pole who had been a prisoner of the Nazis in several concentration camps and who had come to Oświęcim soon after the war to work as a guide in the museum. He still worked part time as a guide, and Rev. Głownia had put me in touch with him. He showed me what remained of the Jewish section. There was a square with a rusting, hand-operated water pump in the middle, at one side of which stood the small synagogue, a simple, rectangular building with a peaked roof and arched

OŚWIĘCIM: The small building with arched windows is a former synagogue. When the picture was taken, it was being used as a wholesale carpet outlet.

windows. It had been converted into a wholesale carpet outlet. Inside, rolls and rolls of carpeting and other heavy fabric were stacked up. On the walls there were still two Hebrew inscriptions—workmen shifted rolls of carpet so that I could see one of them—but otherwise there was no indication of the former function.

"This was a Jewish street," my guide said. The street was named after Berek Joselewicz, a Jewish Polish army colonel who led a Jewish regiment that fought alongside Poles against the Russians in 1794. At one end was a tree-shaded vacant lot, like a little park: Here the main synagogue, the one destroyed by the Nazis, had stood.

The buildings on the narrow street were all shabby; some were in ruins. One, in the middle of the block, was distinguished by three arched windows on the upper floor. This, I was told, had been the Jewish school or another small prayer room. "And this building here was a bakery," my guide said. "People say the bread from here was very good."

Around the corner, beneath the castle and just before the bridge leading over the Soła River, a huge, crumbling mansion attached to a series of other buildings took up nearly an entire block. The mansion looked empty, and the facade, with its decorative stuccowork, was in such bad repair that the sidewalk beneath it had been covered by a protective wooden shield for fear that bits of masonry might fall off onto pedestrians. This, I was told, was the Haberfeld mansion, once owned by the wealthiest Jewish family in town. "This was their home," my guide said, "and that building next door, which is now a beverage bottling plant, that was their liquor factory. They ran a big distillery that was very famous all over Galicia. Young people today in Oświęcim know the Haberfeld name, but not the history."

The Haberfeld distillery was founded in 1804, and I had noticed a picture of this decrepit mansion in the exhibit of old photographs set up in the interfaith center. The photograph showed a big sign atop the then splendid building reading, *"Jakob Haberfeld, Parowa Fabryka Wódek i Likierów."* [Jakob Haberfeld, Vodka and Liquor Distillery]. In Galicia, at whose western edge Oświęcim was located, there were about five thousand distilleries at the time the Haberfeld family set up their shop nearly two hundred years

(Facing page)

OŚWIĘCIM: A man runs down the street past the derelict Haberfeld mansion.

ago. The manufacture and particularly the sale of alcoholic drinks was an overwhelmingly Jewish occupation in Poland—so much so that the role of Jews selling vodka to the peasants and thus contributing to widespread alcoholism became one of the premises for anti-Semitism. In Galicia at the end of the nineteenth century, nine percent of the Jewish population—more than seventy thousand people—worked as tavern keepers or liquor dealers.[17]

Members of the Haberfeld family, I learned, had survived the Holocaust and were currently embroiled in an acrimonious series of lawsuits and claims concerning recovery of their prewar property, including the ruined mansion. The story was both fascinating and depressing, and it shed painful human light on the complex of passions, memory, and painful personal dilemmas involved in sorting out who should own what now in Poland. "How should wrongs be corrected?" wrote Associated Press correspondent Drusilla Menaker in an article about the affair several months before. "What is fair to those who were robbed through unspeakable wartime crimes? Who lost the most? These questions pit Pole against Pole, Poles against émigrés and raise sensitive conflicts of class and religion."[18]

In the summer of 1939, wealthy industrialist Jakob Haberfeld, the current owner of the family distillery, and his wife, Felicia, sailed for the United States to attend the New York World's Fair, leaving their two-year-old daughter, Franuśka, at home in the Oświęcim mansion with her grandmother. Jakob and Felicia were on their way home, crossing the Atlantic on the ocean liner *Piłsudski,* when the Germans invaded Poland on September 1. They never reached Poland and never saw their daughter again. The family of the Haberfelds' chauffeur, Paweł Kotułek—a loyal family retainer who had come to work for the Haberfelds as a boy in the 1920s—tried to hide Franuśka, but they were unable to save her. The toddler and her grandmother were deported from Oświęcim with the rest of the town's Jews; they ended up in the ghetto in Cracow and, according to reports, were last seen in a truck heading back toward Auschwitz, their hometown, where they died in the gas chambers at Birkenau in 1943.

Jakob and Felicia Haberfeld eventually settled in California, where they prospered and had another child, a son named Stephen, who became a lawyer in Los Angeles. But they never forgot their baby daughter, their home, their hometown, and everything else they had been forced to leave behind. After the war, unlike most surviving Polish Jews who severed all ties with Poland, they maintained contact with their hometown and particularly with the Kotułeks, who had managed to rescue some of the Haberfelds' personal belongings—a few pieces of furniture and some oil paintings—and save them from the Nazis. According to the Haberfelds, Paweł Kotułek, who died some years ago, and his wife felt that they were safeguarding these possessions until it was possible to return them. The Haberfelds obtained a handwritten letter from Mrs. Kotułek, signed and witnessed shortly before her death in 1991, listing the specific items that were to be returned to the Haberfelds after she died.

The Kotułeks' four children felt differently, however. After their mother's death they maintained that the furnishings were their property, asserting that the family had bought them legally from the Communist authorities after the war—and that they had receipts to prove it. They insisted that the 1991 letter signed by their cancer-stricken mother had been written when she was too weakened and dazed by morphine to know what she was doing.

The rival claims over what amounted to about fifteen thousand dollars' worth of furniture were bitterly fought out in a stuffy district courtroom in the town of Bielsko Biała, twenty-five miles from Oświęcim, near the Czech border in late 1992.

"The Kotułeks do not deny that the furniture once belonged to the Haberfelds, except for a menorah that one witness said actually had been looted from another emptied Jewish home," Drusilla Menaker wrote in her Associated Press report on the trial.

> Yet they also uphold the right of the Communists to have sold them the plunder. That's how it was after 1945, in the great "liquidation" that assigned owners to property left behind by murdered Jews or expropriated from the upper classes. They say local party apparatchiks would come to the Haberfeld house waving official papers and carry off the bedroom set or a sideboard.

The court ruled in the Haberfelds' favor, but the Kotułeks immediately filed an appeal. One of the Kotułeks told Menaker that the Haberfelds were "rich enough already" and had "been away" so long. "My father helped Mrs. Haberfeld and her husband so much. . . . She should thank us and give us a reward," the woman said. "If I had been away so long, I would accept it." The reasons they had "been away" did not seem to have any bearing on the matter.

During the trial, Mrs. Haberfeld, then a sprightly eighty-one, told the judge that her husband had been "a real Pole." He had died some time before and was buried in the United States, her son said, with a bit of the soil of Oświęcim in his grave.

EARLIER GENERATIONS OF HABERFELDS were buried in Oświęcim's Jewish cemetery, and some of their gravestones are still to be seen. They are not standing at the sites of real graves, though, because the cemetery, the same one Israel Cohen had seen devastated in 1919, was, like hundreds—thousands—of Jewish cemeteries throughout Poland, totally demolished during World War II. All the tombstones were uprooted and heaped in a pile at one end of the enclosure. "There was no fence around the place; all the graves were destroyed," I was told. "The whole area was used as a dump."

Mieczysław Kapała, a big, burly man with a very lined, weathered face and a white fleck of spittle at the corner of his mouth, kept the key to the gate in the high wall that was erected around the cemetery in the 1950s and repaired to pristine condition in 1979 when Pope John Paul II visited Auschwitz. We stepped through the gate into a black and white world. Deep snow covered the undulating ground—there were no tracks on its surface except for traces left by birds. "The only people who usually want to see this place are Israeli journalists," Kapała said. The black trunks and branches of the graceful, leafless trees were burdened by snow that from time to time slid off with a soft whoosh. My feet sank deep, and I felt very cold and wet. "See that little valley?" asked Kapała. "That's where the Nazis made a pond for the use of the firefighters."

All around, over the entire area, tombstones stood arranged in neat rows. They were very neat; too neat. All had been plucked out of the heap of uprooted tombstones left by the Nazis and, in the early 1980s, repaired and re-erected with a symmetry that to me seemed uncomfortable and even alien. Or maybe it was the snow that made everything seem so blank and sterile. I was pleased, of course, to see that there had been restoration work and that the cemetery was cared

OŚWIĘCIM: The Jewish cemetery.

OŚWIĘCIM: Mieczysław Kapała, who tends the Jewish cemetery, at the monument in the center of the grounds, pointing to the memorial stone for Rudolf and Erna Haberfeld.

for. But somehow it reminded me of a woman who had had too many face lifts.

In the center of a clearing at the heart of the cemetery stood a monument built of tombstones. One of them, near the bottom, was that of a Rudolf and Erna Haberfeld. Rudolf was born in 1874 and died in 1921. According to the inscription, he had been a leading Oświęcim citizen, a town assessor, and a council member of the Cracow Chamber of Commerce. He had also been president of the Oświęcim Jewish community. It may have been he who described the attempted pogroms in Oświęcim to Israel Cohen after World War I. Erna, his wife, died in 1919; she was only thirty-one.

THAT NIGHT I HAD DINNER WITH the American woman who had welcomed me to the interfaith center. A devout Catholic, she said a silent grace before eating, standing up with hands clasped and looking toward heaven as she whispered a brief prayer. Prompted perhaps by the Haberfeld saga and the bits and pieces I had been picking up about the long Jewish presence in Oświęcim, I got talking with her about family roots and one's own innate sense of identity. "Do you go home often?" I asked her, conscious that over the many years I myself have lived in Europe, I have made only infrequent visits to the United States—though I never have stopped thinking of it as home.

"Funny you should put the question like that," she replied, "because I felt the moment I got to Poland in 1988 that I *was* home, that I was *finally* home, that I *am* home."

She explained that both her parents had been born in Poland, one in Częstochowa and one in Warsaw, so she is a first-generation American. Her father, she said, made frequent visits back to Poland before he died. "A tree cut off from its roots withers," she said, quoting an old expression. She herself had applied for and received Polish citizenship "because of blood."

"Maybe that makes a difference," I countered. I told her that for me, as a Jew, "I belong to a people who were always moving, and usually not of their own free will." I felt a very strong identity as a Jew, and a strong sense of family, I told her, but I certainly didn't feel that any physical place my ancestors had come from here in Eastern Europe was—or could be—home. The United States was home.

"I have visited the town where my grandparents came from in Romania," I told her. "My grandmother left for America with her whole family when she was a little girl, but my grandfather was the only one of his family to emigrate." It had been moving, yes, to find my great grandmother's grave in the Jewish cemetery and to visit the synagogue where my ancestors once had prayed. But it certainly hadn't felt like going home. "Each time I've visited that town," I told her, "I've thanked God that my grandfather had the sense to get out!"

Day Three

I was awakened before 6 A.M. by the sound of the wind moaning at the windows. Snow was still falling. In the purple half light before dawn it looked colder, deeper, sharply drifted; the roads were totally covered. I heard the early morning sounds of the building—the person in the next room running water, closing a door. I realized I had been dreaming vividly. My family and I were blocked somewhere—at home? By what—the weather? War? Serbs? Vampires? We were fighting some sort of monster or outer space alien, yes. Little by little survivors arrived, and we made them coffee. Some of us were at a wine exhibit (with the Haberfelds at the World's Fair?). Many were dazed and disheveled, except for an old friend of the family, an elderly woman, eighty-nine years old. . . .

I turned on my shortwave radio to catch the BBC news at six o'clock. There were graphic reports from war-torn Bosnia. Two thousand refugees had been evacuated from the besieged Muslim town of Srebrenica to Tuzla, a sixty-mile trip, described as grueling, that took all day. The refugees, women and children mainly, "wounded, sick and undernourished refugees," the report said, were packed so close into U.N. trucks that they had to stand the entire way. Some of the trucks had no tops, so they faced the full force of the weather. Some of the refugees were reported to have died en route, and many were reported by the correspondent as looking "close to death" on arrival. When the back of one truck fell open, many refugees crashed to the ground. One baby was killed. One woman was described as being "too weak to cry." The trucks had been held up for five hours at a

Serbian check point. A video cassette showing conditions in Srebrenica had been confiscated.

I was lying in bed here in Auschwitz—in *Auschwitz*—listening to
this. I couldn't bear it. I thought of a phrase I had read somewhere:
"History doesn't repeat itself, it rhymes." I turned off the radio and
drifted uneasily back to sleep, back to my dreams.

"IN THE PUBLIC IMAGINATION here in Oświęcim, there is no Jewish history of this town," local journalist Jurek Bebak told me. A wiry
twenty-six-year-old with acne scars, black-rimmed glasses, and a troubled expression, he frowned and lighted a cigarette. "If people think
of Jews here before the war, they may know some names—Haberfeld, etc.—because the buildings these people owned are still standing but are in ruins. They're eyesores; that's how they look at the situation. Only three to five percent of people living here know
anything of the local Jewish history."

In the fall of 1992, Jurek and a score or so other young people in
Oświęcim formed a local chapter of the Polish-Israeli Friendship Society, a nationwide organization with headquarters in Warsaw. The
group had eager ambitions to encourage dialogue between young
Poles in Oświęcim and young Jews from Israel and elsewhere, and to
bring the town's forgotten Jewish history to light. Jurek told me they
wanted to transform the little synagogue, the one that had been
turned into a carpet outlet, into a Jewish museum, for example, and
wanted to take part in the conservation and maintenance of the Jewish cemetery. In this, I was told, they had run up against resistance
from Mieczysław Kapała, the current custodian, who saw them as
potential competition.

"Why am I interested?" Jurek said. "Because I want to try to
change things here. I was born here, and I'm interested in everything
about the town."

His friend Mirek Ganobis, the president of the new Polish-Israeli
Friendship Society chapter, encouraged this interest based on his own
fascination with local history.

"My grandmother told me a lot about the Jews," Mirek, a tall
youth with curly blond hair, told me. "When I was a little boy, I

asked her, 'What is a Jew?' I got interested—they once lived here, and now they don't. Grandmother told me a lot about the situation. She and my grandfather were friendly with Jews in town; Grandfather worked with Jewish people at the local courthouse."

Mirek has combed local records for information on Jewish history and maintains contact with former Oświęcim Jews who survived the war and now live in Israel and the United States. He attended the Haberfeld furniture trial and took assiduous notes. He has also cultivated relations with the man described to me as the one Jew left in Oświęcim—a man in his sixties named Szymon Klueger who lives as a semirecluse in the house next to the little synagogue, which was his family home before the war.[19]

I was interested in meeting Klueger. I wanted to talk with him about how it was that he remained in Oświęcim, how it felt to be the last representative of the centuries-old Jewish community in a town so identified with the Shoah. He once, I learned, told a local newspaper that he felt it his duty to stay, to watch over the synagogue. "I think he feels that he must stay here as a last witness," Jurek remarked.

Klueger had no telephone, and I was reluctant simply to turn up at his door. An older Oświęcim man had told me that Klueger "doesn't want to speak much" and that, although he has a brother and sister in the United States who visit him frequently in Oświęcim, he refuses to take up their invitations to go to the United States. Others said that he appears on first sight to be mentally disturbed, that he doesn't like to meet people, that he acts crazy, that he refuses even to let Jewish charity workers from Cracow into his house. I had been told, too, that once one gets past the barrier, breaks down his suspicions and talks with him, he opens up as an intelligent, insightful person.

"It's a defense he puts up, I think," said Mirek. "He returned to the town after the war. Now he lives alone and doesn't work, but he won't leave. He's very attached to the town, to the place where his family lived. His brother and sister come often to visit and help him out a lot, but he won't leave."

Mirek said he himself was on good terms with Klueger but did not want to take me to see him; he was very protective of the man's privacy. It was clear, too, that he did not want to have his own relationship with Klueger jeopardized by a foreigner.

"He is very closed," Mirek said. "He doesn't want to talk. He doesn't trust people. It took me two years to establish a rapport of trust with him, and it's still very fragile."

So I stood alone by the gate to Klueger's house, set back behind a low picket fence next to the former synagogue, beneath the castle rising on its hill, around the corner from the crumbling Haberfeld mansion. I stood alone there looking up the narrow path through the snow, at the closed door, the closed windows. I debated with myself about walking up that path and knocking on the door and confronting—for it could only be a confrontation—the man who so easily fit into a set of quotation marks: "The Last Jew in Auschwitz."

I chose to walk away.

THE FORMATION OF A BRANCH of the Polish-Israeli Friendship Society in Oświęcim was part of two connected broader movements that, I found, had been growing—at least among certain circles in the town—over the past few years. These included what I had already noted as a concerted effort to use the tragic symbolism of Auschwitz as a basis for dialogue and reconciliation among religions and peoples. In addition to the Catholic Church–run interfaith center, an International Youth Center had been opened near the Auschwitz camp in 1986, sponsored by a guilt-fueled German charitable organization, *Aktion Sühnezeichen* (Action Reconciliation). Its main aim was to teach German young people about the Nazi past and foster contacts between young Germans and Poles. "Action Reconciliation was founded by the Protestant Church in the 1960s [by people who felt that] the Protestant Church in Germany had failed during the war to protect the victims of the Nazis," Jutta Renner, a young German woman who was the youth center's director, told me. "Feeling this guilt, that they failed, they searched for reconciliation with oppressed people. They started to do volunteer work with [Nazi] victims in Poland, France, Israel, and other places. And in Poland they started to send groups of young Germans to the camps to do volunteer work and to learn the history."

In addition to efforts at promoting dialogue, there was also a deliberate attempt now to pull the town of Oświęcim, its history and its cultural associations, out from under the overwhelming shadow of the Auschwitz camp, though Oświęcim Deputy Mayor Kazimierz Płonka admitted to me that it was an uphill battle.

"Before the war Oświęcim was a very small town that practically no one knew anything about," he told me in an interview at the town hall. "Unfortunately, the Nazis set up the camp here, and from that moment we became infamous worldwide. Certainly our efforts are directed toward illuminating the eight-hundred-year history of our town, but this history has not sunk in to people with whom we have contact. For all people, Oświęcim in their minds is not a town with a long history but a town with a death camp. However much we want to present ourselves as a town with a long history, the brutal truth is that it is impossible to separate it from the recent history of World War II. . . . This newly written history is much more important than the earlier, long history of our town. The influence of this latest part of our history is extremely strong, so that however much we want to change this image, it is almost impossible."

THE DESIRE TO ESCAPE THE INESCAPABLE SHADOW has created a slightly schizophrenic atmosphere. In a bookstore on the main market square, for example, I saw not one book displayed about World War II, the Nazis, or Jews, except a couple of thrillers. Bookstores in other Polish cities generally stock a selection of books on these topics. In the town hall itself, the mayor's office was devoid of any reference to the concentration camp or the town's wartime history; it was decorated with an amateurish oil painting of the market square and a few testimonial plaques. A city guidebook I was given concentrates on the general history of the town and devotes less than a fifth of its seventy-five pages—and just one of its more than a dozen illustrations—to the death camp or the World War II period.

"The town authorities are aware of the special significance of the town," Jutta Renner told me. "They can't change its name, so they have to live with the name Auschwitz. But I don't think the ordinary people have any special feeling about the camp. For most of them, living in Auschwitz isn't anything special. After all, most of them are newcomers who settled here after the war because of the chemical industry.

"Oświęcim is a quiet, normal town," she went on. "The camp is there, outside the town, and if you want books or slides, etc., about these topics you can go there and buy them. Otherwise they don't want the camp looking at you from everywhere. They want to be a normal, lively town. They show the camp to people who are interested, but they don't push it to people who are not interested."

Jurek Bebak agreed. He told me that he had recently worked for two weeks with a Japanese monk who had come to Oświęcim because he wanted to build a "peace pavilion." The town council, after much debate, gave approval to the plan, but, Jurek said, "the reaction of the people was strange. They say, we are living in the shadow of the camp, we don't need anything more. We don't want to just do things that center on the camp."

Jurek, however, said it was impossible to ignore realities, to escape the shadow, no matter how hard one might try. "When I travel somewhere, and people ask me where I'm from and I answer Oświęcim," he said, "they say, 'Oh, no—you live in a concentration camp.'"

LATE THAT NIGHT I SAT TALKING with one of the night watchmen at the interfaith center as I waited to put through a telephone call. He was an older man, rather garrulous, and looked like a retired factory worker or farmer.

"You're Jewish, aren't you?" he asked. "The American woman who works here is Jewish too, you know. She converted; she's a very devout Catholic, but she's Jewish."

Day Four

It was still snowing at daybreak, but the forecast called for sunny skies and warmer temperature by the afternoon. If all went well, I thought, I'd be able to leave the next morning. Once again, a simple thought boomeranged into the past: I found it impossible not to think of the people who fifty years ago had not been able to leave this place at all, whatever the weather.

That morning was an important one for the young people of the Polish-Israeli Friendship Society. For the first time, they were going to meet formally with a group of Israeli students, in what they felt would be a step toward breaking through the barriers of suspicion, indifference, wariness, and ingrained mistrust built up between Poles and Israelis over the decades.

It was not that Israeli young people have no experiences in Poland. Since the mid-1980s, throughout the year, but particularly in the spring, around the commemoration of *Yom HaShoah*—Holocaust Remembrance Day—in mid-April, groups of Israeli students are brought by the planeload, by the busload, to tour the Holocaust sites of Poland.[20] It is in a way a rite of passage.

Włodek Goldkorn, a Polish-born Jew in his early forties who emigrated to Israel with his family during the Polish Communists' anti-Semitic purges of 1968 and later left Israel to settle in Italy, once explained it to a mixed group of Italians and Poles this way: "The trips are organized by the Israelis with little if any participation by the Poles—not on account of the Poles but on account of the Israelis. Reporters for Israeli newspapers go along on these trips and send back articles. What is striking is the image presented of Poland. The image is that of a cemetery. The young Israelis rarely have contacts with young Poles; their trips are closed, their groups virtually sealed off because of security, too. And they do not see a living country— only a dead one, a place of martyrs."

These hermetically sealed tours, Goldkorn asserted, encourage the development of what he termed "almost a religion of the Shoah. . . . There is an attempt to make some sense out of the Shoah," he said. "That is, that six million Jews died, but their deaths led to the birth of Israel, so it can seem as if they died for a reason, that they didn't die in vain. But that isn't true; their deaths were senseless." Imbuing the horrible deaths of six million innocent people with a deeper, religious meaning is more a Christian rather than a Jewish way of thinking, he said.

Jewish theologians have debated this and related issues—the meaning of the Holocaust, the role of God in the Holocaust, the theological relationship between the Holocaust and the birth of Israel, and so on—ever since the war. Rabbis, scholars, and ordinary Jews spoke and wrote of such concerns even while the Holocaust was raging. In a discussion in 1990 of the wide range of Jewish theological response and thought after the Holocaust, Geoffrey Wigoder, a scholar at

Jerusalem's Hebrew University and editor-in-chief of the *Encyclopaedia Judaica,* touched on the various forms of linkage many people see between the Holocaust and the birth of Israel.

"A historical connection is obvious, but a theological link becomes problematical if based on *post hoc ergo propter hoc* [something happens after something else, therefore it happens because of that something else]," he said. "The obvious question is: Did God need the suffering and death of the six million in order to re-establish Jewish sovereignty in its land? I have read Christian theologians who have, with all due reservations, cited the sequence of Crucifixion and Resurrection as a parallel to recent Jewish history, and while Jewish thinkers do not, of course, use such a comparison, some have seen in the chain of events a divine mystery which brings to mind some Christian thought."[21]

He quoted philosopher and theologian Emil Fackenheim, who has written much on the meaning of the Holocaust, as believing that "it is sacrilegious to seek direct cause and effect in a theological context between the Holocaust and the State of Israel. But while it is impossible to find meaning in the Holocaust, it does demand a response—and Israel is that response. Or, in other words, the cataclysm of the Holocaust has become inseparably bound with the epiphany of Israel."[22]

A few days before I became snowbound in Auschwitz, in another part of Poland, I met an Israeli man in his fifties. He was troubled, confused. He, the son of Polish Jews who had moved to Israel after the war, was visiting Poland for the first time and was somewhat amazed that the image of a grim, hostile country he had grown up with was not correct; that he had met friendly people, that he was actually enjoying himself. "I know I am going to have a lot to talk over with my parents when I go back," he told me. He criticized what he called the "martyrology" tours—going so far as to say that they were part of a "brainwashing" process. "The Israeli tours take young people to see Holocaust sites and that's it," he said. "One such tour operator was even quoted as advising that the groups should be taken on the tours in October, November, and February, as the somber, gray weather in Poland during those months creates a 'better' atmosphere, that is, more depressing. These young people do not see anything of the real Poland." Włodek Goldkorn had compared this type of trip to pilgrimages of religious Christians who tour the Holy Land and see it only in terms of the life and death of Jesus.

Even during the height of the snowstorm I saw at least one or two Israeli groups a day touring Auschwitz. Many of the young people carried small, plastic, blue and white Israeli flags. Some wrapped themselves in big flags like cloaks; one boy had stuck two small flags in his hat, like feathers. They were Israelis and proud of it; the blue Stars of David on the flags were a vividly defiant antithesis to the yellow Stars of David worn by Jews in countless ghettos, and of the Stars of David sewn on the uniforms of Jewish prisoners in the Nazi camps. It was thrilling, somehow, to see them; it did indeed seem like life rising from the ashes. I was therefore all the more shocked when I came across an Israeli boy urinating in the snow outside one of the wooden barracks at Birkenau.

In 1988, a biennial international martyrology tour, the March of the Living, was initiated, gathering young Jews from around the world to experience Holocaust sites firsthand. The 1992 march, during the last week of April, brought five thousand Jews of high school and college age to Poland. They arrived on 150 flights from forty-two different countries and included eighteen hundred North Americans, four hundred and fifty South Africans, one thousand Israelis, and seven hundred foreign students studying in Israel. Convoys of buses, closely guarded by Israeli security men and Polish police, took participants to the death camps at Treblinka and Majdanek and to the historic Jewish cemetery in Warsaw, most of whose sprawling expanse is neglected and overgrown with weeds and shrubs. All five thousand participants were taken to Oświęcim; here, en masse, they walked the two miles from the Auschwitz I camp to Birkenau, where they held a memorial service. After touring the death camps, the group then flew to Israel, to celebrate Israeli Independence Day. The point was clear: from the death camps and cemeteries of Poland to the vibrancy and life of Israel.

The young people who participated in the March of the Living had an emotional, deeply moving experience that will remain with them for the rest of their lives. One young Englishwoman who took part, however, felt very uncomfortable. "It was Zionist propaganda to show the Poles that young Jews are alive," she told me. Local people in Oświęcim—at least those who are hopeful of furthering contacts and dialogue between Poles and Jews—also told me that they were disappointed, possibly a little resentful, too, that the young Jews on that trip and others remained so segregated in tragic memory.

"It was very hard to meet any of the young Jews who took part in the March of the Living," Marek Głownia, the director of the interfaith center, told me. "The police kept them separate. People were told that they needed permission from the police to meet them."

He told me that in general people on Jewish tours to Auschwitz had little desire to meet with Poles. Jutta Renner, at the International Youth Center, also said that she felt the lack of Jewish participation in meetings between various groups of young people at her center.

"Up to now, cooperation with Jewish groups in this center has been missing," she said. "It's been difficult. For two years we have been trying to develop a program involving Jewish, German, Israeli, and Polish young people."

She said the Polish-Israeli Friendship Society also had negative reactions to attempts to arrange formal meetings and sessions with Israeli youngsters in Oświęcim. "They came up against a lot of skepticism," she said. In short, she said, "they were told that it was not a good idea to have youth meetings in this place because of the connotations. Anywhere else in Poland, but not here."

Therefore Mirek, Jurek, and their earnest young friends in the society were excited that a group of 180 Israeli students had agreed to meet with them.

The first session took place in the morning, in the cinema of the Auschwitz museum, before the young Israelis began their tour of the death camp. It was a formal encounter, little more than an exchange of greetings. A young Pole and a young Israeli each gave a speech expressing the hope for dialogue, understanding, and friendship. Israeli security men attached to the group guarded the doors, murmuring into their walkie-talkies. I couldn't help comparing the Israelis with the Poles. The Israelis were all robust, healthy-looking, extremely attractive young people; their skin was clear, their hair was shiny, and they dressed in fashionable clothes. They exuded self-confidence and a teenage arrogance that comes of well-being. I felt a little sorry for the Poles; they looked like poor relations at a party, earnest and very sincere, a little unsure of themselves. They were good-looking young men, but they did not glow the way the Israelis did, nor did they radiate the same robust, earthy healthiness.

Late that afternoon, after the Israelis had toured both Auschwitz and Birkenau, they came in three busloads to the interfaith center for a longer, less formal question-and-answer session with the Poles. There were so many people that the meeting had to take place in two shifts.

Some of the Israeli students—and some of their teachers—were openly hostile and seemed predisposed to discount or even despise the Poles and everything Polish.

"I didn't know what to reply when they asked what was the use of having Polish-Israeli contacts," Jurek said. After all, he said, he was well aware that there was still anti-Semitism in Poland, even in Oświęcim. There were small groups of skinheads here, as elsewhere in the country; anti-Jewish slogans, he was ashamed to admit, had even been scrawled on buildings at the Auschwitz camp. And I recalled what had happened once here to a friend of a friend, a Polish-Jewish survivor of Auschwitz making his first trip back along with several other survivors. At the very gate of Birkenau, he had overheard a group of Poles making derisive anti-Semitic comments about him and his companions, thinking they would not be able to understand what they said.

Out in the hall, surrounded by the exhibit of old photographs of Oświęcim, Jurek and I became involved in an animated conversation with a twenty-two-year-old Israeli girl whose father was a Holocaust survivor from Poland.

"How can you speak of the future and talk about the past?" she asked, referring to discussions of the centuries-old Jewish history of Oświęcim and all Poland. "For us, history here is dead, finished. Israel has wonderful artists—why do you talk about the past and not the future?"

I replied that I thought it was essential to study history and then to learn from that history. As we spoke, I gradually realized that we were speaking different languages; "history," "Auschwitz," maybe even "Jew" meant different things or were interpreted from very different perspectives. I realized, too, that I had never discussed anything like this with a young, native-born Israeli. She was bright, attractive, and—as she put it herself—politically to the left. But it became clear that, whereas former Israeli Prime Minister Yitzak Shamir had once declared that Poles take in anti-Semitism with their mothers' milk, this Israeli girl, despite herself, had taken in anti-Polish feeling in much the same way.

"I can't blame these young Poles here for what their father or grandfather might have done," she said, clearly implying that it was a given that whatever they had done had been bad. "My father is sixty, and he is still afraid of Doberman pinschers because his Polish neighbors set such dogs on him. . . . This guy Jurek here is nice and all that—but he and the others are talking about youth exchanges; how could I invite a Pole to visit our home?"

She admitted that her image of Poland had been very negative before she came on the trip and that she was very surprised to find that Poles are normal people. "They have McDonald's and everything," she said. "We were expecting a gray expanse."

I was taken aback by her rejection of any history before World War II; I realized then that for her, history—what she understood as history—literally began with the Holocaust. The thousand-year saga of Jewish presence in Poland and elsewhere in East-Central Europe; the rival nationalisms and economic competition that had contributed to international conflict and also to the rise of anti-Semitism; the events leading up to World War I, World War II, and the Holocaust—none of this was important, none of it had any meaning for her, except as a prelude to the Shoah. None of the millions of Jews who had lived through hundreds of years in this part of the world meant anything, except as the ancestors of descendants who were killed by the Nazis. She seemed unaware of any historical events aside from the existence of anti-Semitism and the Holocaust, just as she seemed scarcely aware that anyone but Jews had died or suffered in World War II. When I mentioned nationalism and broader underlying conflicts, she responded, "Oh, yes," but then went on simply to put everything in terms of who had also been put into ghettos and camps, rather than broader implications. "Oh yes, gays and Gypsies were killed in the camps, too."

I realized that I was shocked by the conversation. It shook me. Most of my research work and writing over the past few years had dealt with Eastern and Central European Jewish history—not the Holocaust but what had come before the Holocaust, what the Holocaust had erased. I was well aware that when people today think of Jews and this part of the world, they think primarily in terms of their destruction. They think in time-scale terms of less than a decade. I had grown to feel that there was an urgent need to broaden the awareness of Jewish history. The millions killed in the Holocaust must never be forgotten—but neither should the Jewish civilization that was here before. Jewish experience in Eastern and Central Europe, I felt very strongly, must not solely be defined or remembered in terms of death. To do so, I had come to believe, paid a disservice to—even denigrated—the millions of Jews who had *lived* here over many centuries, who despite anti-Semitism, despite pogroms, despite poverty, despite plagues, despite waves of persecution, had created a rich culture; had kept the faith, or variations thereof; had produced lofty achievements in scholarship, fine arts, music, literature, and commerce; had lived the humble lives of ordinary people.

My talk with the Israeli girl intensified this feeling. I was concerned, too, that deliberate lack of knowledge or awareness or interest in the historical dynamics that had led to the Holocaust could be dangerous in today's world. All one had to do was listen to the radio news to hear the echoes of past history making themselves known in the Balkans, in the former Soviet Union, even in Germany. History is a continuum; *it rhymes*.

She was a very intelligent young woman, nonetheless, and I like to think that the conversation we three had—and she was just about the only one of the 180 Israeli students to make a point of having a one-on-one discussion with one of the young Poles—gave her cause for reflection. Indeed, it was she, a little embarrassed, who brought up the question of Israeli treatment of Palestinians; the sealing off of the occupied territories, the deportations, the violence, the razing of houses, the reprisals, the moral ambiguity. "I can admit this, that I question it, that I don't like it," she said, "but I'm politically quite on the left. People on the right won't admit to questions about anything."

"Read history," I again advised her, and left her to exchange addresses with Jurek.

Mirek was pleased and excited about the meetings. There had been questions, arguments, interaction. "It's a step, a little step," he said. "Very delicate. But it's an opening. We now have established contact."

A NEW GUEST WAS CHECKING IN when I went down to dinner. He looked about the same age as the young Poles and Israelis, but he looked—I have to say it—Aryan. He could almost have been a poster boy for the Hitler Youth: tall, blond, blue-eyed, short-haired, well scrubbed. Clean. He was American. As I had been asked, the Polish-Catholic, once Jewish-American, woman at the reception desk asked him if he ate everything. "Well, as long as it's kosher," he said.

He was, in fact, Jewish.

Jewish, sort of, he said. "My mother is Jewish, but my father isn't. He went along with raising the family Jewish, though; and my mother kept a kosher home. I'm not at all religious, but I have real difficulty eating nonkosher food: pork; dairy products together with meat. It's not that I have anything against it, but I simply can't eat it; there's a block; my friends can't understand at all."

We three Americans sat over dinner together, the only people in the immense dining hall. The student, Steve, toyed with his spaghetti—he'd found some bits of ham in it. "Here I am at Auschwitz. . . . I can imagine all my ancestors rolling in their graves," he said. He was studying in Scotland and was on vacation, touring the continent. He had made a point of taking the train all the way to Białystok, in eastern Poland, the city his grandparents had come from, just to see it.

I decided it was the moment to ask the woman if it was true that she was originally Jewish, "from a Jewish family," I put it. I didn't like putting her on the spot if it was something she didn't want to discuss. After all, in our conversations over the past few days there had been ample openings for her to bring up the topic herself. I kept thinking of how we had discussed national identity and the sense of home and how I had contrasted my feelings as a Jew with hers as a Pole.

"Yes," she replied. "But I knew I wanted to become a Catholic from the time I was four years old. My parents gave me their permission to do so when I was seventeen."

From the way she described her family, it sounded as if they had been highly assimilated, possibly among that small minority of Polish Jews who considered themselves "Poles of the Mosaic persuasion." "My father always said he was of Polish nationality but Jewish religion," she said.

And as for her own conversion to Catholicism, "I don't feel that Catholicism and Judaism are mutually exclusive," she said. "I'm

Catholic, but I'm still a daughter of Abraham. Just because I accept the New Testament doesn't mean I reject the Old."

Being a Jew or coming from a Jewish background can still be very uncomfortable for a Pole. The attitudes of many Poles are still, as they were before World War II, similar to those of many white people toward blacks. Jews, as Aleksander Hertz described it, formed a caste that was generally looked down upon, and very hard to escape.[23] Not long before I was in Oświęcim I met a Polish man aged about sixty who had recently discovered that one of his grandparents had been Jewish; the discovery threw him into a crisis not only of identity but of shame and anxiety. Mindful of Polish attitudes historically toward converts and assimilated Jews, mindful of the anti-Semitism that still exists in the country, the stereotypes, the superstitions, I wondered

OŚWIĘCIM: Leaving town. The slash through the name of the town on the sign indicates the town limits.

about how this Polish-Jewish-Catholic-American woman fared here; about identity and *perceived* identity, about whether she, despite being a devout Catholic and working for a Church-run organization, still encountered anti-Semitism.

And she admitted that, yes, she did have, as she put it, "trouble with some Poles who won't accept me as Polish." The worst examples of anti-Semitism, she said, she found among doctors.

WE SAT THERE AT DINNER, in the interfaith center a few hundred yards from the *Arbeit Macht Frei* gate leading into Auschwitz. Myself, an American Jew who was not religious but who had never doubted nor felt uncomfortable with my Jewish identity. Steve, the "Aryan," Jewish under Jewish law because his mother was Jewish, ambivalent about his Jewish identity, but still unable to shake the dietary laws he had been brought up to observe. The woman from the center, a devoutly Catholic convert but still unable to relinquish—or be released from—identification as a Jew.

We were so very different in attitudes, experiences, and self-awareness, so very similar in our East European Jewish origins. Fifty years ago none of it would have mattered; we would all three have been on the other side of the gate.

The roads were clear the next morning, and I left.

Notes

INTRODUCTION

1. Jerome Rothenberg, *Khurbn and Other Poems*. New York: New Directions, 1989, p. 38.

CHAPTER 1: *A Circle Game*

1. This photo was not visible when I visited Prague in October 1993.
2. Historical evidence indicates that the massacre took place not in the Altneu Synagogue but in the Old Synagogue nearby, which was torn down in 1867.
3. I. L. Peretz, "The Golem," in Eliezer Greenberg and Irving Howe, eds., *A Treasury of Yiddish Stories*. New York: Schocken, 1973, p. 246.
4. Ctibor Rybár, *Jewish Prague, Guide to the Monuments*. Prague: TV Spektrum, 1991, p. 219.
5. See Vladimír Sadek, "Stories of the Golem and Their Relation to the World of Rabbi Löw," *Judaica Bohemiae* XXIII/2, Prague, 1987.
6. Ibid., p. 90.
7. For a recent imaginative retelling of the golem tale, see Marge Piercy, *He, She and It*. New York: Fawcett Crest, 1991.
8. Rothenberg, op. cit., p. 43.
"The poem was written in 1982 or maybe in early '83 in the aftermath of a trip to Europe the previous fall & early winter," Rothenberg told me years later in a letter. "I found Prague very spooky & the several artists we met in varying stages of despair. . . . There was from the start a sense that I had—in no way uniquely—that this was Kafka's city and

Rabbi Loew's; & the expressionistic grimness (& beauty) of the old town tended in a hokey sort of way to reenforce it."

Rothenberg told me that he had long kept a postcard of the Old Jewish Cemetery, sent by a friend, on his desk as inspiration. "So that was in my mind, too, along with all the golem stories I had ever come across . . . which was almost too inevitably something I would have had in mind on my first trip to Prague."

The image of a goddess had been running through his head, too, "along with a Kali-like (graveyard goddess) image that seemed in line with premonitions of holocaust horrors, etc., rather than anything more satisfying," he said. "Anyway, all of that came together in Prague & with it, in a silly sort of way, a temptation to sit in what was described as Rabbi Loew's throne, which I did & then went out & visited the graves."

9. See Israel Abrahams, *Jewish Life in the Middle Ages*. New York: Atheneum, 1981, p. 248.

10. Six months after Adam's visit, new rules regulating entrance to the cemetery and limiting tourists to certain paths were instituted.

11. The Pinkas Synagogue became less of a respite after the new entry regulations for the Old Jewish Cemetery, instituted in 1993, channeled tourists through the synagogue.

12. In October 1993, I found a new sign in the synagogue, which read: "Following the Six Day War in 1967, all relations between Czechoslovakia and Israel were broken off, and the synagogue was closed by Communist officials. Sometime after 1975, the walls were replastered and the names were covered over, allegedly in the process of 'restoration.' When the building was finally reopened in 1989 [sic], repairs began in earnest." This is somewhat misleading as it implies that restoration was not needed.

13. Quoted in Jan Herben, "Thomas G. Masaryk: Jews and Anti-Semitism," in *T. G. Masaryk and the Jews,* a collection of essays translated by Benjamin R. Epstein. New York: B. Pollak, 1945, p. 3.

14. Ernst Pawel, *The Nightmare of Reason: A Life of Franz Kafka*. London: Collins Harville, 1984, p. 12.

15. Franz Kafka, "Letter to His Father," in *Wedding Preparations in the Country and Other Stories*. London: Penguin, 1978, pp. 56–58.

16. Quoted in Pawel, op. cit., p. 90.

17. Not long after we spoke, Kulstadt took up a post as an aide to President Havel.

18. A year or so after this conversation, I indeed found less Kafka kitsch apparent in Prague.

19. Jiří Fiedler, *Jewish Sights of Bohemia and Moravia*. Prague: Sefer, 1991.

20. His tomb was restored as part of commemorations, in May 1993, marking the two hundredth anniversary of his death.
21. William O. McCagg, Jr., *A History of the Habsburg Jews: 1670–1918*. Bloomington: Indiana University Press, pp. 75, 76, 78.
22. As quoted by Hillel J. Kieval in *Where Cultures Meet, The Story of the Jews of Czechoslovakia*, Natalia Berger, ed. Tel Aviv: Beth Hatefutsoth, 1990, p. 46.
23. Rybár, op. cit.

CHAPTER 2: *Wine Merchants and Wonder Rabbis*

1. Traditional; from Jerome Rothenberg and Harris Lenowitz, eds., *Exiled in the World*. Port Townsend, WA: Copper Canyon Press, 1989.
2. Some commentators think the spilling of wine when the plagues are enumerated may have originated as a superstitious safeguard against evil when mentioning such calamities.
3. As quoted in "Wine and Liquor Trade," *Encyclopaedia Judaica*, Vol. 16, p. 542. Jerusalem: Keter, 1972.
4. This practice continued until the Holocaust. Marika Rapcsak, a Hungarian Jewish woman living in Szeged (southern Hungary), told me that her father, who kept a tavern in the northern town of Salgótarján before the war, used to purchase entire vineyard productions the same way. "It was the same with plums, for making plum brandy," she said.
5. Solomon Maimon, *An Autobiography*, Moses Hadas, ed./trans. New York: Schocken, 1947, pp. 51–52.
6. Meir Sas, *Vanished Communities in Hungary: The History and Tragic Fate of the Jews in Újhely and Zemplén County*. Toronto: Memorial Book Committee, 1986, pp. 26–27.
7. Salo W. Baron, *A Social and Religious History of the Jews*, Vol. XVI. Philadelphia: Jewish Publication Society, 1976, p. 233.
8. Ber of Bolechów, *The Memoirs of Ber of Bolechów*, M. Vishnitzer, ed. New York: Arno Press, 1973, pp. 68–69.
9. Sas, op. cit.
10. Ber of Bolechów, op. cit., p. 129.
11. Ibid., pp. 129–130.
12. Translation by Rabbi Tzvi Rabinowicz, in *Chassidic Rebbes from the Baal Shem Tov to Modern Times*. Southfield, Mich.: Targum/Feldheim, 1989, pp. 123–124.
13. Martin Buber, *Tales of the Hasidim: The Early Masters*. New York: Schocken, 1947, 1975 (renewed), pp. 52–53.

14. Maimon, op. cit., pp. 54–55.
15. Epitaph translation from an unpublished study of the cemetery by a group of Israeli students, provided to me by Lajos Lőwy.
16. Ibid.
17. Elie Wiesel, *Night*. London: Penguin, 1981, p. 18.
18. Martin Buber, *Tales of the Hasidim: The Later Masters*. New York: Schocken, 1947/1975, pp. 191–192.
19. Sas, op. cit., p. 76.
20. Iakovos Kampanellis, "Song of Songs," from Nicholas De Lange, *Atlas of the Jewish World*. Oxford: Phaidon, 1984, p. 71.
21. Sas, op. cit., pp. 83, 153.
22. Ber of Bolechów, op. cit., p. 138.
23. From interviews shortly before Gertrude's death in 1992, recorded by her daughter, Susan Birnbaum, who has kindly allowed me to quote them.
24. Klánský has detailed his early memories and also the hardships and adventures he underwent in surviving the Holocaust in an autobiography, *Přežil Jsem Hitlera* (*I Survived Hitler*), published in Prague by Svícen in 1992 on the fiftieth anniversary of the deportation of Jews from Slovakia.
25. Buber, *Tales of the Hasidim, The Later Masters*, p. 127.

CHAPTER 3: *Synagogues Seeking Heaven*

1. Carol Herselle Krinsky, *Synagogues of Europe*. New York: The Architectural History Foundation, 1985, p. 181.
2. Ibid., p. 89.
3. Israel Cohen, *Travels in Jewry*. New York: Dutton, 1953, pp. 175–178.
4. Krinsky, op. cit., p. 181.
5. Anikó Gazda, ed., *Magyarországi Zsinagógák*. Budapest: Műszaki Könyvkiadó, 1989. It is the book in which I first saw pictures of the synagogue in Mád (see Chap. 2).
6. My translation of an entry in the *Guida d'Europa—Cecoslovacchia*. Milan: Touring Club Italiano, 1991, p. 94.
7. Krinsky, op. cit., p. 428.
8. When I visited Liptovský Mikuláš two years earlier, I had no idea that Baumhorn had had anything to do with the synagogue there, a neoclassical building that, when I saw it, was in an abandoned, partially ruined state awaiting funds for restoration. When I revisited it in June 1993, I found that the restoration was well under way. At that time, I was able

to note "typical" Baumhorn features incorporated into the exterior—his trademark arched windows, for example. Also, I was able to look inside and see the extremely elaborate interior decoration, which bore all the hallmarks of Baumhorn's eclectic style.

9. János Gerle, Attila Kovács, and Imre Makovecz, *A Századfordulo Magyar Építészete*. Budapest: Szépirodalmi Könyvkiadó, 1990.

10. According to Gerle, Baumhorn maintained his office on the ground floor and lived in an apartment on the second and third floors. At some point, he sold the building and moved to an apartment on the fourth floor after losing money in a bad business deal involving one of his former co-workers, Károly Kovács. Kovács apparently induced Baumhorn to participate in a construction business that failed, and he also forged Baumhorn's name on bills.

CHAPTER 4: *What's to Be Done?*

1. Henryk Halkowski, "Cracow—City and Mother of Israel." In *Cracow: Dialogue of Traditions*. Cracow: ZNAK, 1991.

2. Marvin Lowenthal, *A World Passed By*. New York: Behrman's Jewish Book House, 1938, p. 363.

3. Grace Humphrey, *Poland the Unexplored*. Indianapolis: Bobbs-Merrill, 1931, pp. 273–274.

4. Rafael Scharf, "Cracow—Blessed Its Memory." In Stanisław Markowski, *Krakowski Kazimierz; Dzielnica żydowska 1870–1988*. Cracow: Arka, 1992, p. 15.

5. Christopher Wellisz, "The Perils of Restitution." In *Report on Eastern Europe*. Radio Free Europe/Radio Liberty Research Institute, vol. 2, no. 32, August 9, 1991, p. 1. The article provides a detailed discussion of the problem. For a discussion of specifically Jewish aspects of this issue, see *Jewish Restitution and Compensation Claims in Eastern Europe and the Former USSR*, Research Report. London: Institute of Jewish Affairs, 1993.

6. See Aviva Kempner, "Jewish Woodstock in Cracow." In *Washington Jewish Week*, July 16, 1992.

7. One of the Venice synagogues was restored by the World Monuments Fund.

8. Lowenthal, op. cit., p. 361.

9. Traditionally, the most honored men of the community had their own seats along the eastern wall of the synagogue, flanking the Ark.

10. Israel Cohen, *Travels in Jewry*. New York: Dutton, 1953, p. 55.

11. Isaac Grynbaum, "Osias Thon: Statesman of Polish Jews." In Lucy S. Dawidowicz, ed., *The Golden Tradition*. New York: Schocken, 1967, p. 484.

12. Later, Levine was instrumental in organizing a concert at the Vatican, in the presence of Pope John Paul II, to commemorate Jewish Holocaust victims on Holocaust Remembrance Day, in April 1994.

13. My translation of a Polish translation of the poem by Jerry Ficowski in Markowski, op. cit., p. 90.

14. In a speech at the Joint Distribution Committee Board's semiannual meeting in New York, May 12, 1993.

15. From "SWOT Analysis of Kazimierz Area," kindly provided by the International Culture Center, Cracow.

16. English translation taken from Monika Krajewska, *A Tribe of Stones*. Warsaw: Polish Scientific Publishers, 1993, p. 16.

17. Adapted from the translation in Krajewska, op. cit.

18. Lowenthal, op. cit., p. 359.

CHAPTER 5: *Snowbound in Auschwitz*

1. As quoted in Jack Kugelmass and Jonathan Boyarin, eds., *From a Ruined Garden*. New York: Schocken, 1983, p. 19.

2. The nuns began moving out of the contested convent about two months after my visit.

3. Philip Ward, *Polish Cities: Travels in Cracow and the South, Gdańsk, Malbork, and Warsaw*. Gretna, LA: Pelican Publishing Company, 1989.

4. Jewish Telegraphic Agency, April 7, 1943.

5. A new guidebook to Poland issued by Italy's Touring Club Italiano (Milan) in 1992 does not mention the word "Jew" in its entry on Auschwitz.

6. From the Afterword to Primo Levi, *If This Is a Man*. London: Abacus Books, 1987.

7. As quoted in Celia Heller, *On the Edge of Destruction: Jews of Poland Between the Two Wars*. New York: Schocken, 1977, p. 113.

8. Konstanty Gebert, "Anti-Semitism in the 1990 Polish Presidential Election," *Social Research*, Vol. 58, no. 4 (Winter 1991); and elsewhere.

9. Ibid., p. 741.

10. Neal Ascherson, *The Struggles for Poland*. London: Pan, 1987.

11. Jan Karski, *Story of a Secret State*. Boston: Houghton Mifflin, 1944, p. 8.

12. Israel Cohen, *Travels in Jewry*. New York: Dutton, 1953, pp. 78–79.

13. Jacob Apenszlak, ed., *The Black Book of Polish Jewry*. The American Federation for Polish Jews, 1943, pp. 86–87.
14. Isaiah Trunk, ed., *Jewish Responses to Nazi Persecution*. New York: Stein and Day, 1979, pp. 174–176.
15. Karski, op. cit., pp. 2–6.
16. It has been estimated that as many as three million Germans fled from former German territories incorporated into Poland after the war and that another three million were forced from their homes. See Ascherson, op. cit., p. 134. See also Paul Robert Magocsi, *Historical Atlas of East Central Europe*. Seattle and London: University of Washington Press, 1993, pp. 164–168.
17. Raphael Mahler, "The Economic Background of Jewish Emigration from Galicia to the United States." In Deborah Dash Moore, ed., *East European Jews in Two Worlds*. Evanston, IL: Northwestern University Press/YIVO, 1989, p. 128.
18. I am indebted to Drusilla Menaker for sharing with me her AP reports and comments on this affair, which I have used as source material.
19. One or two women of Jewish ancestry were still in the town, I was told, but were from families converted to Catholicism.
20. For a detailed discussion of this issue, see the chapter "What Does It Do to Me?" in Tom Segev, *The Seventh Million*. New York: Hill and Wang, 1993.
21. Geoffrey Wigoder, "Jewish Thought After the Holocaust," a paper presented at a Jewish-Catholic meeting on interreligious dialogue in Prague, September 1990.
22. Ibid.
23. See Aleksander Hertz, *The Jews in Polish Culture*. Evanston, IL: Northwestern University Press, 1961/1988.

Glossary

Aron ha Kodesh (Ark) The often highly decorated niche or cabinet at the eastern wall of the synagogue where the scrolls of the Torah are kept.

Ashkenazic Jews and their traditions originating in Germany and Eastern, Central, and Western Europe; from *Ashkenaz,* the medieval Hebrew name for Germany.

bar mitzvah The ceremony that marks the initiation of a thirteen-year-old boy into the adult world of the Jewish community.

Bet ha Midrash Study house; a small room or separate building where adult men gather to study the Torah and other sacred texts and commentaries.

Bet Hayyim Literally, in Hebrew, "House of the Living"; a Jewish cemetery.

bimah The platform from which the Torah is read during services in a synagogue.

blood libel The slanderous accusation, often used as a pretext for pogroms or other anti-Jewish persecution, that Jews kidnapped and killed Christians, particularly Christian children, in order to drain their blood for use in the preparation of Passover matzo or other ritual.

ceremonial hall Also *mortuary* or *preburial hall.* The building at the cemetery where the dead are prepared for burial and funeral services are held.

challah Braided egg bread used for Sabbath dinner and other festive occasions.

cheder A religious school for children.

ghetto An enclosed area for Jews, separated from the rest of a town or city. Starting in the Middle Ages, in much of Europe Jews were required to live in such separate streets or neighborhoods, which were often locked at night. The word comes from the Venetian dialect for "foundry," because the

Jewish section in Venice was located near a foundry. The Nazis also set up Jewish ghettos in many towns and cities.

golem   In Jewish folklore, an artificial being without a soul, made of clay and brought to life by a magic word or amulet. Several famous rabbis, including Rabbi Löw of Prague, are associated with the golem legend.

Hasidism   A Jewish religious revival movement that was originated in the Ukraine in the eighteenth century by the legendary Ba'al Shem Tov and spread rapidly throughout Eastern Europe. Based on joy, mysticism, and love of God, it was a reaction to rabbinical Judaism, which stressed dry scholarship. Hasidic worship involves much singing and dancing and centers on influential rabbis who are believed to work wonders.

judenrein   In German, "clean of Jews." The term was used by the Nazis to indicate a place where all Jews had been killed or deported.

Kabbalah   Jewish mysticism and mystic tradition.

Kiddush   The blessing over wine; also, the wine and refreshments served following Sabbath services.

kosher   Ritually clean; usually refers to food prepared according to Jewish dietary laws.

kvittel   A small slip of paper left at the tomb of a great rabbi or sage on which a prayer or supplication is written.

Lubavitcher   A follower of the Lubavitch or Chabad movement of Hasidism, which stresses study and intellectualism as well as spiritual fulfillment. Lubavitch rebbe Menachem Mendel Schneerson, who became Chabad leader in 1950, encouraged his followers to reach out to the Jewish world in general to bring Jews back to Orthodoxy. Chabad outreach programs became highly organized and widespread.

matzo   Unleavened bread eaten during the Passover holiday.

mazzevah   Tombstone in the form of an upright slab, one of whose faces is generally decorated with an epitaph and ornamentation.

memory book   Books or pamphlets of histories and recollections of Jewish communities that were destroyed in the Holocaust, put together after the Holocaust by Jews from those towns.

menorah   The seven-branched candelabrum used in the Temple in Jerusalem, which became one of the most important Jewish symbols. Also, the eight-branched candelabrum, with one single ninth candle, used on the festival of Hanukkah.

mezuzah   Literally, "doorpost." The small case containing prayers written on parchment, which Jews affix to the right-hand doorposts of their homes.

mikvah   Ritual bath.

minyan   The quorum of ten adult Jewish men required for a communal Jewish service.

mohel   The man qualified to perform a circumcision according to Jewish ritual.

Moorish   Flamboyant architectural and decorative style popular with synagogue designers in the late nineteenth and early twentieth centuries, incorporating Islamic and Middle Eastern elements such as horseshoe arches, fancy domes, spires resembling minarets, and complicated arabesques.

Neolog   Hungarian Reform Judaism.

ohel   Literally, in Hebrew, "tent." A little building or protective structure erected around the tomb of a revered sage or, particularly, a Hasidic rebbe.

Orthodoxy   Strictly traditional Jewish observance.

Passover (or Pesach)   an eight-day festival in springtime commemorating the Jews' exodus from Egypt. A ceremonial dinner, the seder, which follows a strict ritual order set forth in books called *Haggadahs,* is eaten on the first two evenings of the festival; matzo, or unleavened bread, is eaten during the entire eight days; and no other leavened products are eaten during that time.

rabbi   Traditionally, a teacher or sage who completed studies at a yeshiva. Today, the ordained religious leader of a Jewish congregation.

rebbe   A Hasidic rabbi, often at the head of a devoted court of followers and disciples. Rebbes are often believed to be direct intermediaries with God and to be able to work miracles.

Reform Judaism   Judaism modified and modernized to fit the conditions of contemporary life. It grew out of the enlightenment movement of the late eighteenth and early nineteenth centuries. Innovations included the adaptation of clothing to modern styles, the use of local languages in services and for sermons, and the use of an organ and choir in the synagogue.

Sephardic   Jews tracing their ancestry and traditions to Spain or Portugal; derived from *Sepharad,* the Hebrew word for Spain.

Shabbat (or Shabbos)   The Sabbath, beginning Friday at sundown and lasting until sundown on Saturday. A day of prayer, rest, and contemplation.

shammas   Sexton or beadle at a synagogue.

Shema   The prayer beginning with the verse "Hear, O Israel, the Lord thy God, the Lord is One," which states the key belief of Jews in one God, and also sets out other commandments.

Shoah   In Hebrew, "catastrophe"; the Holocaust.

shochet A person qualified to slaughter animals according to Jewish ritual.

shofar The ram's-horn trumpet blown in a ritual fashion on Rosh Hashanah and Yom Kippur.

shtetl "Little town" in Yiddish; an East European Jewish small-town community.

shul Synagogue.

Shulchan Aruch The codification of Jewish law and practice, elaborated in the sixteenth century by the Sephardic Rabbi Joseph Caro and adapted for Ashkenazic use by Rabbi Moses Isserles Remuh of Cracow, which became the guide to Orthodox Jewish life.

synagogue A Jewish house of prayer and meeting.

tallis The fringed shawl, white with blue or black stripes, worn by men while praying.

Talmud Two great collections of Hebrew and Aramaic writings encompassing commentaries, debates, discussions, and explanations by numerous sages, scholars, and rabbis on the entire sphere of Jewish teaching.

tefillin Phylacteries; two small leather boxes with prayers inside that men strap to their foreheads and left arms during morning prayers.

Torah Literally, "law." The handwritten parchment scroll containing the Pentateuch, or the first five books of Moses, which is read in the synagogue and kept in the Aron ha Kodesh. Torah can also mean the entire corpus of traditional Jewish scriptures and teaching.

tzaddik An extremely pious, just man, revered for his saintliness and wisdom and believed to have a special relationship with God; often refers to a Hasidic rebbe or leader.

yarmulke (or **kippah)** Skullcap.

yeshiva An advanced Jewish religious school, particularly devoted to the study of the Talmud.

Yiddish The language, derived from German and written in Hebrew characters, traditionally spoken by Ashkenazic Jews.

Yiddishkeit The world of Jewish (particularly Ashkenazic) tradition.

Zionism The movement that developed in the nineteenth century advocating Jewish return to the Holy Land. The father of political Zionism and founder of the World Zionist Organization was Theodore Herzl, who put forth his ideas in the book *The Jewish State* in 1895–1896.

Selected Bibliography

ᘿᕲᕗ

Abrahams, Israel, *Jewish Life in the Middle Ages*. New York, Atheneum, 1981.

Aleichem, Sholom, *From the Fair*. New York, Penguin Books, 1985–1986.

Apenszlak, Jacob (ed.), *Black Book of Polish Jewry*. The American Federation for Polish Jews, 1943.

Ascherson, Neal, *The Struggles for Poland*. London, Pan, 1987.

Baran, Zbigniew (ed.), *Cracow: Dialogue of Traditions*. Cracow, ZNAK, 1991.

Baron, Salo W., *A Social and Religious History of the Jews*. New York, Columbia University Press/Jewish Publication Society of America, 1976.

Ber of Bolechow, *The Memoirs of Ber of Bolechow* (M. Vishnitzer, ed.). New York, Arno Press, 1973 (originally London, Oxford University Press, 1922).

Berger, Natalia (ed.), *Where Cultures Meet: The Story of the Jews of Czechoslovakia*. Tel Aviv, Beth Hatefutsoth, 1990.

Bilski, Emily D., *Golem! Danger, Deliverance and Art*. New York, The Jewish Museum, 1987.

Buber, Martin, *Tales of the Hasidim*. New York, Schocken Books, 1947/1975.

Burchard, Przemysław, *Kultury Żydowskiej W Polsce*. Warsaw, "Reprint" Piotr Protrowski, 1990.

Chazan, Robert, and Marc Lee Raphael (eds.), *Modern Jewish History: A Source Reader*. New York, Schocken Books, 1969.

Cohen, Israel, *Travels in Jewry*. New York, Dutton, 1953.

Dawidowicz, Lucy S. (ed.), *The Golden Tradition: Jewish Life and Thought in Eastern Europe*. New York, Schocken Books, 1967.

Dobroszycki, Lucjan, and Kirshenblatt-Gimblett, Barbara, *Image Before My Eyes*. New York, Schocken Books, 1977.

Duda, Eugeniusz, *A Guide to Jewish Cracow*. Warsaw, Our Roots, 1990.

Encyclopaedia Judaica. Jerusalem, Keter, 1972.

Epstein, Benjamin R. (trans.), *Thomas G. Masaryk and the Jews, A Collection of Essays*. New York, B. Pollak, 1945.

Éri, Gyöngyi, and Zsuzsa Jobbágyi (eds.), *A Golden Age: Art and Society in Hungary 1896–1914*. Miami, Corvina/Barbican Art Gallery/Center for Fine Arts, 1990.

Fenyvesi, Charles, *When the World Was Whole: Three Centuries of Memories*. New York, Viking, 1990.

Fiedler, Jiří, *Jewish Sights of Bohemia and Moravia*. Prague, Sefer, 1991.

Gazda, Anikó (ed.), *Magyarországi Zsinagógák*. Budapest, Műszaki Könyvkiadó, 1989.

Gerle, János, Attila Kovács, and Imre Makovecz, *A Századforduló Magyar Építészete (Turn of the Century Hungarian Architecture)*. Budapest, Szépirodalmi Könyvkiadó, 1990.

Gilbert, Martin, *The Holocaust*. London, William Collins, 1986.

Gitelman, Zvi, *A Century of Ambivalence: The Jews of Russia and the Soviet Union*. New York, Schocken Books, 1988.

Glückel of Hameln, *The Memoirs of Glückel of Hameln* (Marvin Lowenthal, trans.). New York, Schocken Books, 1932, 1977.

Greenberg, Eliezer, and Irving Howe (eds.), *A Treasury of Yiddish Stories*. New York, Schocken Books, 1973.

Gruber, Ruth Ellen, *Jewish Heritage Travel: A Guide to Central and Eastern Europe*. New York, John Wiley & Sons, 1992.

Gutman, Yisrael, E. Mendelsohn, J. Reinharz, and C. Shmeruk, eds., *The Jews of Poland Between Two World Wars*. Hanover, NH, University Press of New England, 1989.

Heller, Celia, *On the Edge of Destruction: Jews of Poland Between the Two World Wars*. New York, Schocken Books, 1977.

Hertz, Aleksander, *The Jews in Polish Culture*. Evanston, IL, Northwestern University Press, 1988.

Humphrey, Grace, *Poland the Unexplored*. Indianapolis, Bobbs-Merrill, 1931.

Hoffman, Charles, *Gray Dawn: The Jews of Eastern Europe in the Post-Communist Era*. New York, HarperCollins, 1992.

Kafka, Franz, *Wedding Preparations in the Country and Other Stories* (including "Letter to His Father"). London, Penguin Books, 1978.

Karski, Jan, *Story of a Secret State*. Boston, Houghton Mifflin, 1944.

Katz, Jacob, *From Prejudice to Destruction: Anti-Semitism, 1700–1933*. Cambridge, MA, Harvard University Press, 1980.

Klánský, Josef, *Přežil Jsem Hitlera*. Prague, Svičen, 1992.

Krajewska, Monika, *A Tribe of Stones: Jewish Cemeteries in Poland*. Warsaw, Polish Scientific Publishers, 1993.

Krejčová, Helena, "The Eyes of Europe Are Upon Us." In Lewis Weiner (ed.), *The Review of the Society for the History of Czechoslovak Jews*, Vol. 5. New York, Society for the History of Czechoslovak Jews, 1992–1993.

Krinsky, Carol Herselle, *Synagogues of Europe*. New York, The Architectural History Foundation, 1985.

Kuděla, Jiří, and Jiří Všetečka, *The Fate of Jewish Prague*. Prague, Grafoprint, 1993.

Kugelmass, Jack, and Jonathan Boyarin, *From a Ruined Garden: The Memorial Books of Polish Jewry*. New York, Schocken Books, 1983.

Levi, Primo, *If This Is a Man/The Truce*. London, Abacus, 1987.

Lindemann, Albert S., *The Jew Accused: Three Anti-Semitic Affairs: Dreyfus, Beilis, Frank; 1894–1915*. Cambridge, Cambridge University Press, 1991.

Lowenthal, Marvin, *A World Passed By*. New York, Behrman's Jewish Book House, 1938.

Maimon, Solomon, *An Autobiography* (Moses Hadas, ed.). New York, Schocken Books, 1947.

Marcus, Jacob R., *The Jew in the Medieval World: A Source Book*. New York, Atheneum, 1973.

Markowski, Stanisław, *Krakowski Kazimierz: Dzielnica Żydowska 1870–1988*. Cracow, Arka, 1992.

McCagg, William O., Jr., *A History of the Habsburg Jews 1670–1918*. Bloomington and Indianapolis, Indiana University Press, 1989.

McCagg, William O., Jr., *Jewish Nobles and Geniuses in Modern Hungary*. New York, Columbia University Press, 1972.

Mendelsohn, Ezra, *The Jews of East Central Europe Between the World Wars*. Bloomington, Indiana University Press, 1983.

Miller, Judith, *One by One by One: Facing the Holocaust*. New York, Touchstone/Simon & Schuster, 1990.

Moore, Deborah Dash (ed.), *East European Jews in Two Worlds: Studies from the YIVO Annual*. Evanston, IL, Northwestern University Press, 1946–1990.

Niezabitowska, Małgorzata, and Tomasz Tomaszewski, *Remnants: The Last Jews of Poland*. New York, Friendly Press, 1986.

Orbán, Ferenc, *Magyarország Zsidó Emlékej Nevezetességej*. Budapest, Panorama, 1991.

Pařik, Arno, and Pavel Stecha, *The Jewish Town of Prague*. Prague, Oswald, 1992.

Pawel, Ernst, *The Nightmare of Reason: A Life of Franz Kafka*. London, Collins Harville, 1984.

Poll, Solomon, *The Hasidic Community of Williamsburg*. New York, Free Press of Glencoe, 1962.

Polonsky, Antony (ed.), *My Brother's Keeper?* London, Routledge, 1990.

Rabinowicz, Tzvi, *Chassidic Rebbes: From the Baal Shem Tov to Modern Times*. Southfield, MI, Targum Press, 1989.

Ripellino, Angelo Maria, *Praga Magica*. Torino, Einaudi, 1973.

Rothenberg, Jerome, *Khurbn and Other Poems*. New York, New Directions, 1983–1989.

Rothenberg, Jerome, *Poland 1931*. New York, New Directions, 1960–1974.

Rothenberg, Jerome, and Harris Lenowitz (eds.), *Exiled in the Word: Poems & Other Visions of the Jews from Tribal Times to the Present*. Port Townsend, WA, Copper Canyon Press, 1989.

Rybár, Ctibor, *Jewish Prague*. Prague, TV Spektrum, 1991.

Sadek, Vladimír, "Social Aspects in the Work of Prague Rabbi Löw," *Judaica Bohemiae* 19(1), Prague, 1983.

Sadek, Vladimír, "Stories of the Golem and Their Relation to the Work of Rabbi Löw of Prague," *Judaica Bohemiae* 23(2), Prague, 1987.

Samuel, Maurice, *The World of Sholom Aleichem*. New York, Alfred A. Knopf, 1943.

Sas, Meir, *Vanished Communities in Hungary: The History and Tragic Fate of the Jews in Ujhely and Zemplén County*. Toronto, Memorial Book Committee, 1986.

Segev, Tom, *The Seventh Million*. New York, Hill and Wang, 1993.

Society for the History of Czechoslovak Jews, *Review,* Vols. 4 and 5. New York, 1991, 1992.

Trunk, Isaiah, *Jewish Responses to Nazi Persecution: Collective and Individual Behavior in Extremis*. New York, Stein and Day, 1979.

Ward, Philip, *Polish Cities: Travels in Cracow and the South, Gdańsk, Malbork, and Warsaw*. Gretna, LA, Pelican, 1989.

Wiesel, Elie, *Night*. London, Penguin Books, 1981.

Wiesel, Elie, *Souls on Fire and Somewhere a Master*. London, Penguin Books, 1984.

Wirth, Péter, *Itt Van Elrejtve*. Budapest, Európa Könyvkiadó, 1985.

Wisse, Ruth R. (ed.), *The I. L. Peretz Reader*. New York, Schocken Books, 1990.

Zborowski, Mark, and Elizabeth Herzog, *Life Is with People*. New York, Schocken Books, 1952.

Index

ᮇᮦᮔᮘ